STAR WARS

WAR OF THE BOUNTY HUNTERS

BOUNTY HUNTERS

D1429751

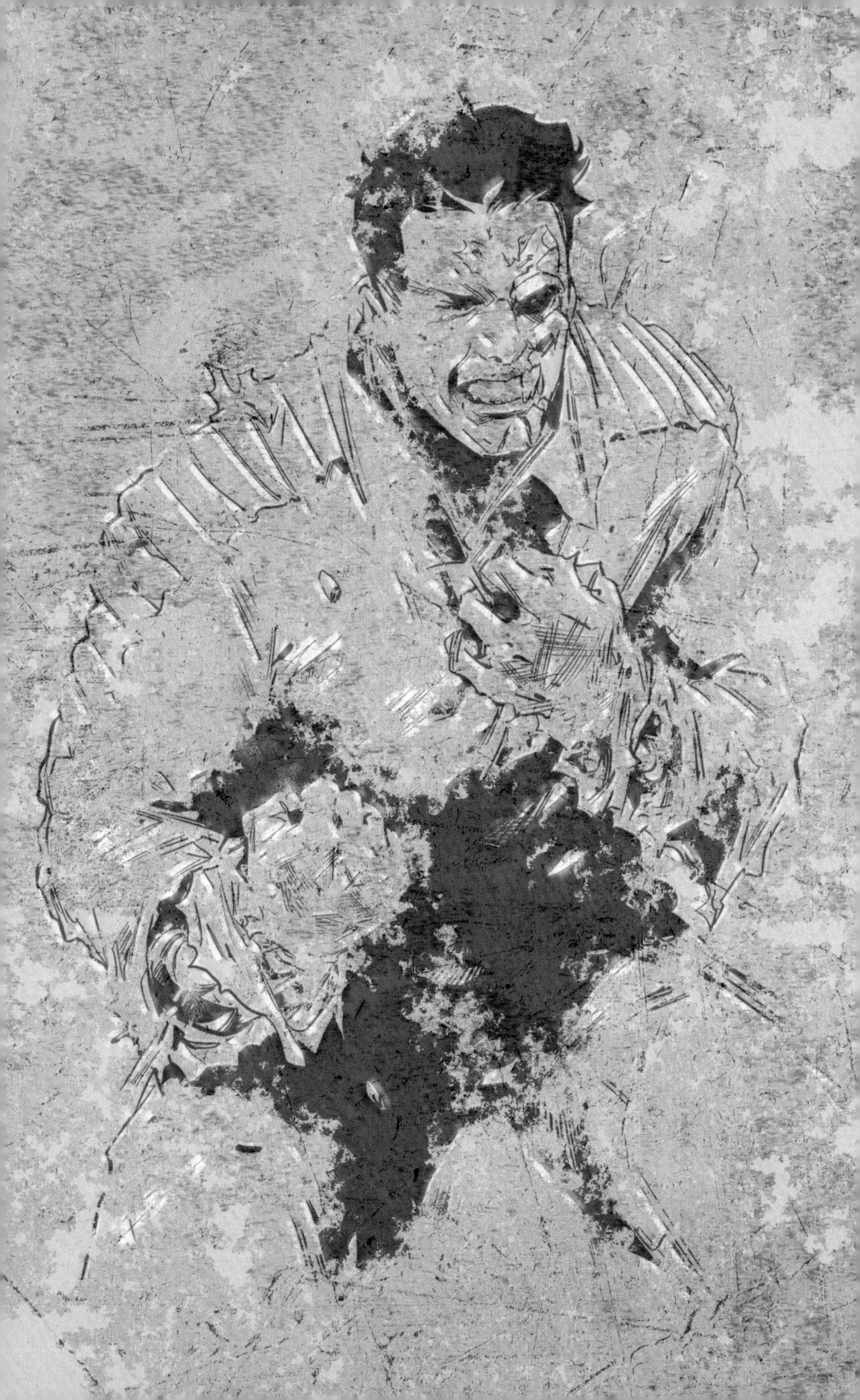

STAR WARS

WAR OF THE BOUNTY HUNTERS

BOUNTY HUNTERS

Writer
ETHAN SACKS

Artist
PAOLO VILLANELLI

Color Artists
ARIF PRIANTO WITH
JESUS ABURTOV (#17) & EDAR DELGADO (#17)

Letterer
VC's TRAVIS LANHAM

Cover Art
MATTIA DE IULIS (#12); GIUSEPPE CAMUNCOLI & MARTE GRACIA (#13-14);
AND GIUSEPPE CAMUNCOLI & NOLAN WOODARD (#15-17)

Assistant Editors
TOM GRONEMAN & DANNY KHAZEM

Editor
MARK PANICCIA

Collection Editor	JENNIFER GRÜNWALD	For Lucasfilm:	
Assistant Editor	DANIEL KIRCHHOFFER	Senior Editor	ROBERT SIMPSON
Assistant Managing Editor	MAIA LOY	Creative Director	MICHAEL SIGLAIN
Assistant Managing Editor	LISA MONTALBANO	Art Director	TROY ALDERS
VP Production & Special Projects	JEFF YOUNGQUIST	Lucasfilm Story Group	MATT MARTIN
Book Designer	ADAM DEL RE		PABLO HIDALGO
SVP Print, Sales & Marketing	DAVID GABRIEL		EMILY SHKOUKANI
Editor in Chief	C.B. CEBULSKI	Creative Art Manager	PHIL SZOSTAK

Disney • LUCASFILM

STAR WARS: BOUNTY HUNTERS VOL. 3 — WAR OF THE BOUNTY HUNTERS. Contains material originally published in magazine form as STAR WARS: BOUNTY HUNTERS (2020) #12-17. First printing 2021. ISBN 978-1-302-92981-0. Published by MARVEL WORLDWIDE, INC., a subsidiary of MARVEL ENTERTAINMENT, LLC. OFFICE OF PUBLICATION: 1290 Avenue of the Americas, New York, NY 10104. STAR WARS and related text and illustrations are trademarks and/or copyrights, in the United States and other countries, of Lucasfilm Ltd. and/or its affiliates. © & TM Lucasfilm Ltd. No similarity between any of the names, characters, persons, and/or institutions in this magazine with those of any living or dead person or institution is intended, and any such similarity which may exist is purely coincidental. Marvel and its logos are TM Marvel Characters, Inc. Printed in Canada. KEVIN FEIGE, Chief Creative Officer; DAN BUCKLEY, President, Marvel Entertainment; JOE QUESADA, EVP & Creative Director; DAVID BOGART, Associate Publisher & SVP of Talent Affairs; TOM BREVOORT, VP, Executive Editor; NICK LOWE, Executive Editor, VP of Content, Digital Publishing; DAVID GABRIEL, VP of Print & Digital Publishing; JEFF YOUNGQUIST, VP of Production & Special Projects; ALEX MORALES, Director of Publishing Operations; DAN EDINGTON, Managing Editor; RICKEY PURDIN, Director of Talent Relations; JENNIFER GRÜNWALD, Senior Editor, Special Projects; SUSAN CRESPI, Production Manager; STAN LEE, Chairman Emeritus. For information regarding advertising in Marvel Comics or on Marvel.com, please contact Vit DeBellis, Custom Solutions & Integrated Advertising Manager, at vdebellis@marvel.com. For Marvel subscription inquiries, please call 888-511-5480. Manufactured between 10/29/2021 and 11/30/2021 by SOLISCO PRINTERS, SCOTT, QC, CANADA.

10 9 8 7 6 5 4 3 2 1

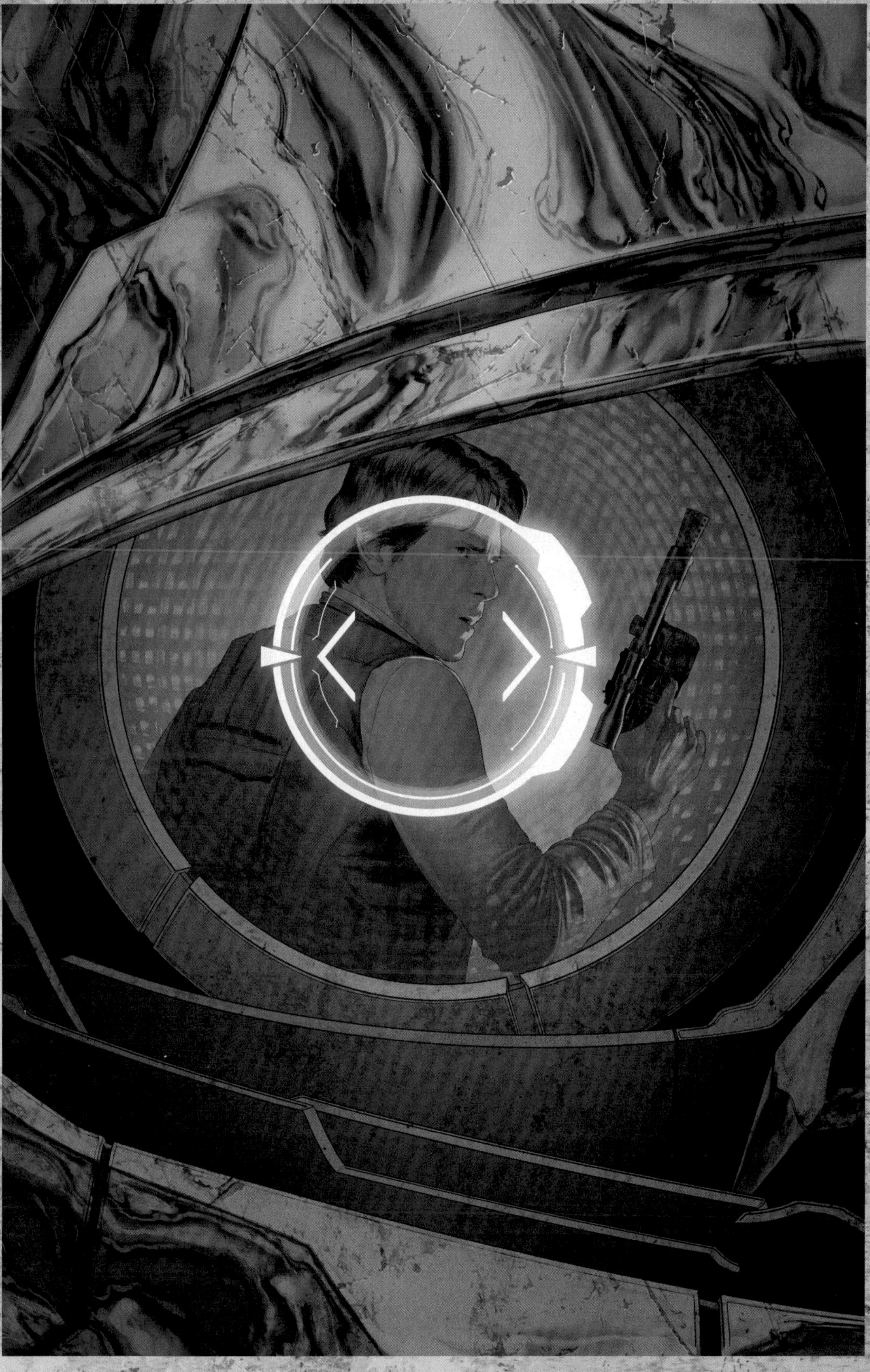

12 – TARGET SOLO

VALANCE

DENGAR

ZUCKUSS

4-LOM

STAR WARS
BOUNTY HUNTERS

WAR OF THE BOUNTY HUNTERS

Cyborg bounty hunter Valance recently rescued a stranded Rebel freighter from marauding pirates.

Dengar let it slip that the notorious Boba Fett captured Valance's old friend, Han Solo. The two rival hunters have come to an understanding in order to find Fett.

Valance now tears through space in a stolen vessel, desperate to pick up the trail before it's too late....

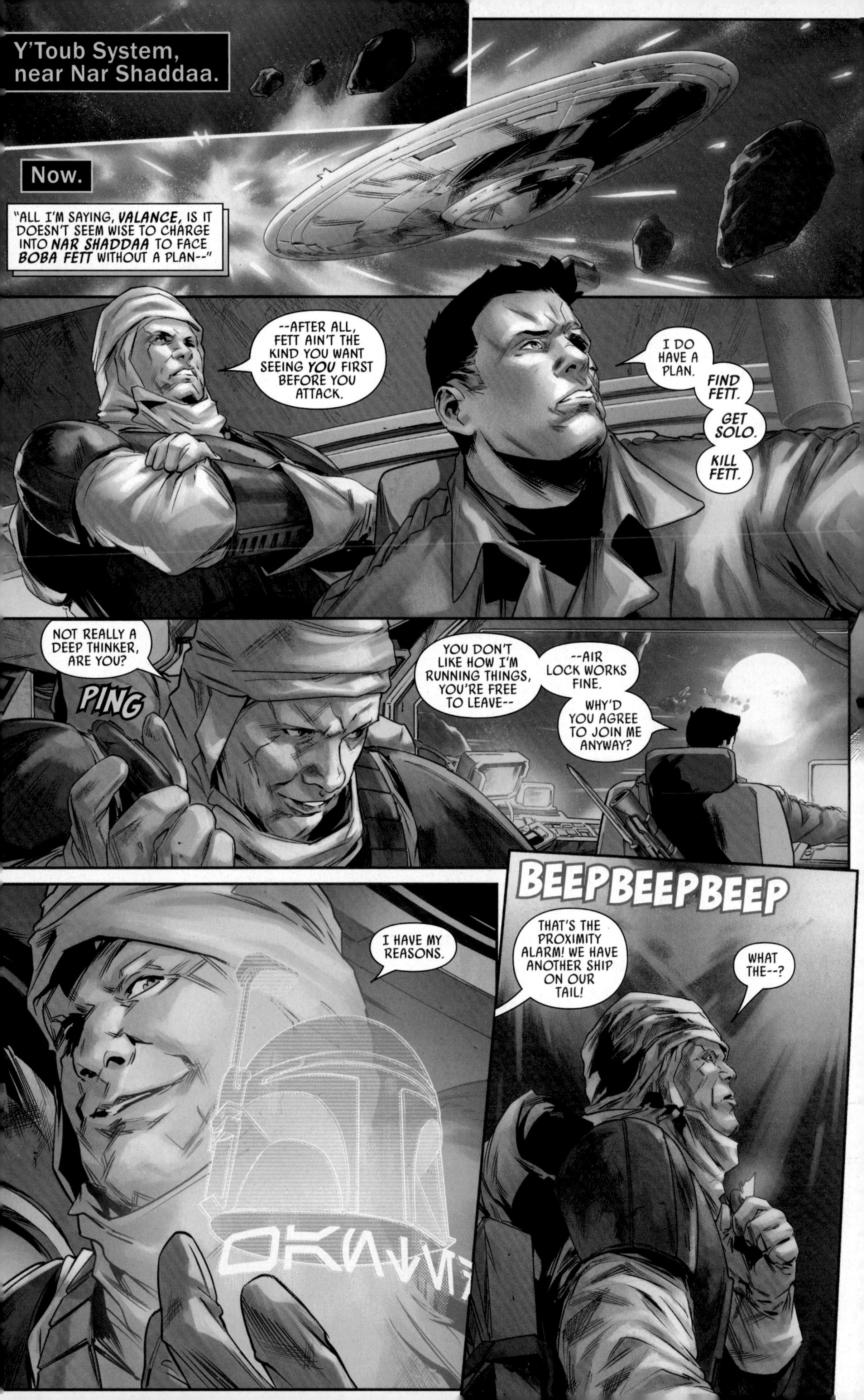

Y'Toub System, near Nar Shaddaa.
Now.
"ALL I'M SAYING, VALANCE, IS IT DOESN'T SEEM WISE TO CHARGE INTO NAR SHADDAA TO FACE BOBA FETT WITHOUT A PLAN--"
--AFTER ALL, FETT AIN'T THE KIND YOU WANT SEEING YOU FIRST BEFORE YOU ATTACK.
I DO HAVE A PLAN.
FIND FETT.
GET SOLO.
KILL FETT.
NOT REALLY A DEEP THINKER, ARE YOU?
PING
YOU DON'T LIKE HOW I'M RUNNING THINGS, YOU'RE FREE TO LEAVE--
--AIR LOCK WORKS FINE.
WHY'D YOU AGREE TO JOIN ME ANYWAY?
I HAVE MY REASONS.
BEEPBEEPBEEP
THAT'S THE PROXIMITY ALARM! WE HAVE ANOTHER SHIP ON OUR TAIL!
WHAT THE--?

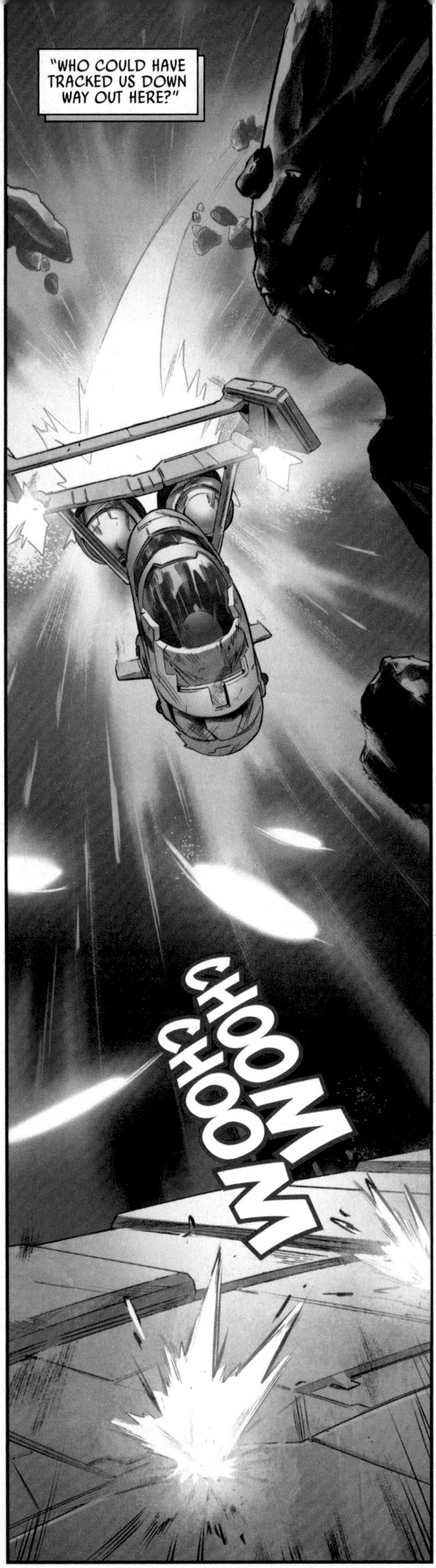
"WHO COULD HAVE TRACKED US DOWN WAY OUT HERE?"
CHOOM CHOOM

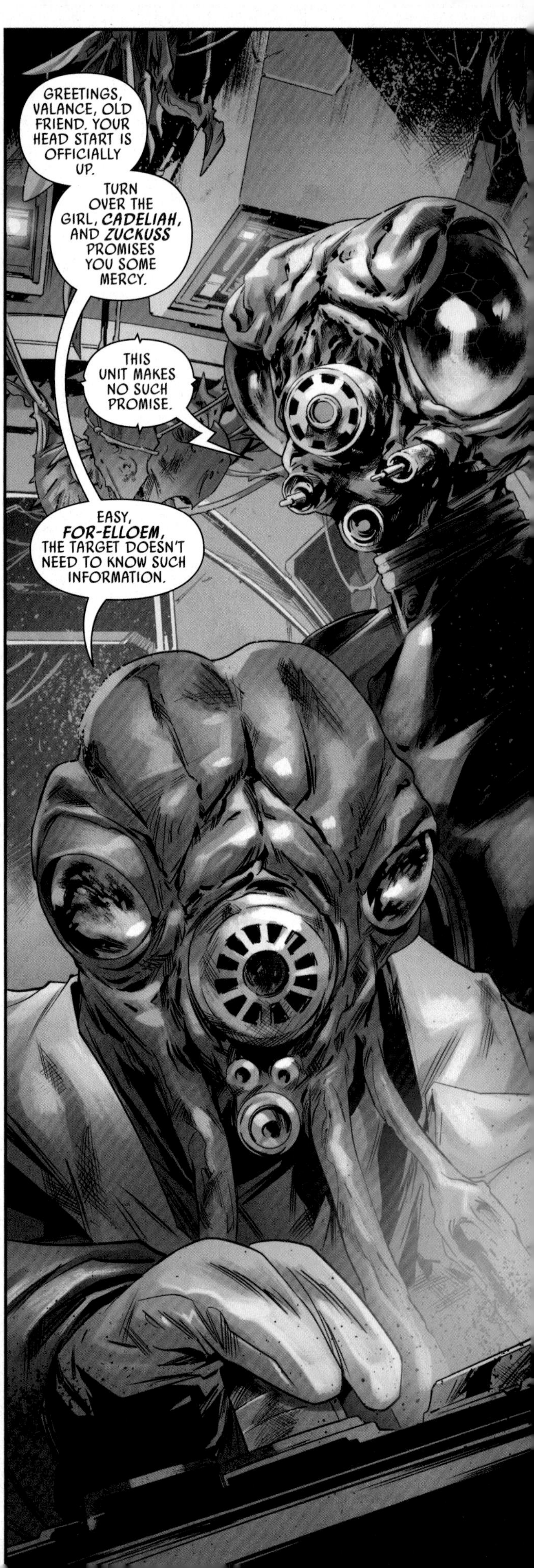
GREETINGS, VALANCE, OLD FRIEND. YOUR HEAD START IS OFFICIALLY UP.
TURN OVER THE GIRL, CADELIAH, AND ZUCKUSS PROMISES YOU SOME MERCY.
THIS UNIT MAKES NO SUCH PROMISE.
EASY, FOR-ELLOEM, THE TARGET DOESN'T NEED TO KNOW SUCH INFORMATION.

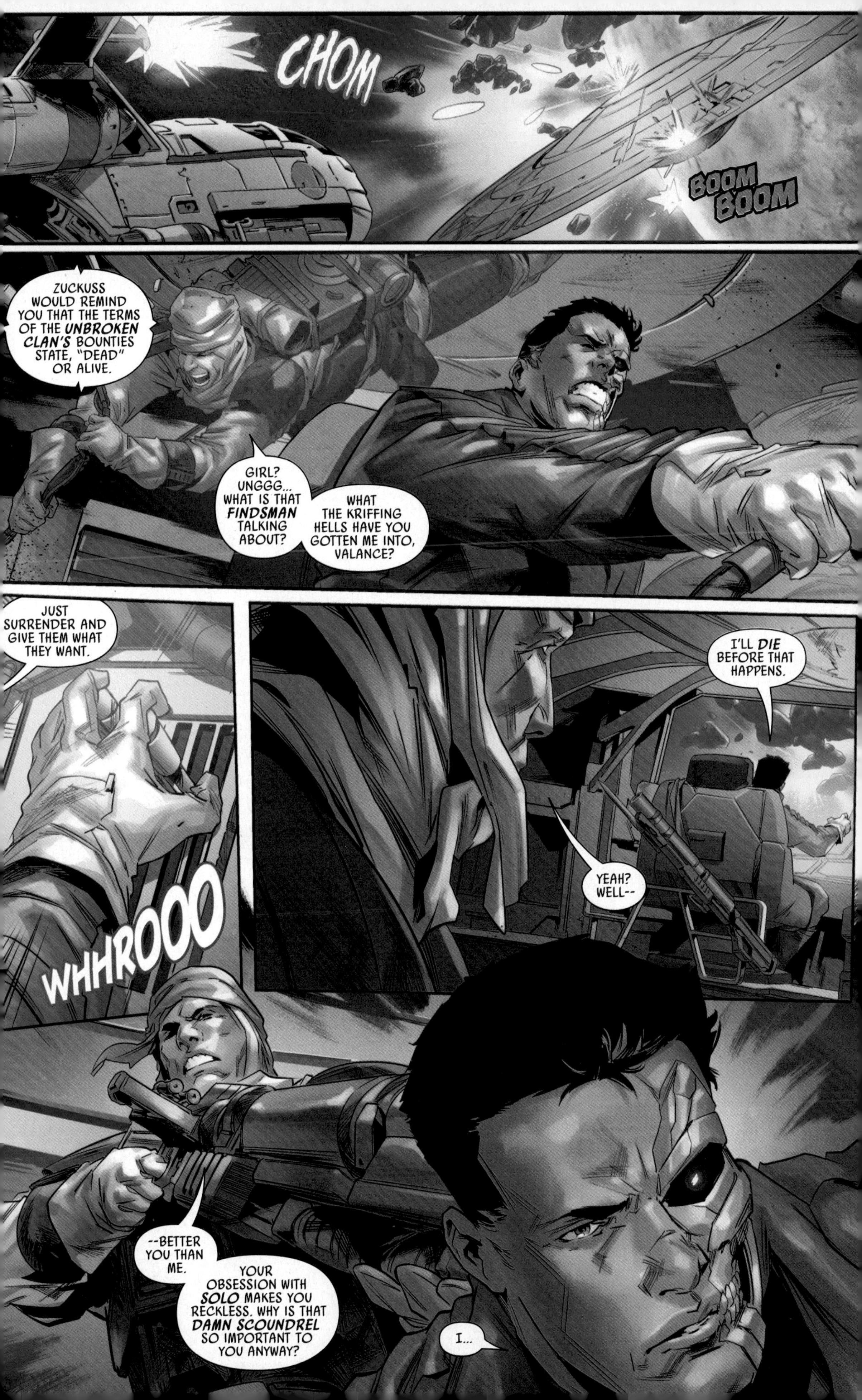
CHOM
BOOM BOOM
ZUCKUSS WOULD REMIND YOU THAT THE TERMS OF THE UNBROKEN CLAN'S BOUNTIES STATE, "DEAD" OR ALIVE.
GIRL? UNGGG... WHAT IS THAT FINDSMAN TALKING ABOUT?
WHAT THE KRIFFING HELLS HAVE YOU GOTTEN ME INTO, VALANCE?
JUST SURRENDER AND GIVE THEM WHAT THEY WANT.
I'LL DIE BEFORE THAT HAPPENS.
YEAH? WELL--
WHHROOO
--BETTER YOU THAN ME.
YOUR OBSESSION WITH SOLO MAKES YOU RECKLESS. WHY IS THAT DAMN SCOUNDREL SO IMPORTANT TO YOU ANYWAY?
I...

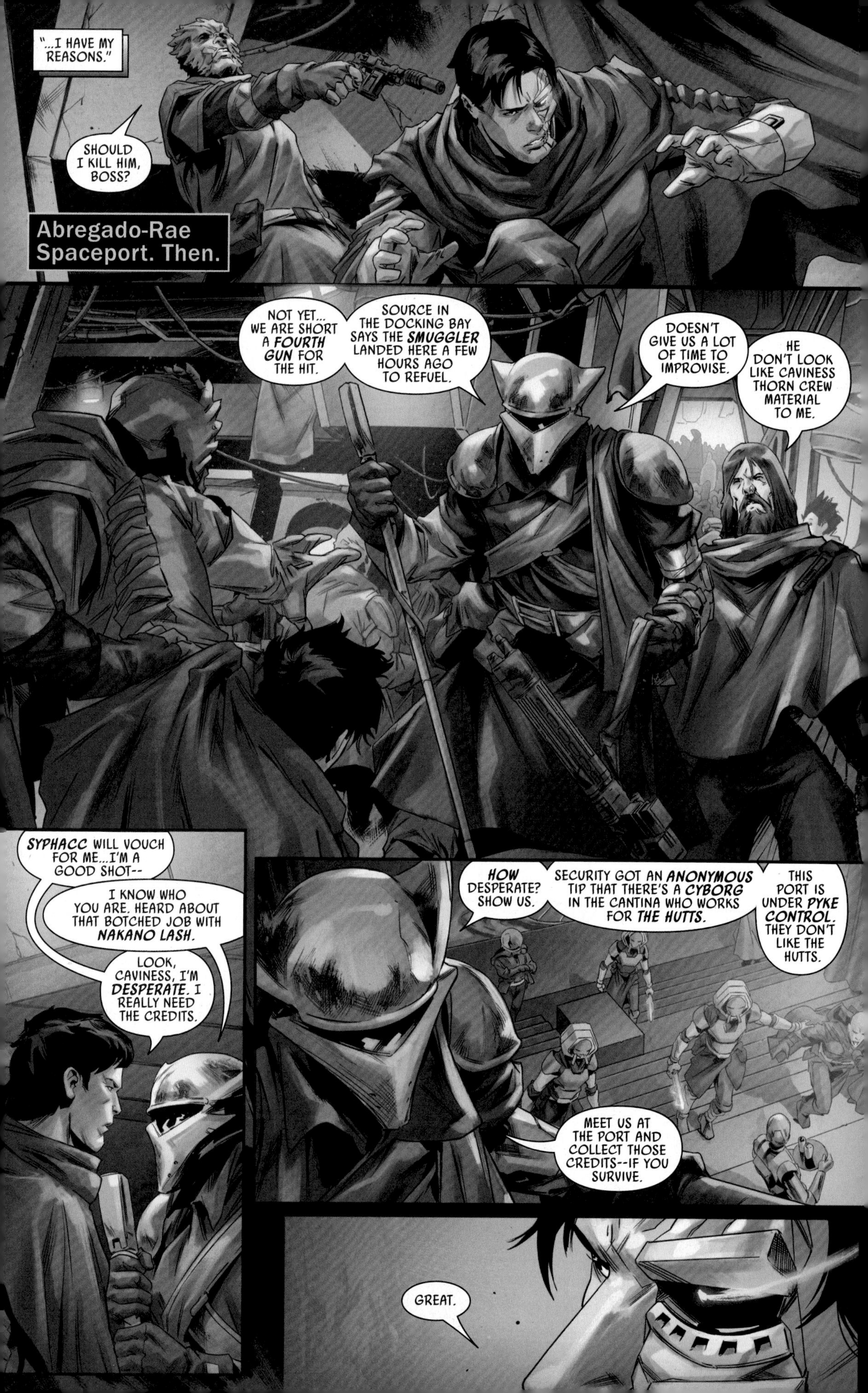
"...I HAVE MY REASONS."
SHOULD I KILL HIM, BOSS?
Abregado-Rae Spaceport. Then.
NOT YET... WE ARE SHORT A FOURTH GUN FOR THE HIT.
SOURCE IN THE DOCKING BAY SAYS THE SMUGGLER LANDED HERE A FEW HOURS AGO TO REFUEL.
DOESN'T GIVE US A LOT OF TIME TO IMPROVISE.
HE DON'T LOOK LIKE CAVINESS THORN CREW MATERIAL TO ME.
SYPHACC WILL VOUCH FOR ME...I'M A GOOD SHOT--
I KNOW WHO YOU ARE. HEARD ABOUT THAT BOTCHED JOB WITH NAKANO LASH.
LOOK, CAVINESS, I'M DESPERATE. I REALLY NEED THE CREDITS.
HOW DESPERATE? SHOW US.
SECURITY GOT AN ANONYMOUS TIP THAT THERE'S A CYBORG IN THE CANTINA WHO WORKS FOR THE HUTTS.
THIS PORT IS UNDER PYKE CONTROL. THEY DON'T LIKE THE HUTTS.
MEET US AT THE PORT AND COLLECT THOSE CREDITS--IF YOU SURVIVE.
GREAT.

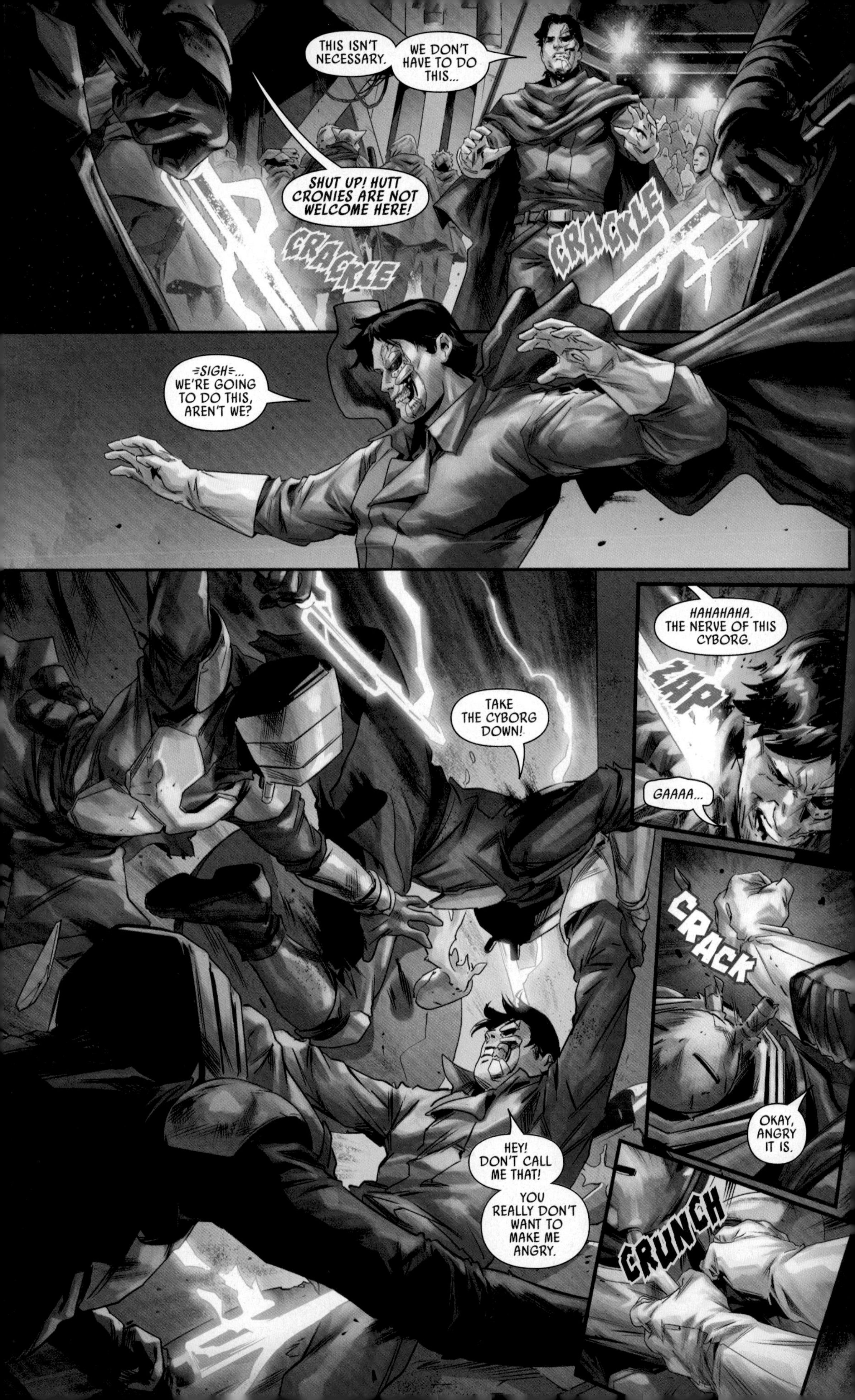
THIS ISN'T NECESSARY.
WE DON'T HAVE TO DO THIS...
SHUT UP! HUTT CRONIES ARE NOT WELCOME HERE!
CRACKLE
CRACKLE
=SIGH=... WE'RE GOING TO DO THIS, AREN'T WE?
TAKE THE CYBORG DOWN!
HEY! DON'T CALL ME THAT!
YOU REALLY DON'T WANT TO MAKE ME ANGRY.
HAHAHAHA. THE NERVE OF THIS CYBORG.
ZAP
GAAAA...
CRACK
OKAY, ANGRY IT IS.
CRUNCH

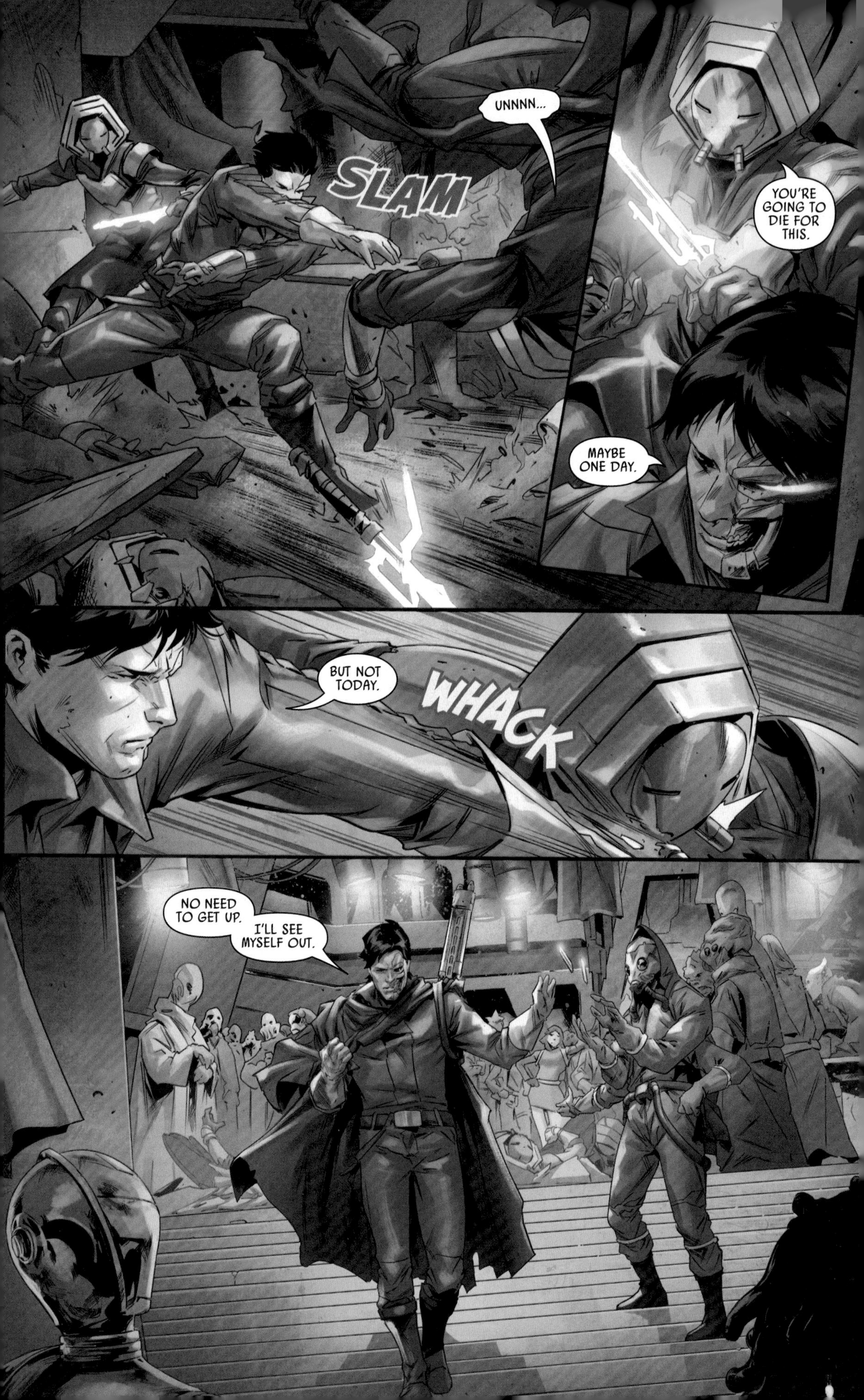
UNNNN...
SLAM
YOU'RE GOING TO DIE FOR THIS.
MAYBE ONE DAY.
BUT NOT TODAY.
WHACK
NO NEED TO GET UP.
I'LL SEE MYSELF OUT.

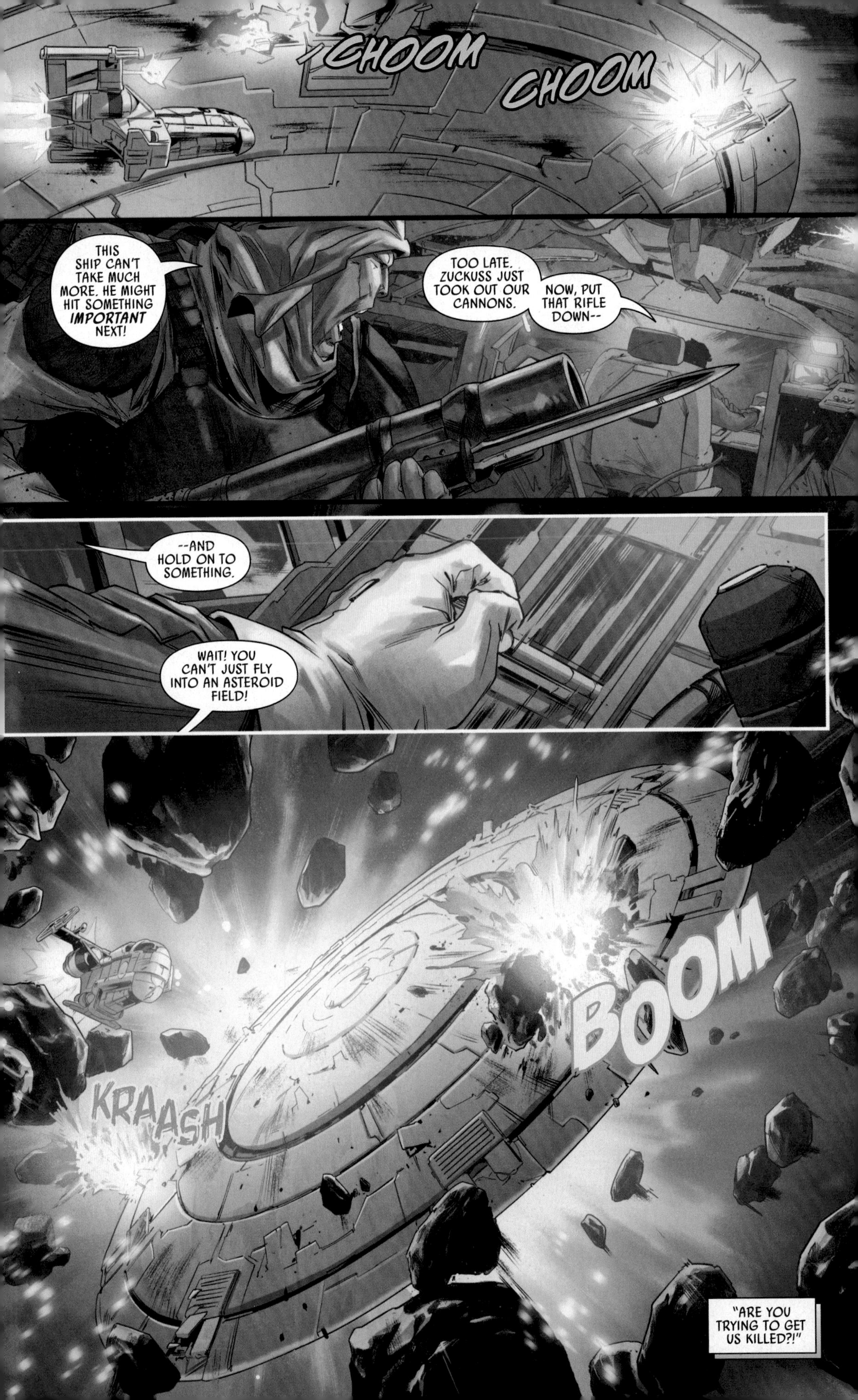
CHOOM
CHOOM
THIS SHIP CAN'T TAKE MUCH MORE. HE MIGHT HIT SOMETHING *IMPORTANT* NEXT!
TOO LATE. ZUCKUSS JUST TOOK OUT OUR CANNONS.
NOW, PUT THAT RIFLE DOWN--
--AND HOLD ON TO SOMETHING.
WAIT! YOU CAN'T JUST FLY INTO AN ASTEROID FIELD!
BOOM
KRAASH
"ARE YOU TRYING TO GET US KILLED?!"

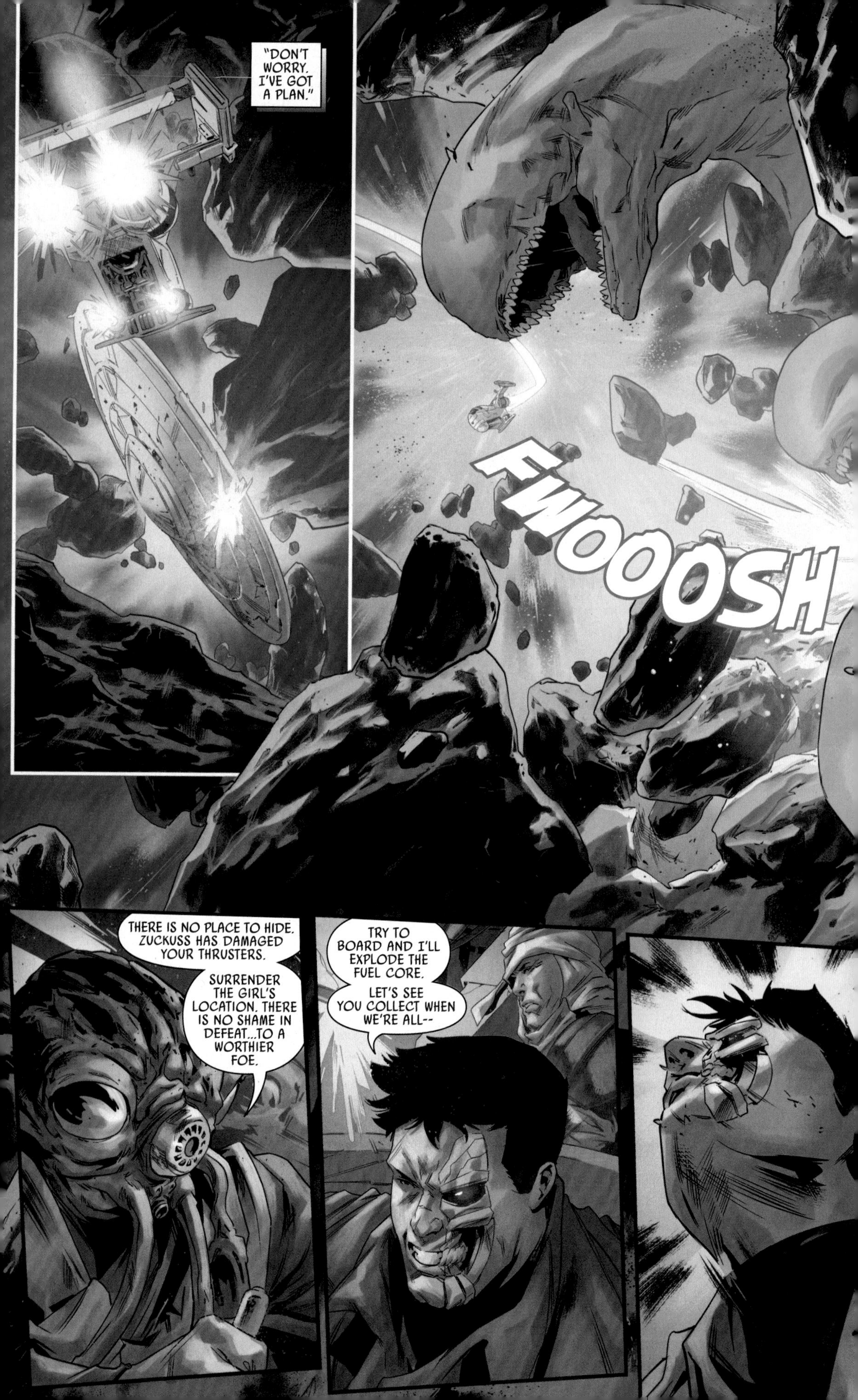
"DON'T WORRY. I'VE GOT A PLAN."
FWOOOSH
THERE IS NO PLACE TO HIDE. ZUCKUSS HAS DAMAGED YOUR THRUSTERS.
SURRENDER THE GIRL'S LOCATION. THERE IS NO SHAME IN DEFEAT...TO A WORTHIER FOE.
TRY TO BOARD AND I'LL EXPLODE THE FUEL CORE.
LET'S SEE YOU COLLECT WHEN WE'RE ALL--

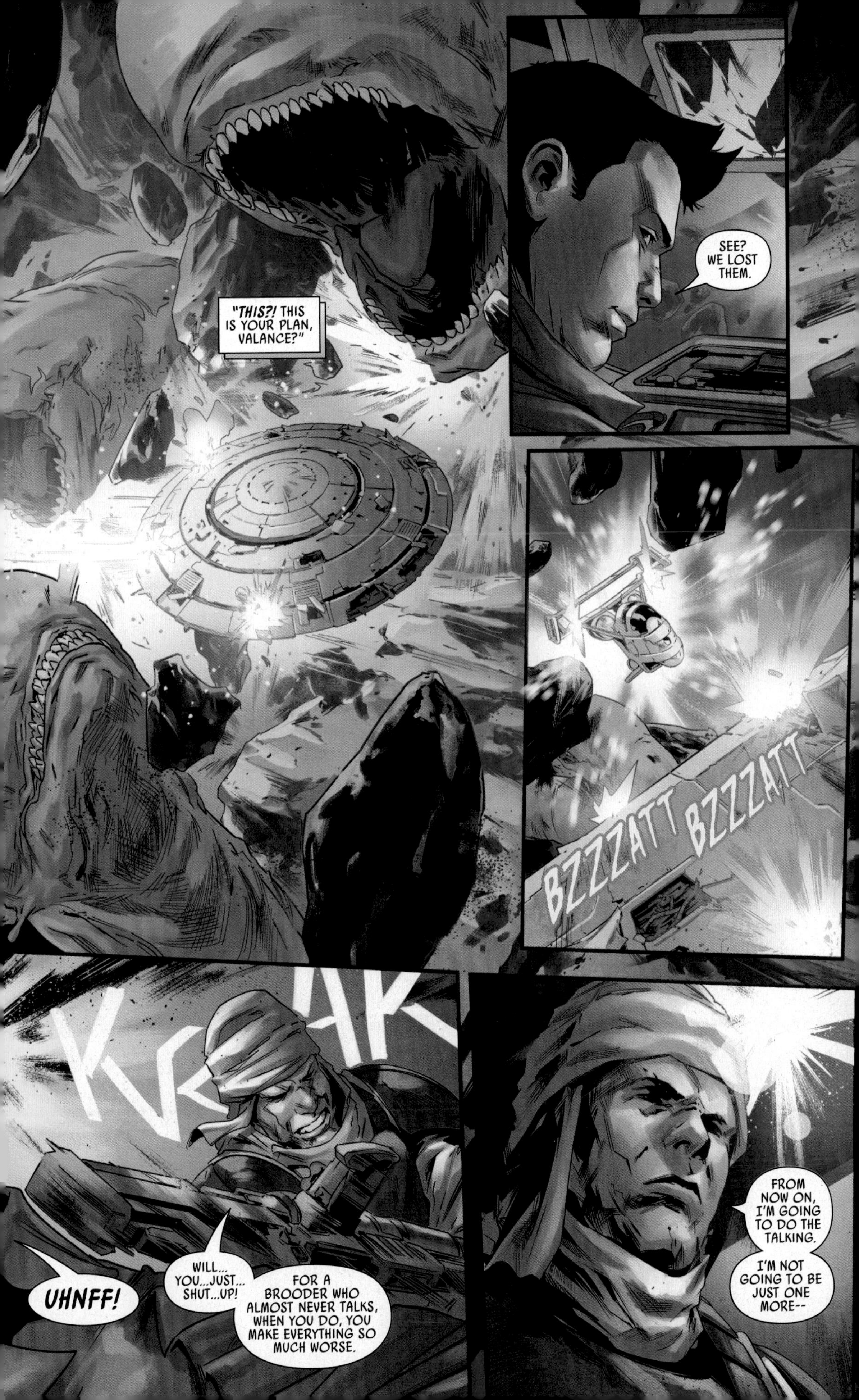
"THIS?! THIS IS YOUR PLAN, VALANCE?"
SEE? WE LOST THEM.
BZZZATT BZZZATT
UHNFF!
WILL... YOU...JUST... SHUT...UP!
FOR A BROODER WHO ALMOST NEVER TALKS, WHEN YOU DO, YOU MAKE EVERYTHING SO MUCH WORSE.
FROM NOW ON, I'M GOING TO DO THE TALKING.
I'M NOT GOING TO BE JUST ONE MORE--

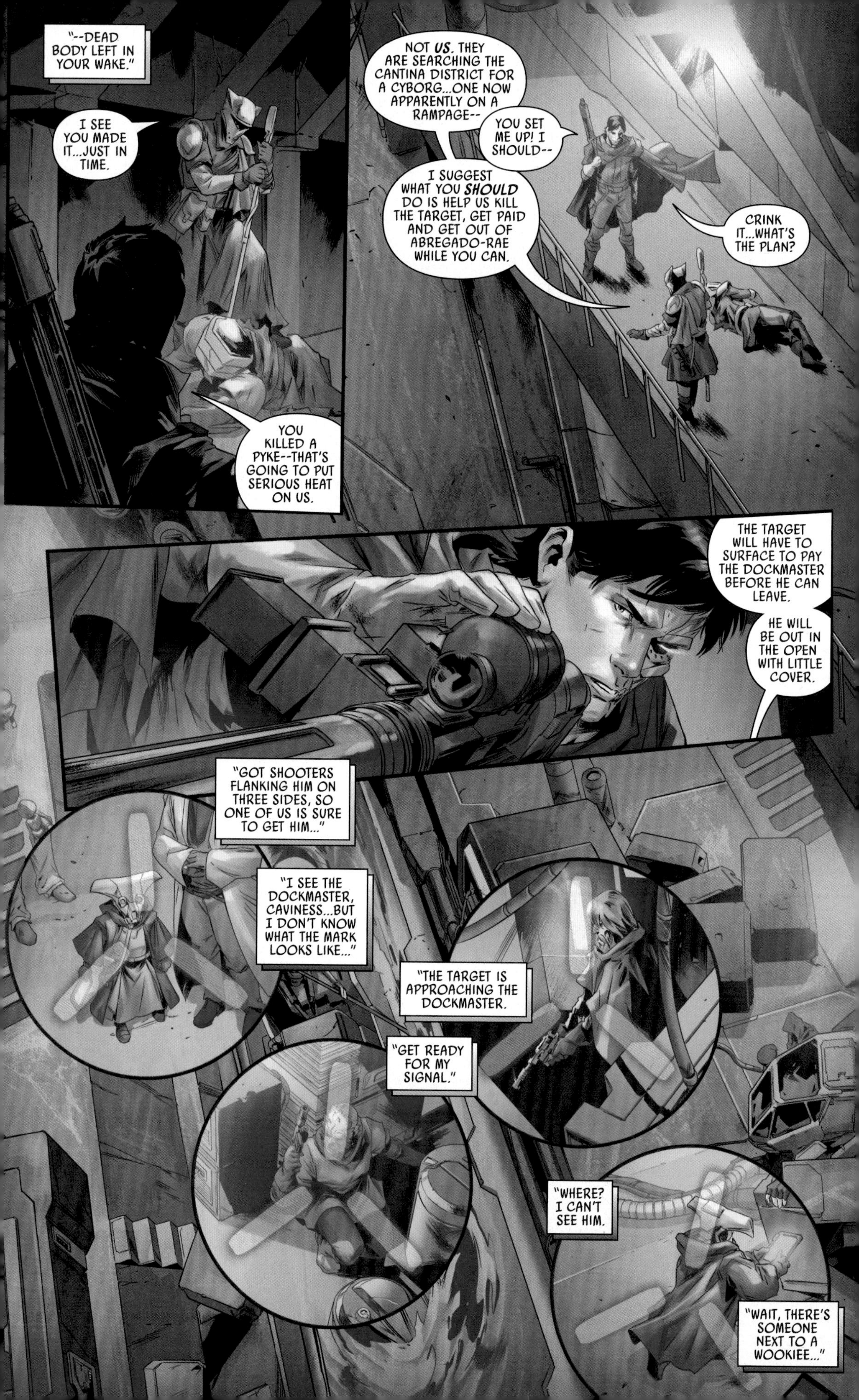
"--DEAD BODY LEFT IN YOUR WAKE."
I SEE YOU MADE IT...JUST IN TIME.
YOU KILLED A PYKE--THAT'S GOING TO PUT SERIOUS HEAT ON US.
NOT US. THEY ARE SEARCHING THE CANTINA DISTRICT FOR A CYBORG...ONE NOW APPARENTLY ON A RAMPAGE--
YOU SET ME UP! I SHOULD--
I SUGGEST WHAT YOU SHOULD DO IS HELP US KILL THE TARGET, GET PAID AND GET OUT OF ABREGADO-RAE WHILE YOU CAN.
CRINK IT...WHAT'S THE PLAN?
THE TARGET WILL HAVE TO SURFACE TO PAY THE DOCKMASTER BEFORE HE CAN LEAVE.
HE WILL BE OUT IN THE OPEN WITH LITTLE COVER.
"GOT SHOOTERS FLANKING HIM ON THREE SIDES, SO ONE OF US IS SURE TO GET HIM..."
"I SEE THE DOCKMASTER, CAVINESS...BUT I DON'T KNOW WHAT THE MARK LOOKS LIKE..."
"THE TARGET IS APPROACHING THE DOCKMASTER.
"GET READY FOR MY SIGNAL."
"WHERE? I CAN'T SEE HIM.
"WAIT, THERE'S SOMEONE NEXT TO A WOOKIEE..."

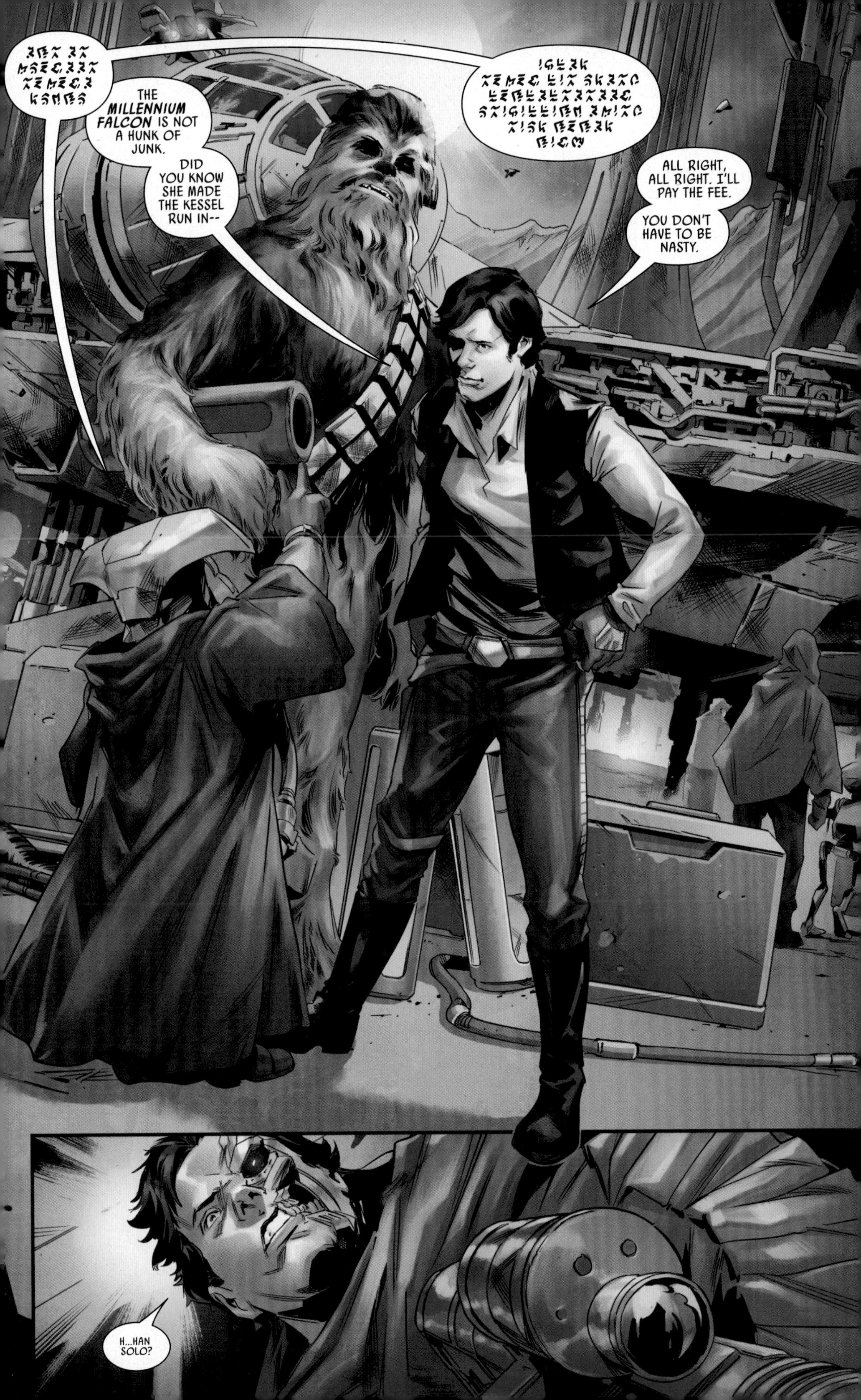
THE MILLENNIUM FALCON IS NOT A HUNK OF JUNK.
DID YOU KNOW SHE MADE THE KESSEL RUN IN--
ALL RIGHT, ALL RIGHT. I'LL PAY THE FEE.
YOU DON'T HAVE TO BE NASTY.
H...HAN SOLO?

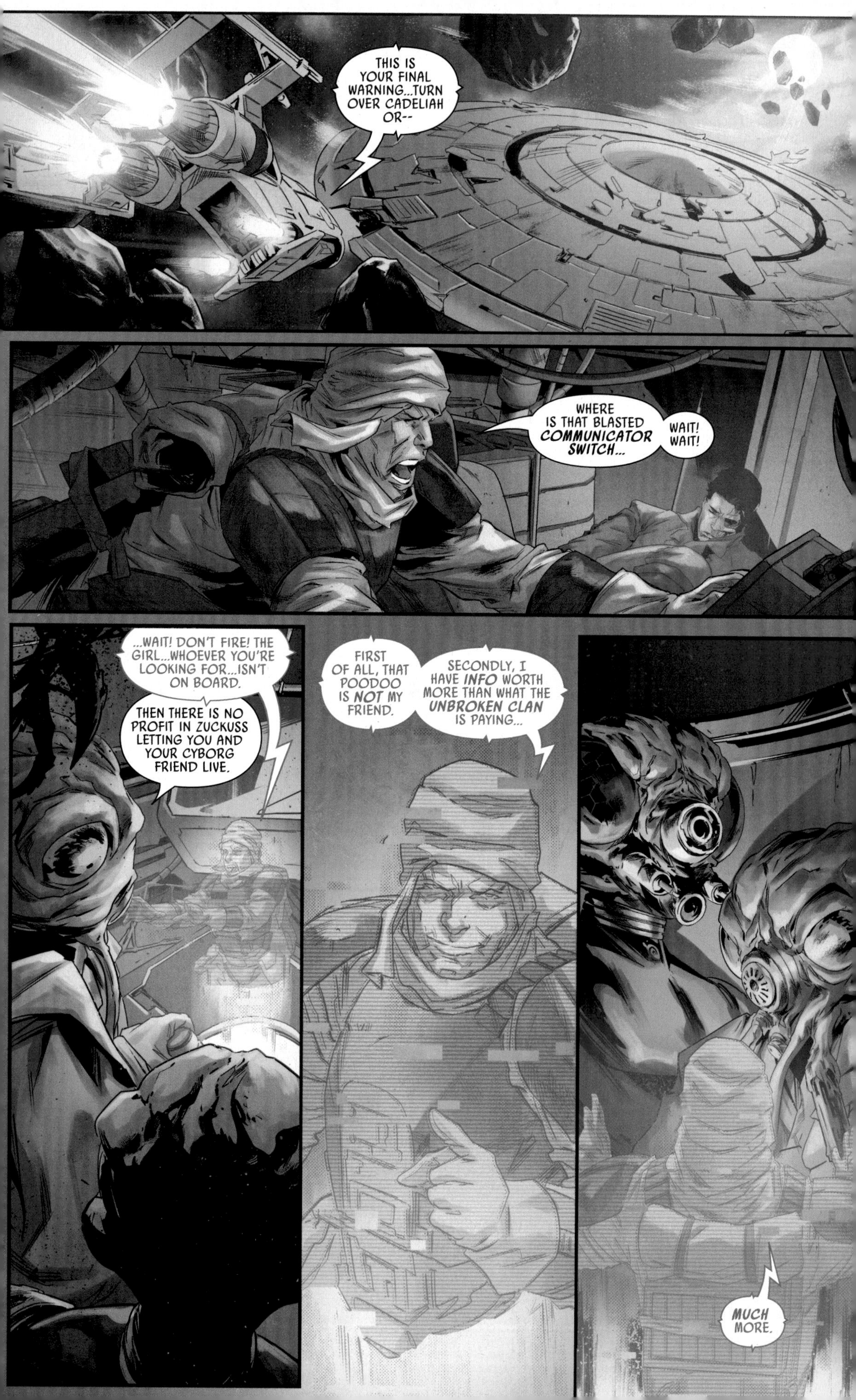
THIS IS YOUR FINAL WARNING...TURN OVER CADELIAH OR--
WHERE IS THAT BLASTED COMMUNICATOR SWITCH...
WAIT! WAIT!
...WAIT! DON'T FIRE! THE GIRL...WHOEVER YOU'RE LOOKING FOR...ISN'T ON BOARD.
THEN THERE IS NO PROFIT IN ZUCKUSS LETTING YOU AND YOUR CYBORG FRIEND LIVE.
FIRST OF ALL, THAT POODOO IS NOT MY FRIEND.
SECONDLY, I HAVE INFO WORTH MORE THAN WHAT THE UNBROKEN CLAN IS PAYING...
MUCH MORE.

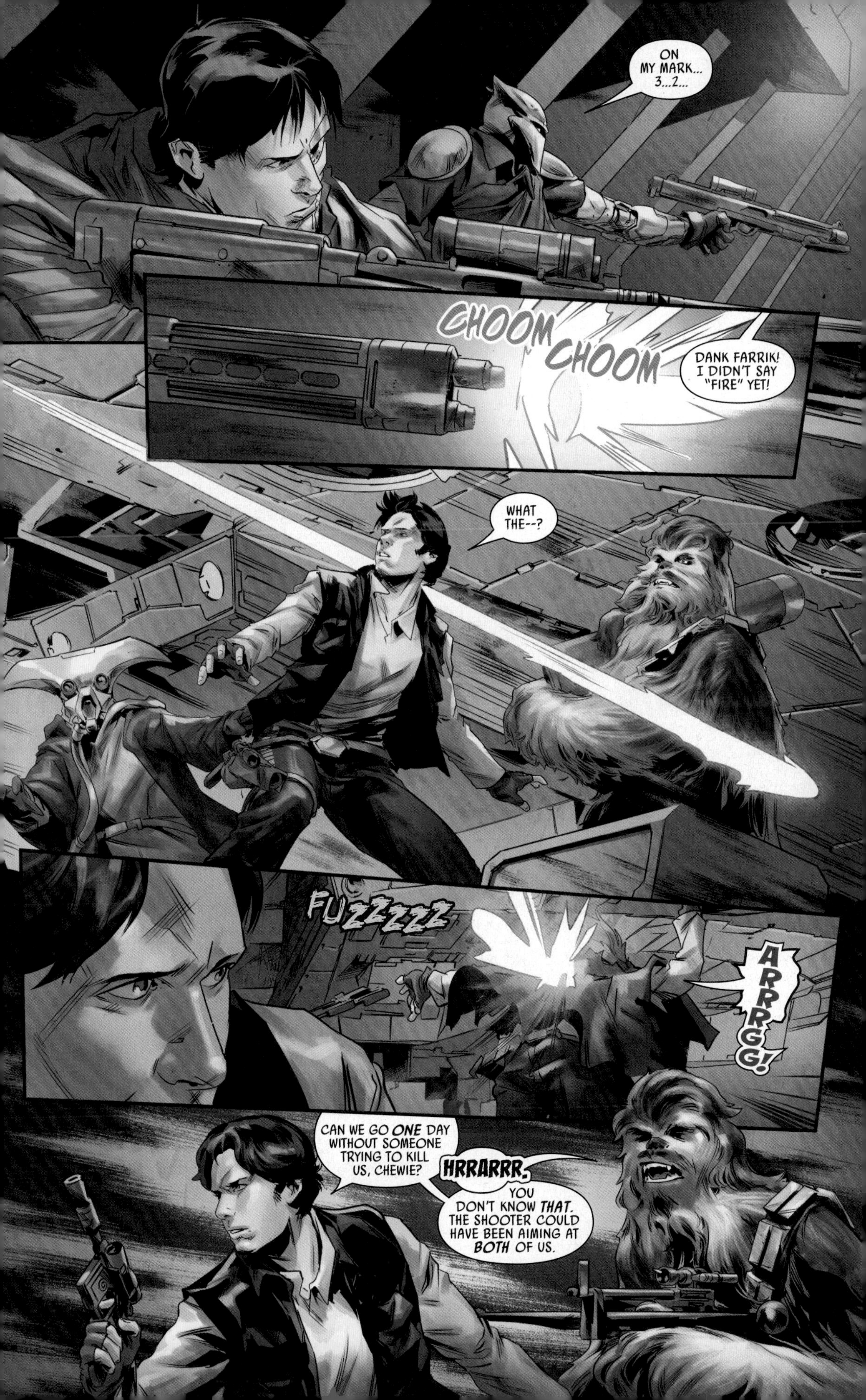

ON MY MARK... 3...2...
CHOOM CHOOM
DANK FARRIK! I DIDN'T SAY "FIRE" YET!
WHAT THE--?
FUZZZZZZ
ARRRRGG!
CAN WE GO ONE DAY WITHOUT SOMEONE TRYING TO KILL US, CHEWIE?
HRRARRR.
YOU DON'T KNOW THAT. THE SHOOTER COULD HAVE BEEN AIMING AT BOTH OF US.

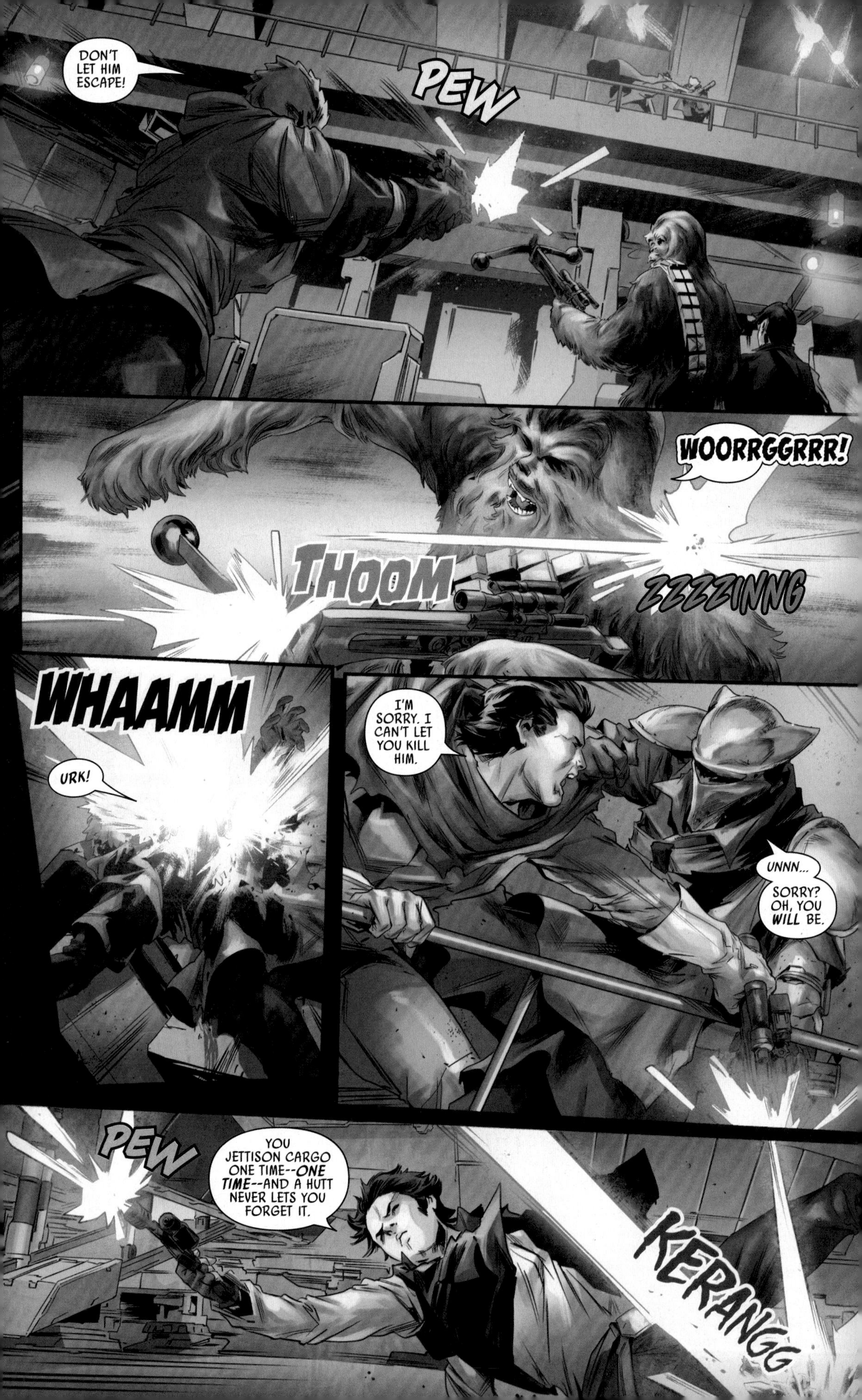
DON'T LET HIM ESCAPE!
PEW
WOORRGGRRR!
THOOM
ZZZZINNG
WHAAMM
URK!
I'M SORRY. I CAN'T LET YOU KILL HIM.
UNNN...
SORRY? OH, YOU *WILL* BE.
PEW
YOU JETTISON CARGO ONE TIME--*ONE TIME*--AND A HUTT NEVER LETS YOU FORGET IT.
KERANGG

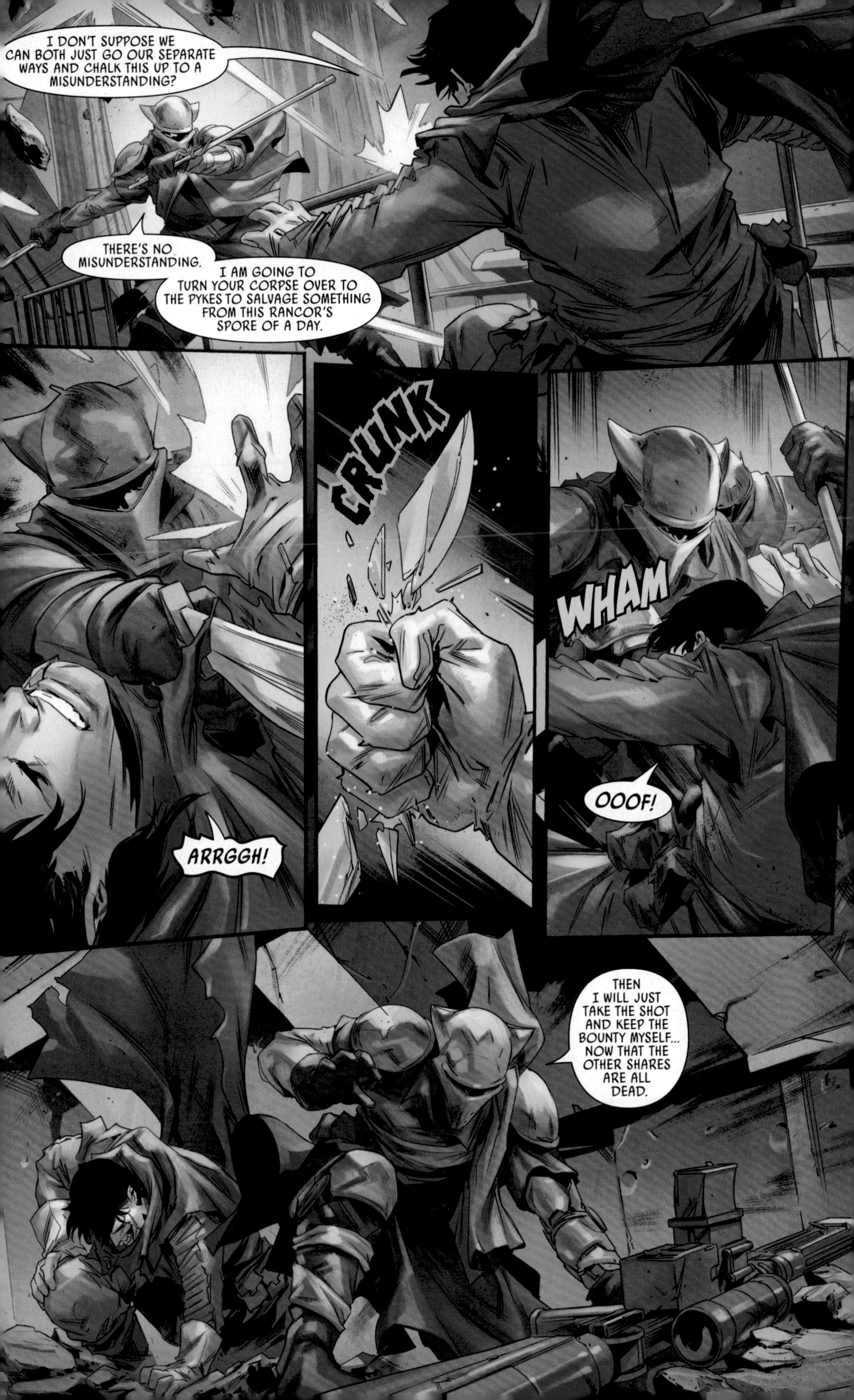
I DON'T SUPPOSE WE CAN BOTH JUST GO OUR SEPARATE WAYS AND CHALK THIS UP TO A MISUNDERSTANDING?
THERE'S NO MISUNDERSTANDING.
I AM GOING TO TURN YOUR CORPSE OVER TO THE PYKES TO SALVAGE SOMETHING FROM THIS RANCOR'S SPORE OF A DAY.
ARRGGH!
CRUNK
WHAM
OOOF!
THEN I WILL JUST TAKE THE SHOT AND KEEP THE BOUNTY MYSELF... NOW THAT THE OTHER SHARES ARE ALL DEAD.

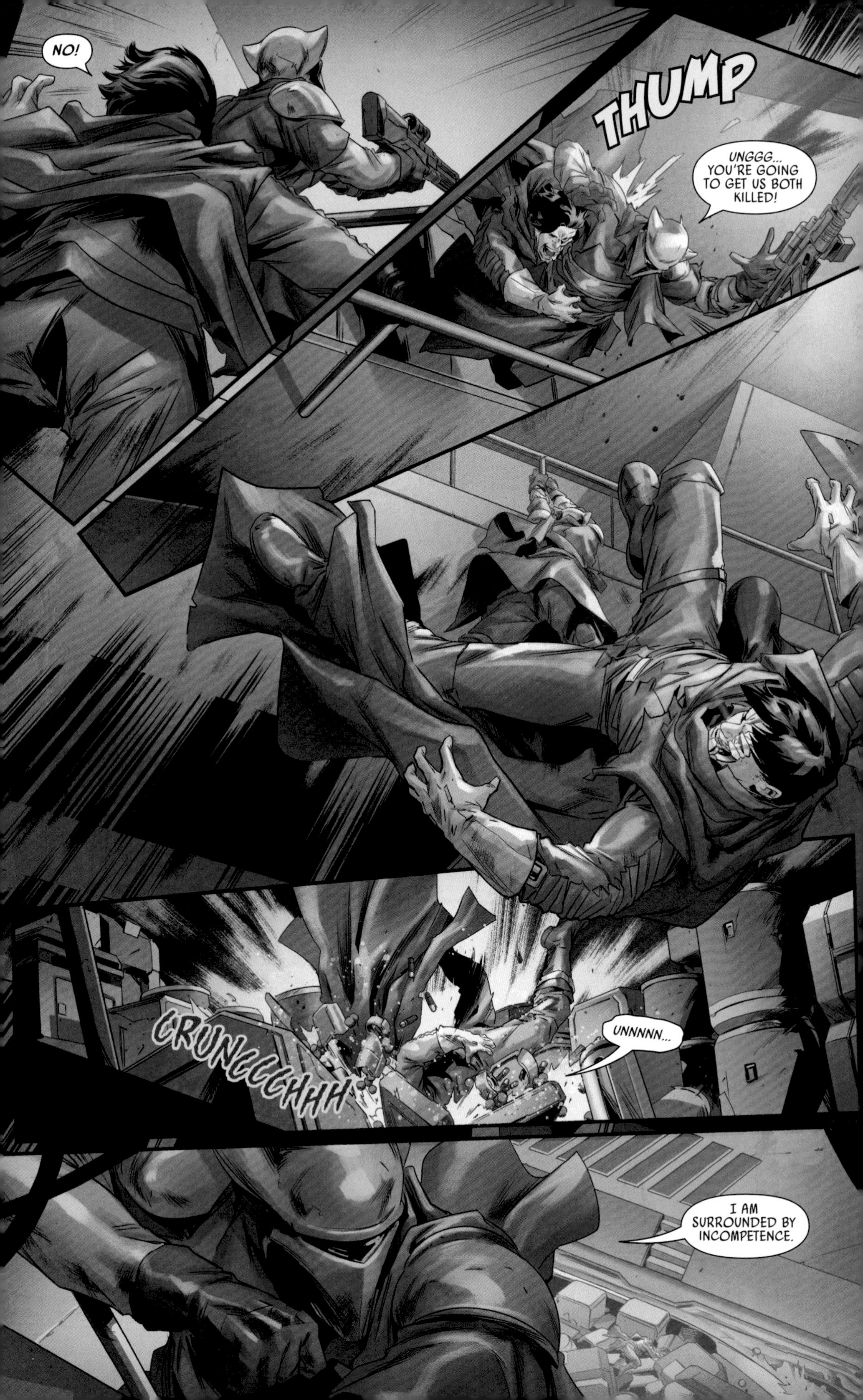
NO!
THUMP
UNGGG... YOU'RE GOING TO GET US BOTH KILLED!
CRUNCCCHHH
UNNNNN...
I AM SURROUNDED BY INCOMPETENCE.

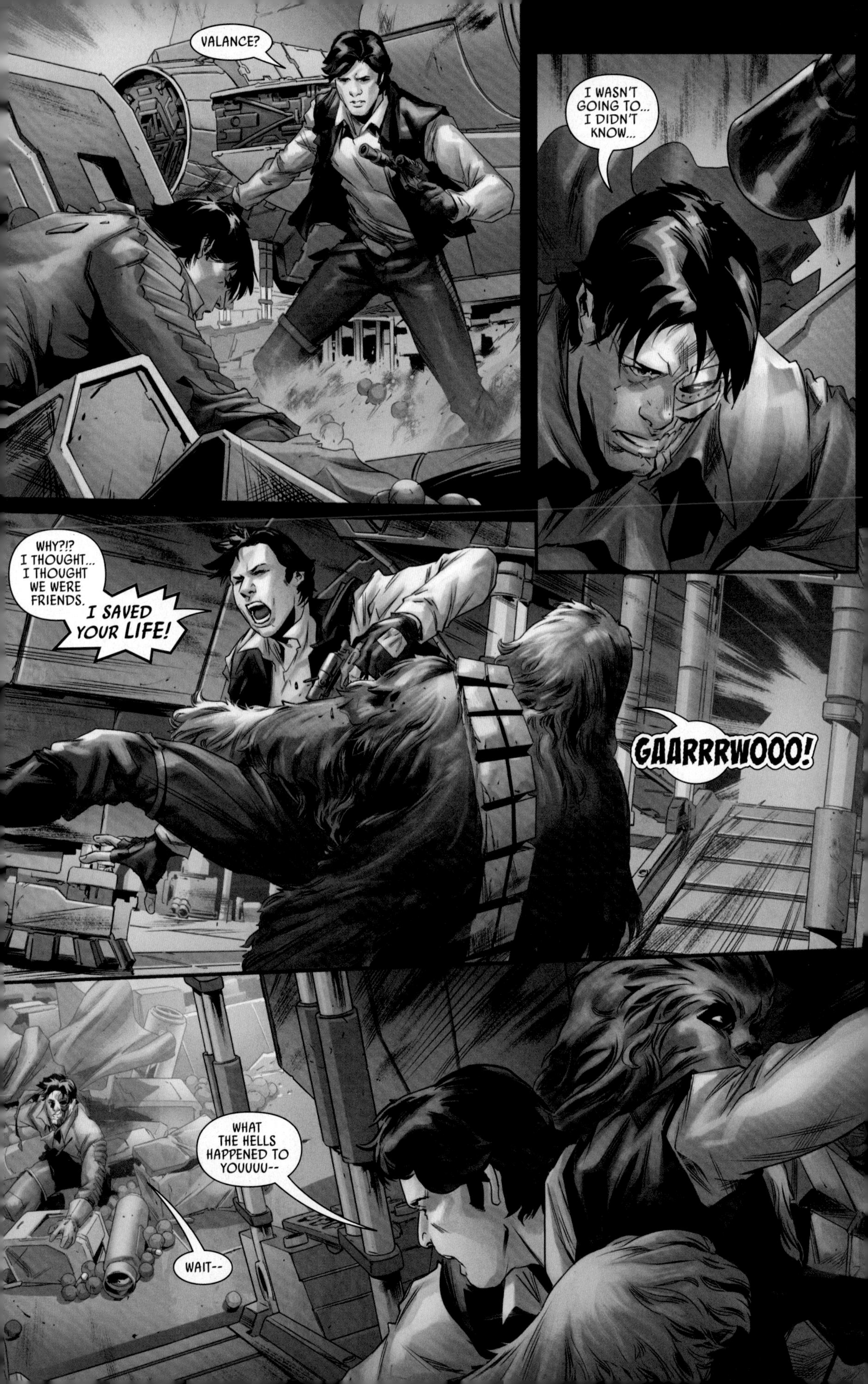
VALANCE?
I WASN'T GOING TO... I DIDN'T KNOW...
WHY?!? I THOUGHT... I THOUGHT WE WERE FRIENDS.
I SAVED YOUR LIFE!
GAARRRWOOO!
WHAT THE HELLS HAPPENED TO YOUUUU--
WAIT--

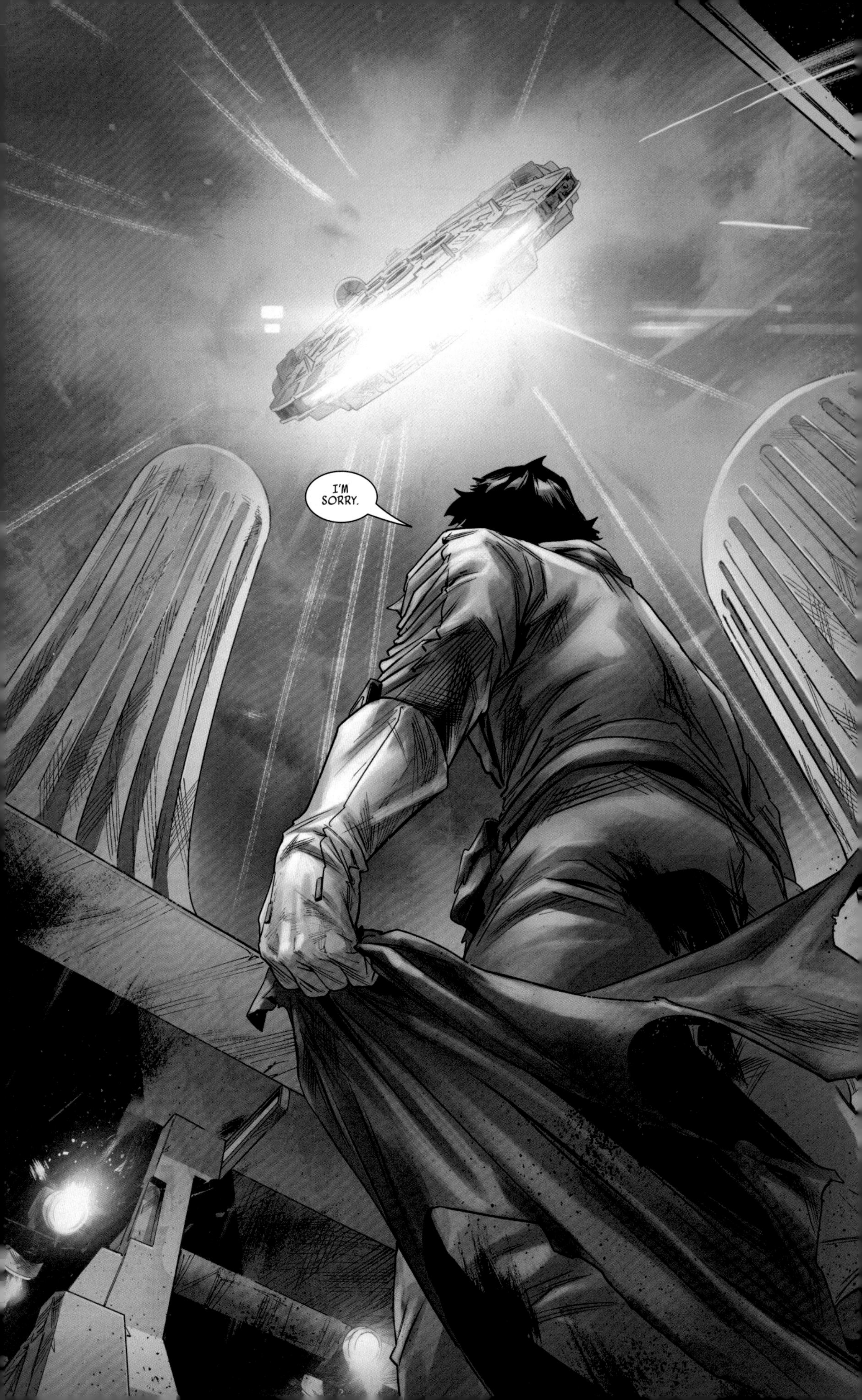
I'M SORRY.

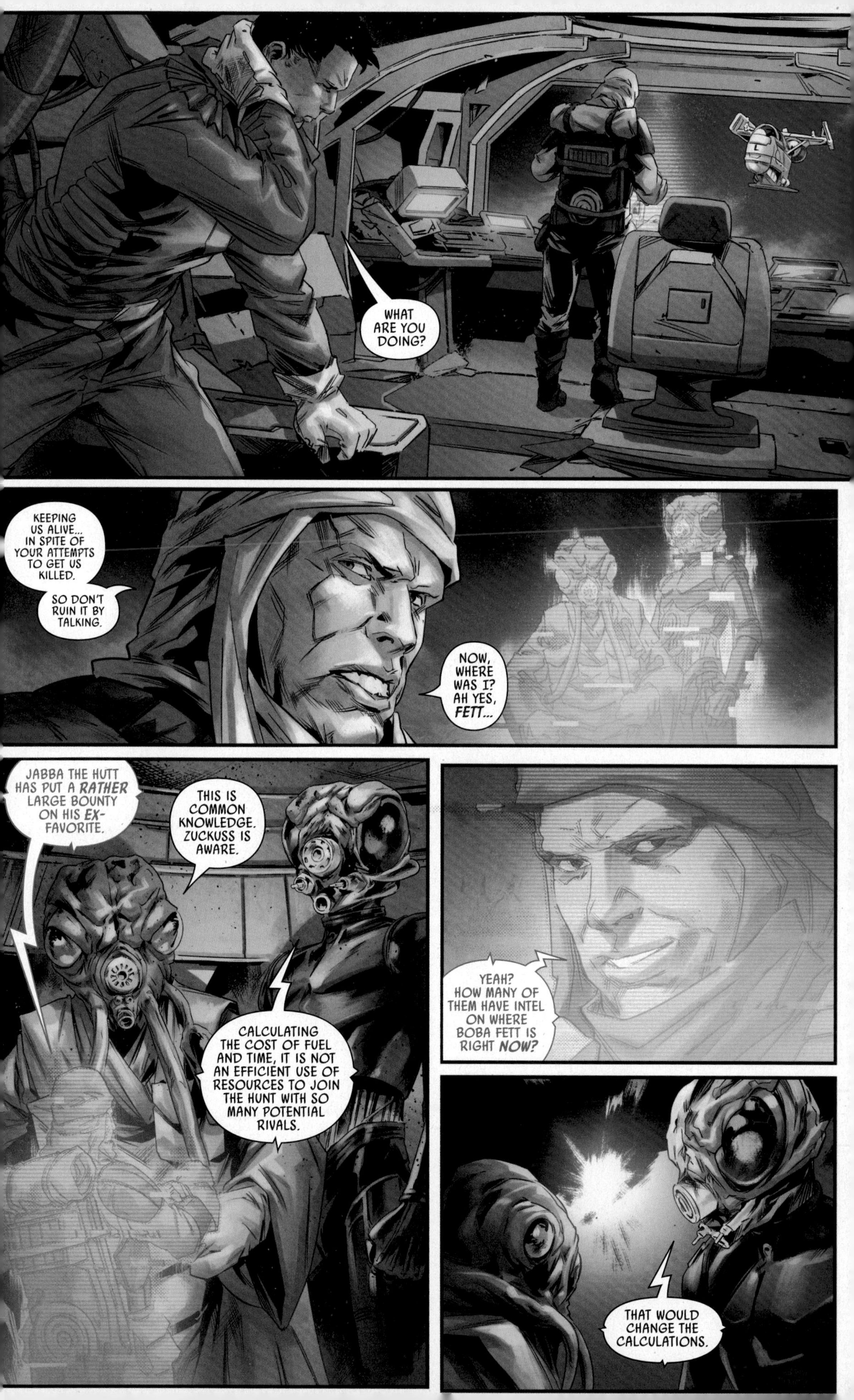
WHAT ARE YOU DOING?
KEEPING US ALIVE... IN SPITE OF YOUR ATTEMPTS TO GET US KILLED.
SO DON'T RUIN IT BY TALKING.
NOW, WHERE WAS I? AH YES, FETT...
JABBA THE HUTT HAS PUT A RATHER LARGE BOUNTY ON HIS EX-FAVORITE.
THIS IS COMMON KNOWLEDGE. ZUCKUSS IS AWARE.
CALCULATING THE COST OF FUEL AND TIME, IT IS NOT AN EFFICIENT USE OF RESOURCES TO JOIN THE HUNT WITH SO MANY POTENTIAL RIVALS.
YEAH? HOW MANY OF THEM HAVE INTEL ON WHERE BOBA FETT IS RIGHT NOW?
THAT WOULD CHANGE THE CALCULATIONS.

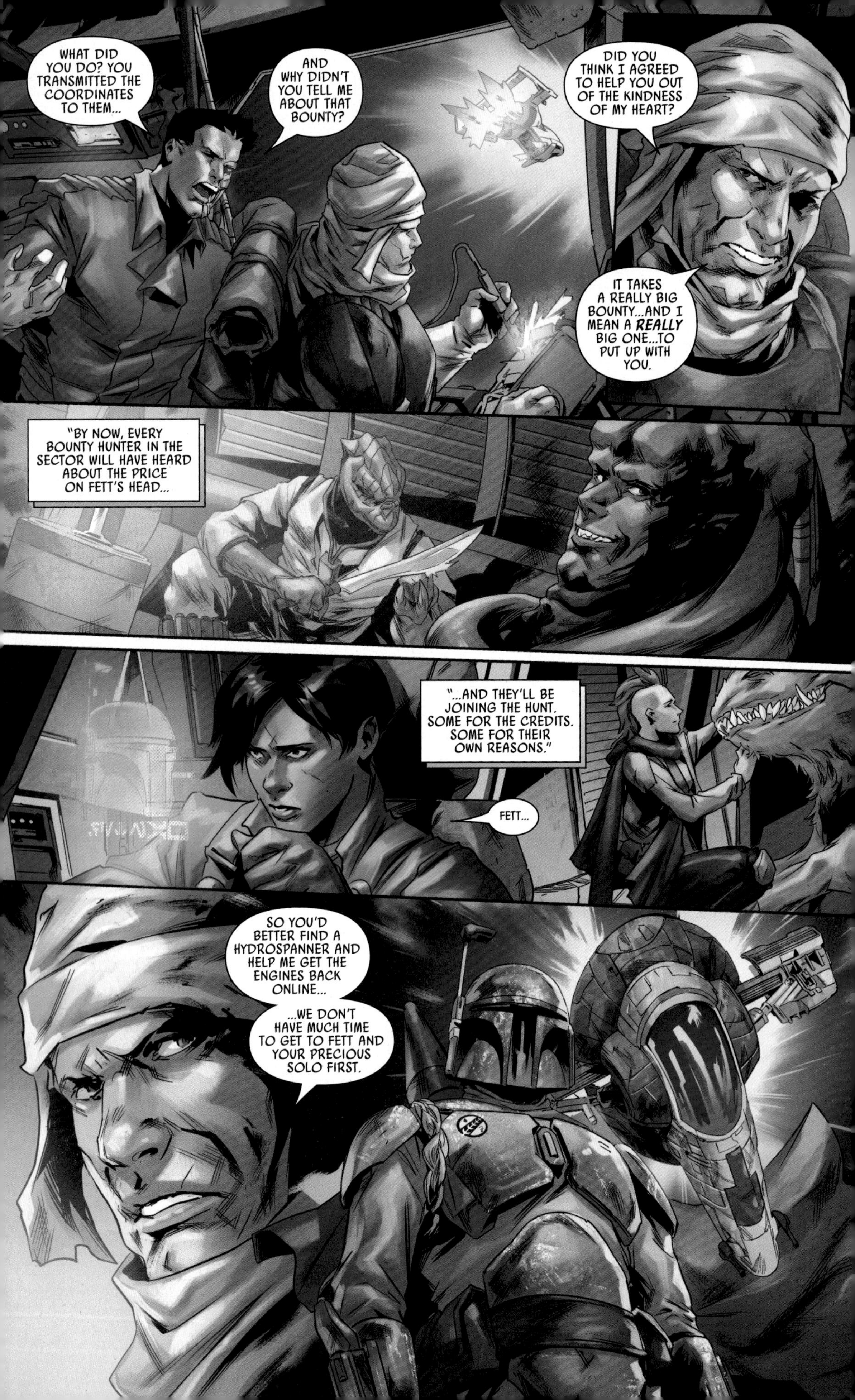
WHAT DID YOU DO? YOU TRANSMITTED THE COORDINATES TO THEM...
AND WHY DIDN'T YOU TELL ME ABOUT THAT BOUNTY?
DID YOU THINK I AGREED TO HELP YOU OUT OF THE KINDNESS OF MY HEART?
IT TAKES A REALLY BIG BOUNTY...AND I MEAN A *REALLY* BIG ONE...TO PUT UP WITH YOU.
"BY NOW, EVERY BOUNTY HUNTER IN THE SECTOR WILL HAVE HEARD ABOUT THE PRICE ON FETT'S HEAD...
"...AND THEY'LL BE JOINING THE HUNT. SOME FOR THE CREDITS. SOME FOR THEIR OWN REASONS."
FETT...
SO YOU'D BETTER FIND A HYDROSPANNER AND HELP ME GET THE ENGINES BACK ONLINE...
...WE DON'T HAVE MUCH TIME TO GET TO FETT AND YOUR PRECIOUS SOLO FIRST.

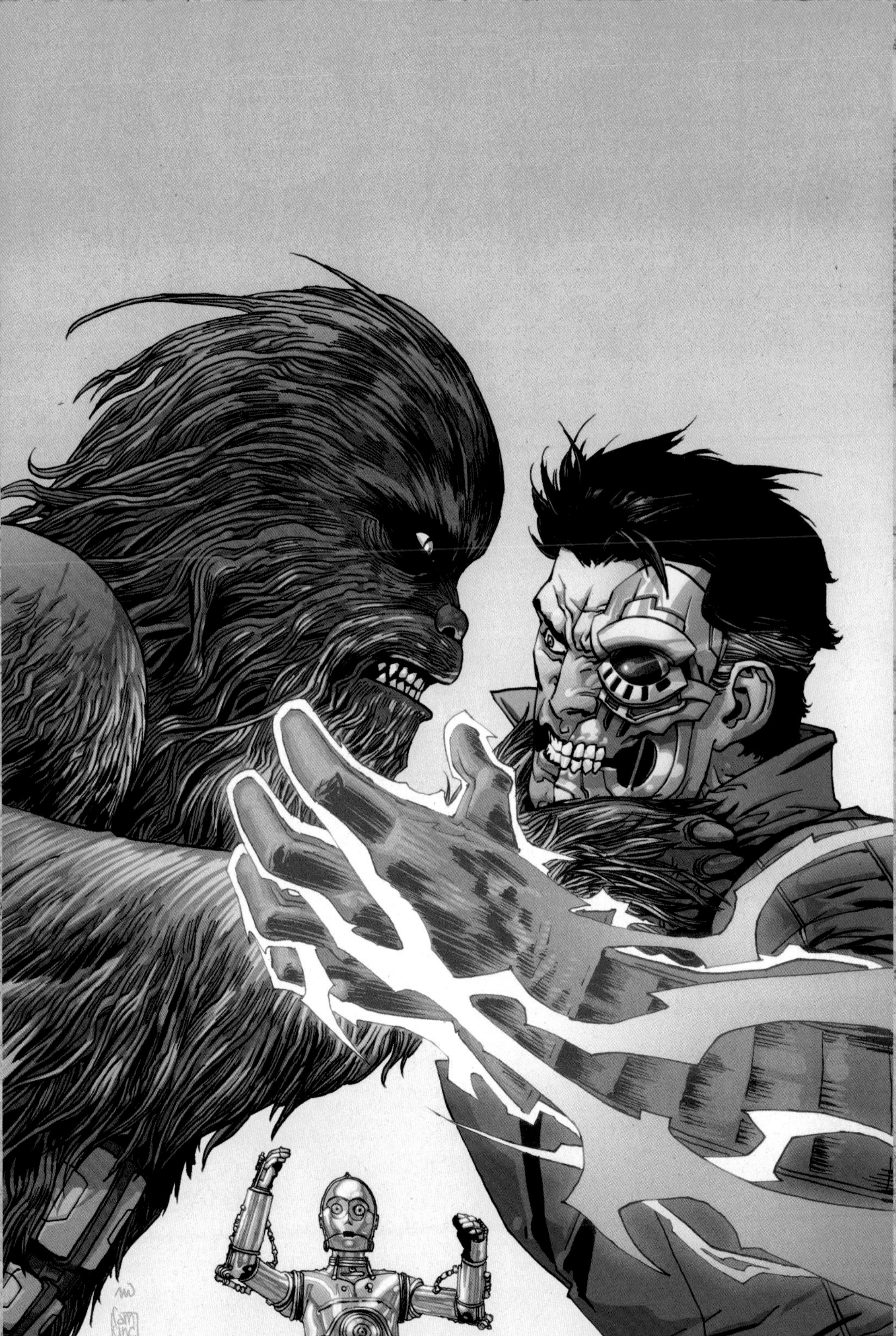

13 – SHOWDOWN ON SMUGGLER'S MOON

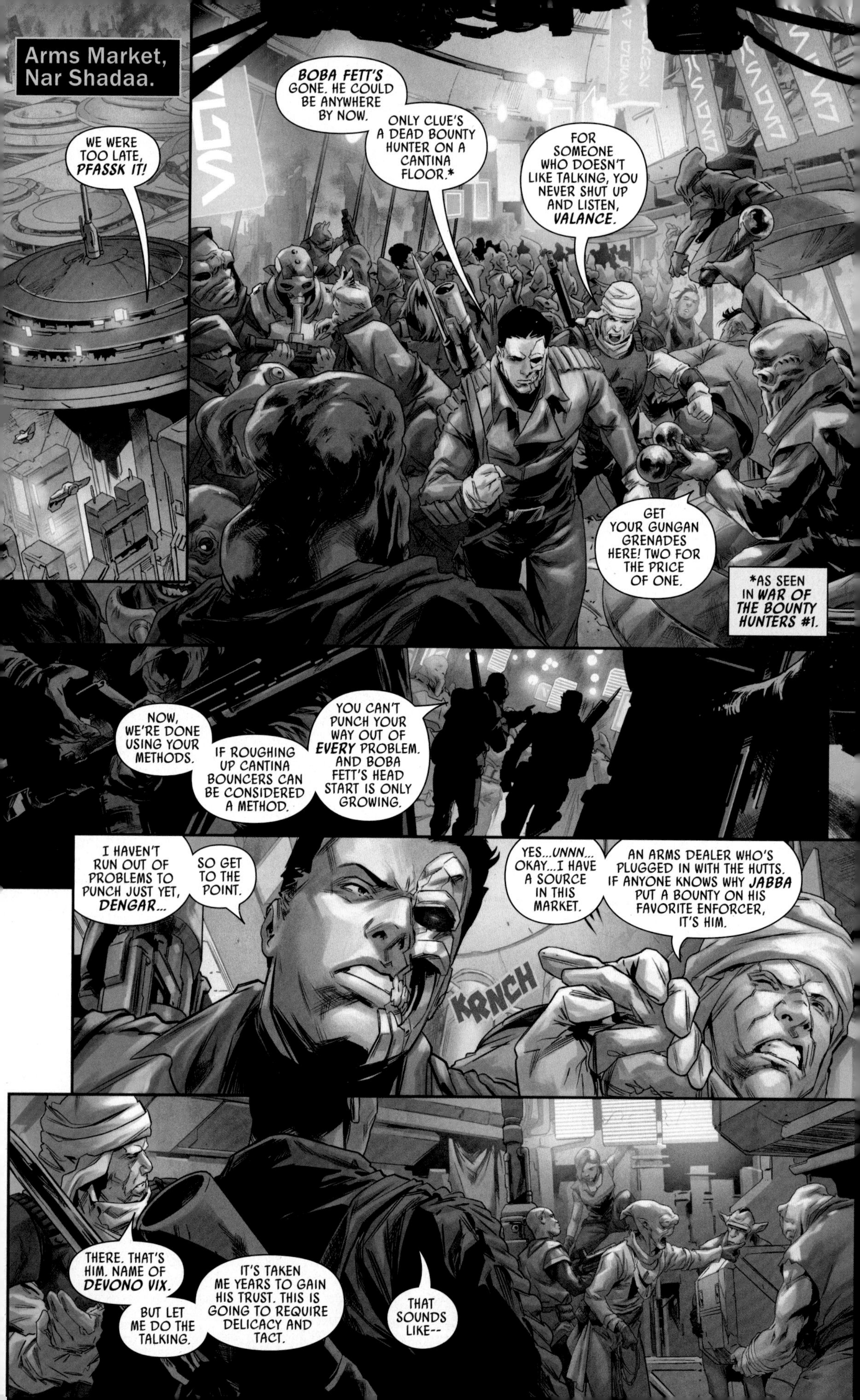
Arms Market, Nar Shadaa.
WE WERE TOO LATE, PFASSK IT!
BOBA FETT'S GONE. HE COULD BE ANYWHERE BY NOW.
ONLY CLUE'S A DEAD BOUNTY HUNTER ON A CANTINA FLOOR.*
FOR SOMEONE WHO DOESN'T LIKE TALKING, YOU NEVER SHUT UP AND LISTEN, VALANCE.
GET YOUR GUNGAN GRENADES HERE! TWO FOR THE PRICE OF ONE.
*AS SEEN IN WAR OF THE BOUNTY HUNTERS #1.
NOW, WE'RE DONE USING YOUR METHODS.
IF ROUGHING UP CANTINA BOUNCERS CAN BE CONSIDERED A METHOD.
YOU CAN'T PUNCH YOUR WAY OUT OF EVERY PROBLEM. AND BOBA FETT'S HEAD START IS ONLY GROWING.
I HAVEN'T RUN OUT OF PROBLEMS TO PUNCH JUST YET, DENGAR...
SO GET TO THE POINT.
YES...UNNN... OKAY...I HAVE A SOURCE IN THIS MARKET.
AN ARMS DEALER WHO'S PLUGGED IN WITH THE HUTTS. IF ANYONE KNOWS WHY JABBA PUT A BOUNTY ON HIS FAVORITE ENFORCER, IT'S HIM.
KRNCH
THERE. THAT'S HIM. NAME OF DEVONO VIX.
BUT LET ME DO THE TALKING.
IT'S TAKEN ME YEARS TO GAIN HIS TRUST. THIS IS GOING TO REQUIRE DELICACY AND TACT.
THAT SOUNDS LIKE--

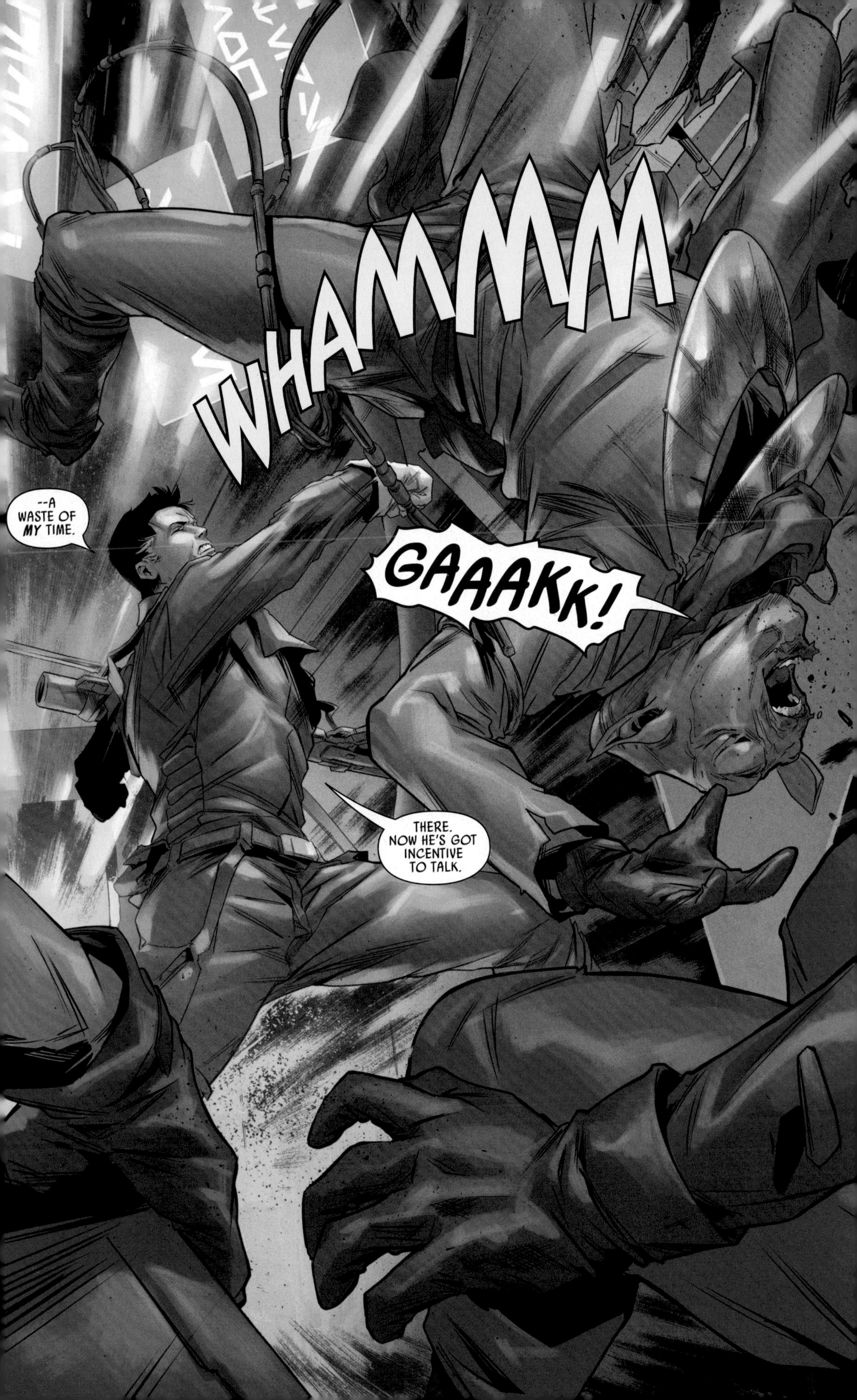
WHAMMMM
--A WASTE OF MY TIME.
GAAAKK!
THERE. NOW HE'S GOT INCENTIVE TO TALK.

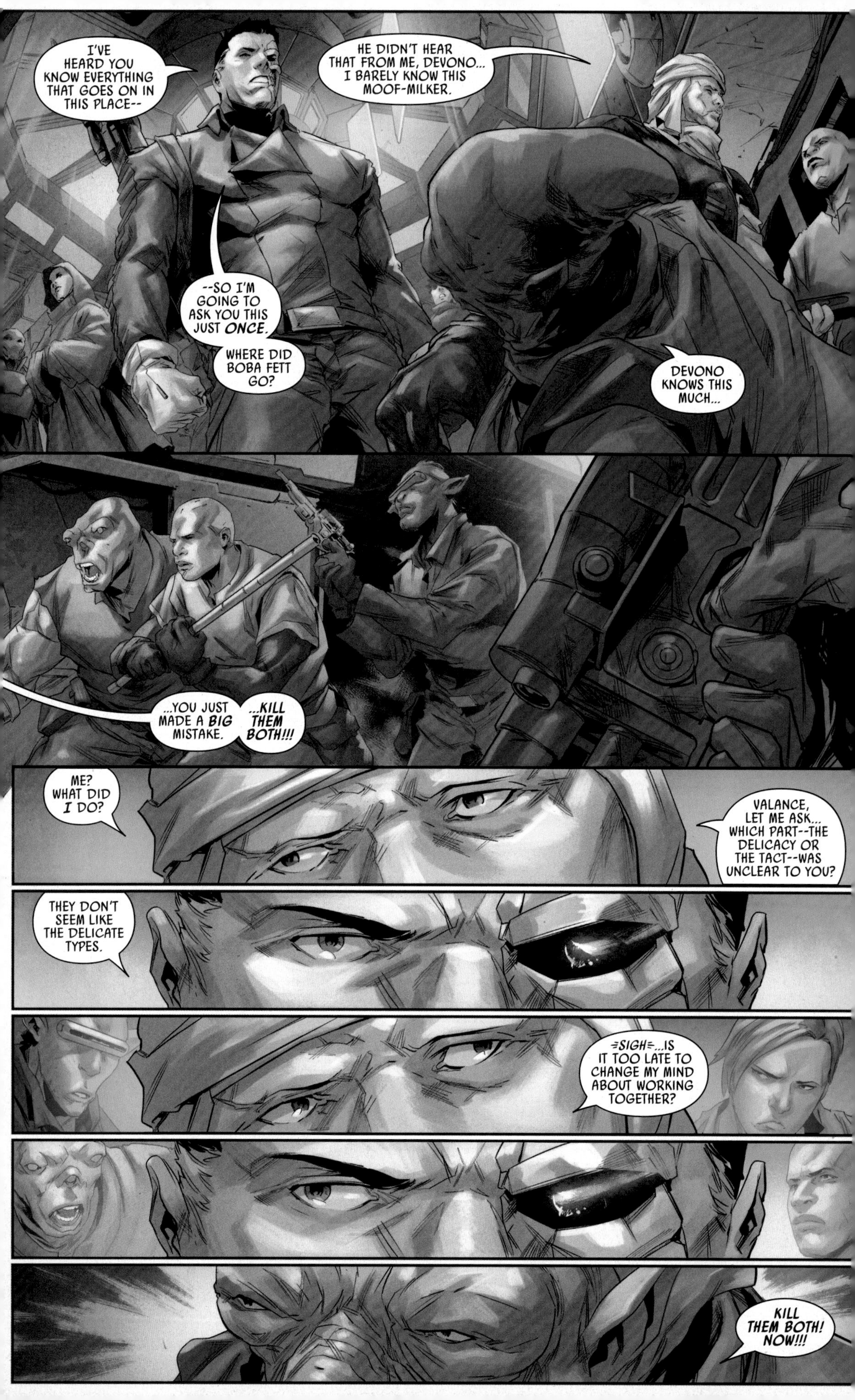
I'VE HEARD YOU KNOW EVERYTHING THAT GOES ON IN THIS PLACE--
HE DIDN'T HEAR THAT FROM ME, DEVONO... I BARELY KNOW THIS MOOF-MILKER.
--SO I'M GOING TO ASK YOU THIS JUST ONCE.
WHERE DID BOBA FETT GO?
DEVONO KNOWS THIS MUCH...
...YOU JUST MADE A BIG MISTAKE.
...KILL THEM BOTH!!!
ME? WHAT DID I DO?
VALANCE, LET ME ASK... WHICH PART--THE DELICACY OR THE TACT--WAS UNCLEAR TO YOU?
THEY DON'T SEEM LIKE THE DELICATE TYPES.
=SIGH=...IS IT TOO LATE TO CHANGE MY MIND ABOUT WORKING TOGETHER?
KILL THEM BOTH! NOW!!!

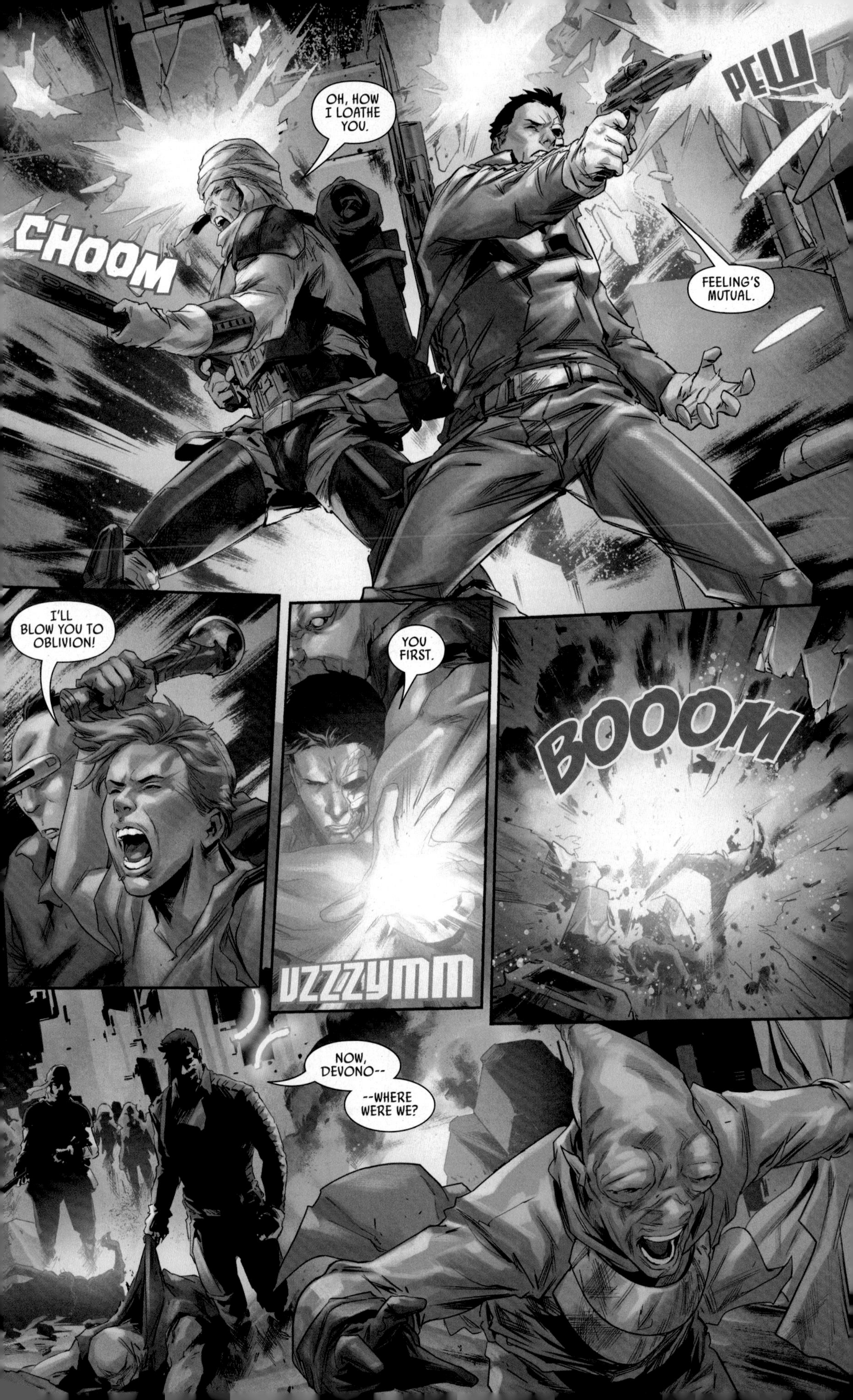
OH, HOW I LOATHE YOU.
CHOOM
PEW
FEELING'S MUTUAL.
I'LL BLOW YOU TO OBLIVION!
YOU FIRST.
VZZZYMM
BOOOM
NOW, DEVONO--
--WHERE WERE WE?

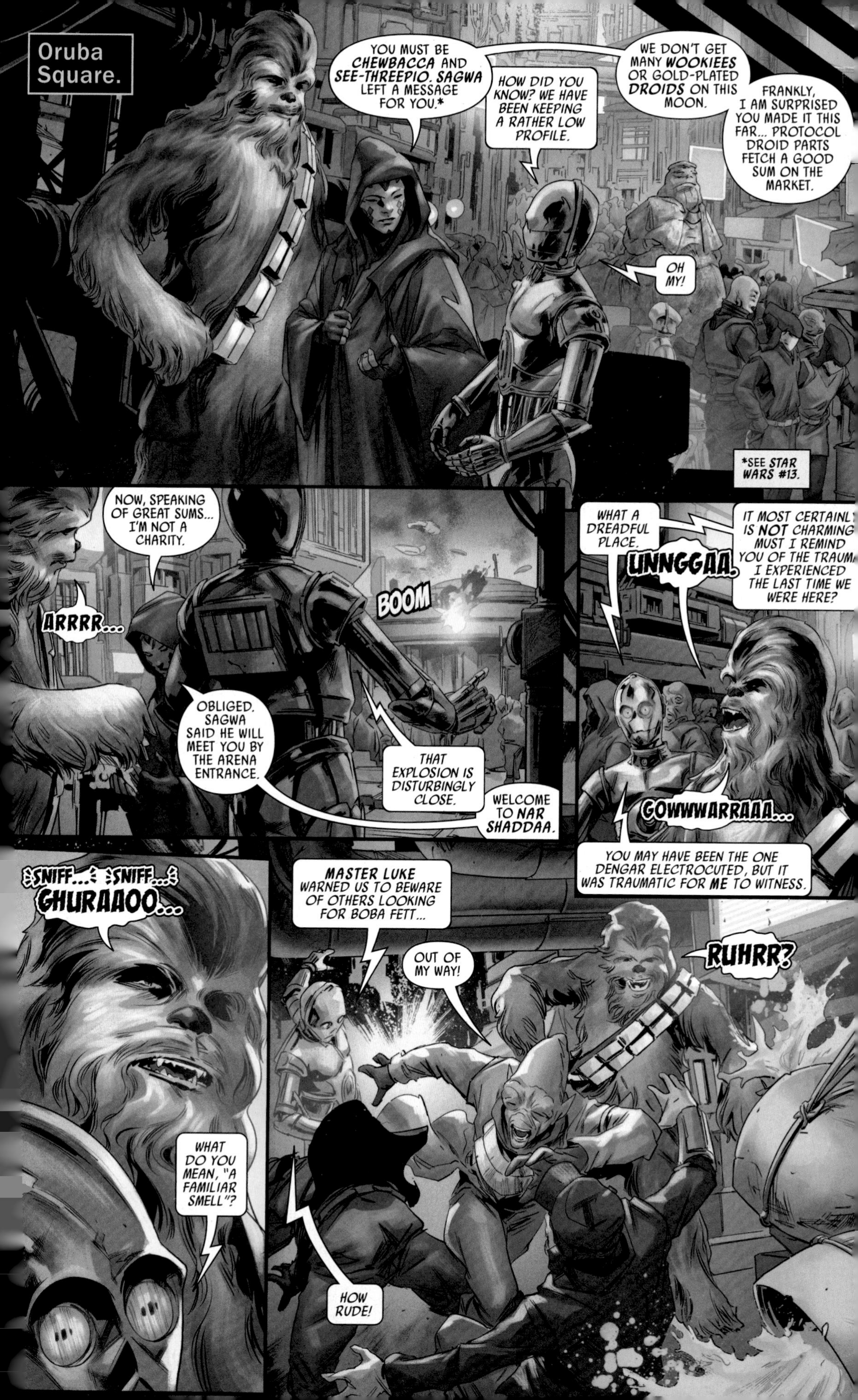

Oruba Square.
YOU MUST BE CHEWBACCA AND SEE-THREEPIO. SAGWA LEFT A MESSAGE FOR YOU.*
HOW DID YOU KNOW? WE HAVE BEEN KEEPING A RATHER LOW PROFILE.
WE DON'T GET MANY WOOKIEES OR GOLD-PLATED DROIDS ON THIS MOON.
FRANKLY, I AM SURPRISED YOU MADE IT THIS FAR... PROTOCOL DROID PARTS FETCH A GOOD SUM ON THE MARKET.
OH MY!
*SEE STAR WARS #13.
NOW, SPEAKING OF GREAT SUMS... I'M NOT A CHARITY.
ARRRR...
BOOM
OBLIGED. SAGWA SAID HE WILL MEET YOU BY THE ARENA ENTRANCE.
THAT EXPLOSION IS DISTURBINGLY CLOSE.
WELCOME TO NAR SHADDAA.
WHAT A DREADFUL PLACE.
UNNGGAA.
IT MOST CERTAINL IS NOT CHARMING MUST I REMIND YOU OF THE TRAUM I EXPERIENCED THE LAST TIME WE WERE HERE?
GOWWWARRAAA...
YOU MAY HAVE BEEN THE ONE DENGAR ELECTROCUTED, BUT IT WAS TRAUMATIC FOR ME TO WITNESS.
SNIFF... SNIFF...
GHURAAOO...
WHAT DO YOU MEAN, "A FAMILIAR SMELL"?
MASTER LUKE WARNED US TO BEWARE OF OTHERS LOOKING FOR BOBA FETT...
OUT OF MY WAY!
RUHRR?
HOW RUDE!

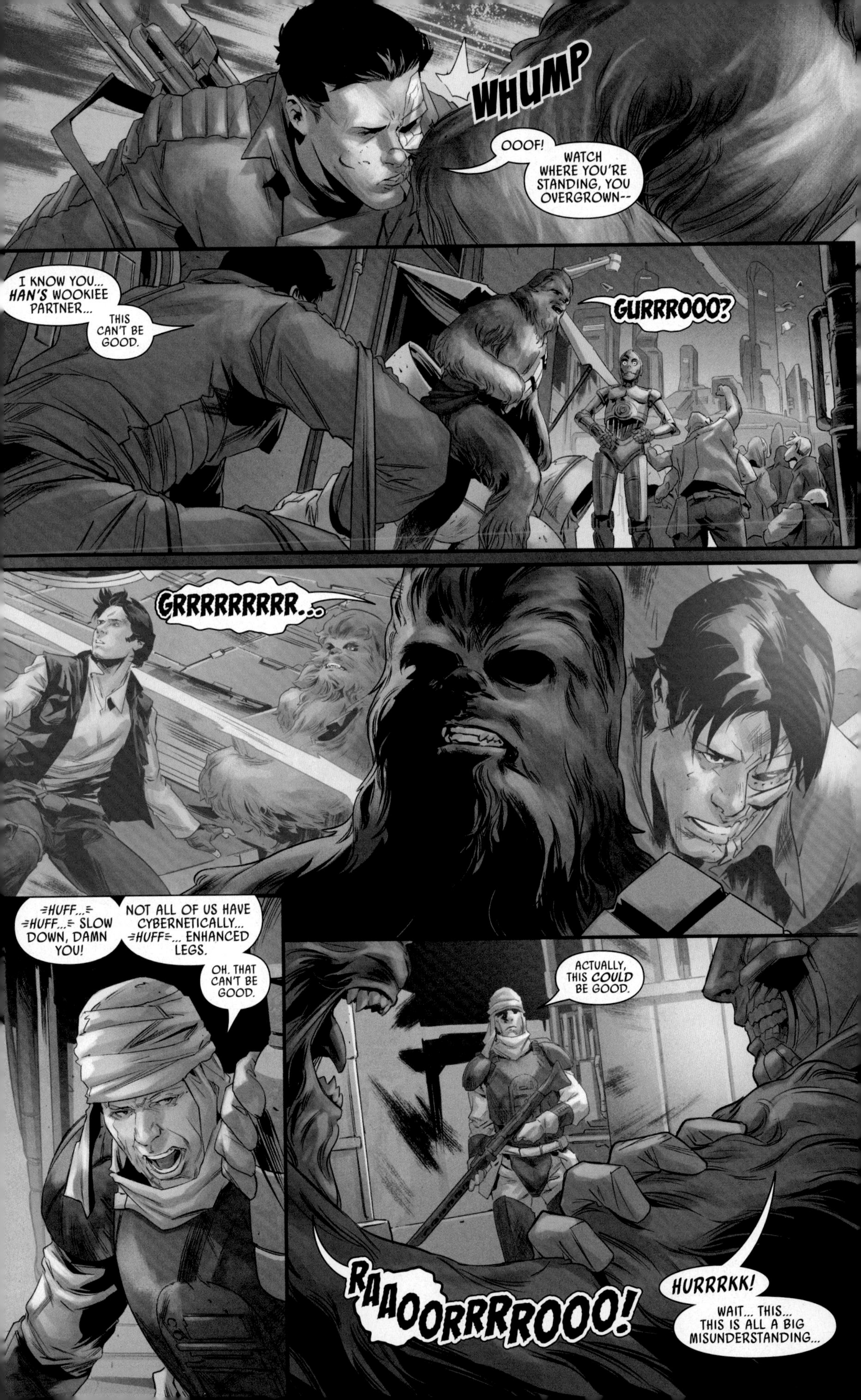
WHUMP
OOOF!
WATCH WHERE YOU'RE STANDING, YOU OVERGROWN--
I KNOW YOU... HAN'S WOOKIEE PARTNER...
THIS CAN'T BE GOOD.
GURRROOO?
GRRRRRRRRR...
=HUFF...= =HUFF...= SLOW DOWN, DAMN YOU!
NOT ALL OF US HAVE CYBERNETICALLY... =HUFF=... ENHANCED LEGS.
OH. THAT CAN'T BE GOOD.
ACTUALLY, THIS COULD BE GOOD.
RAAOORRRROOO!
HURRRKK!
WAIT... THIS... THIS IS ALL A BIG MISUNDERSTANDING...

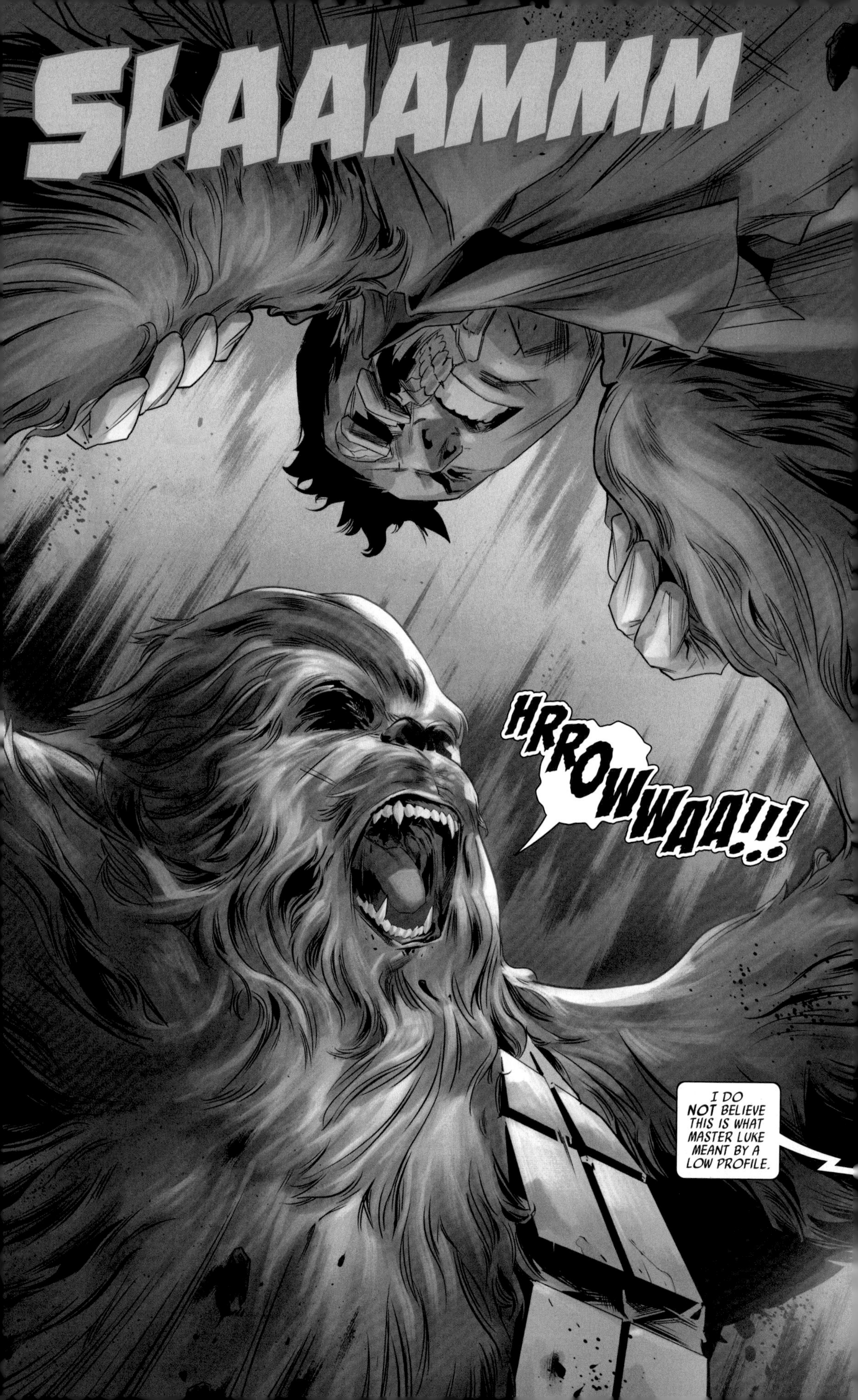
SLAAAMMM
HRROWWAA!!!
I DO NOT BELIEVE THIS IS WHAT MASTER LUKE MEANT BY A LOW PROFILE.

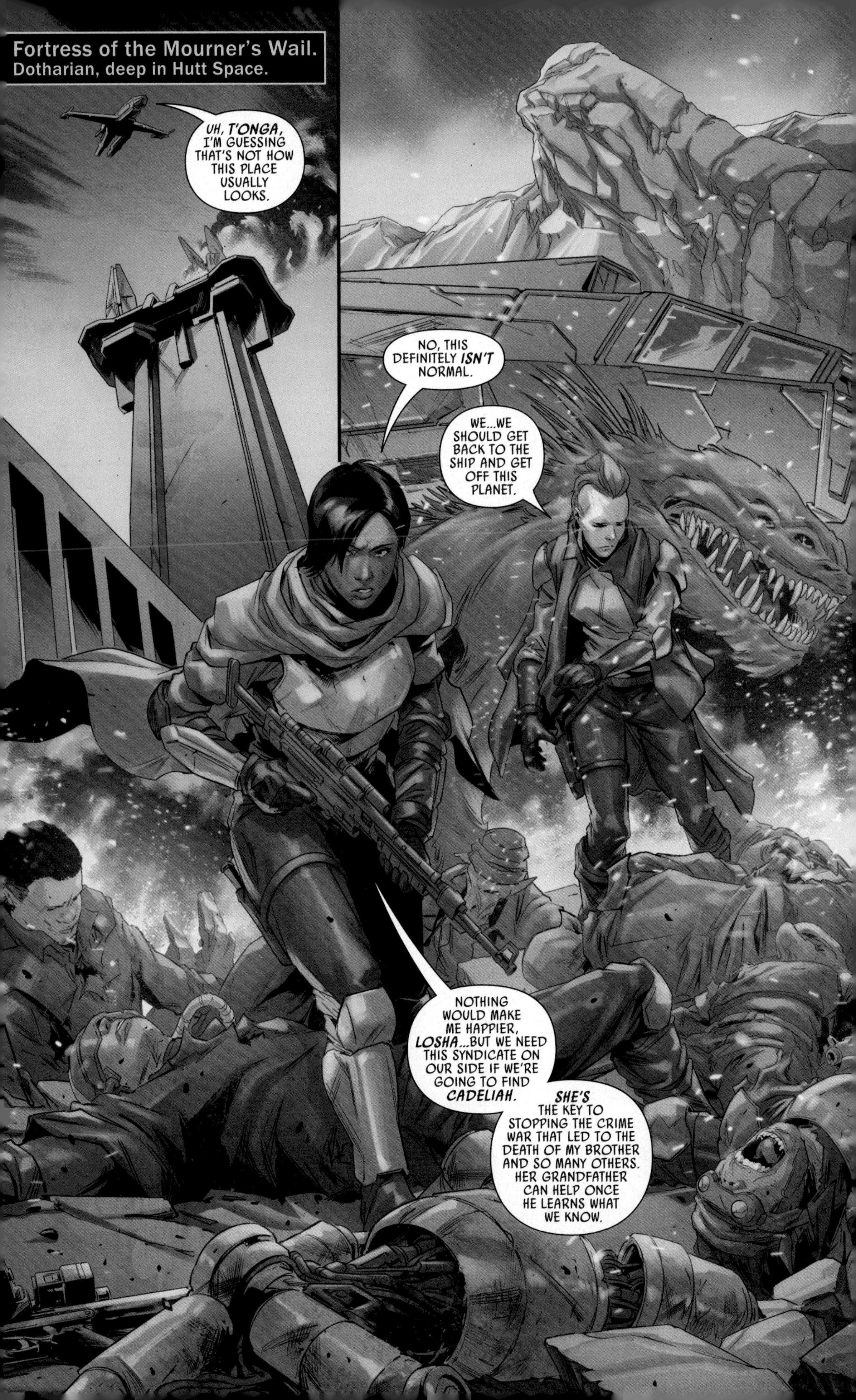
Fortress of the Mourner's Wail.
Dotharian, deep in Hutt Space.
UH, T'ONGA, I'M GUESSING THAT'S NOT HOW THIS PLACE USUALLY LOOKS.
NO, THIS DEFINITELY ISN'T NORMAL.
WE...WE SHOULD GET BACK TO THE SHIP AND GET OFF THIS PLANET.
NOTHING WOULD MAKE ME HAPPIER, LOSHA...BUT WE NEED THIS SYNDICATE ON OUR SIDE IF WE'RE GOING TO FIND CADELIAH.
SHE'S THE KEY TO STOPPING THE CRIME WAR THAT LED TO THE DEATH OF MY BROTHER AND SO MANY OTHERS. HER GRANDFATHER CAN HELP ONCE HE LEARNS WHAT WE KNOW.

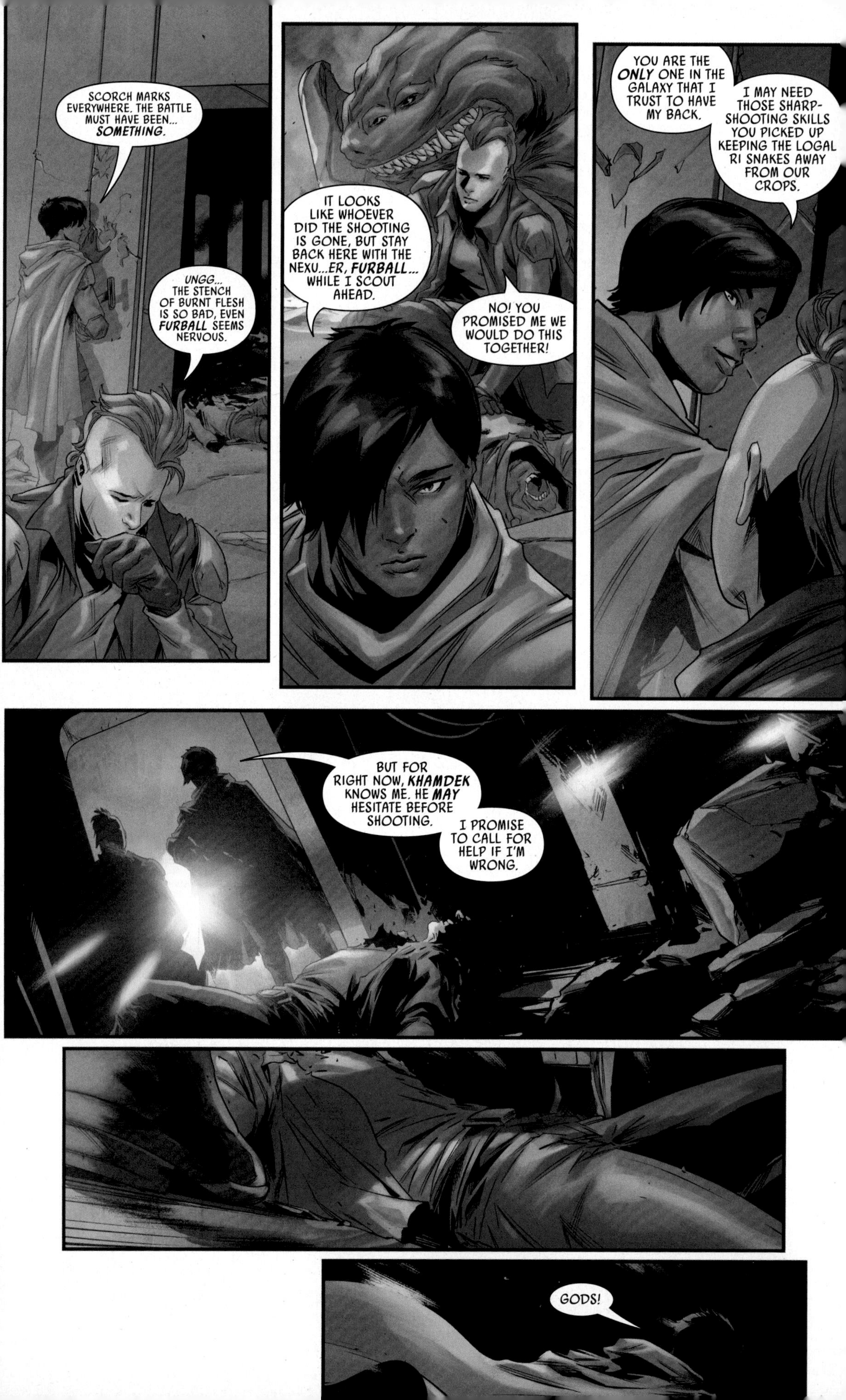
SCORCH MARKS EVERYWHERE. THE BATTLE MUST HAVE BEEN... SOMETHING.
UNGG... THE STENCH OF BURNT FLESH IS SO BAD, EVEN FURBALL SEEMS NERVOUS.
IT LOOKS LIKE WHOEVER DID THE SHOOTING IS GONE, BUT STAY BACK HERE WITH THE NEXU...ER, FURBALL... WHILE I SCOUT AHEAD.
NO! YOU PROMISED ME WE WOULD DO THIS TOGETHER!
YOU ARE THE ONLY ONE IN THE GALAXY THAT I TRUST TO HAVE MY BACK.
I MAY NEED THOSE SHARP-SHOOTING SKILLS YOU PICKED UP KEEPING THE LOGAL RI SNAKES AWAY FROM OUR CROPS.
BUT FOR RIGHT NOW, KHAMDEK KNOWS ME. HE MAY HESITATE BEFORE SHOOTING.
I PROMISE TO CALL FOR HELP IF I'M WRONG.
GODS!

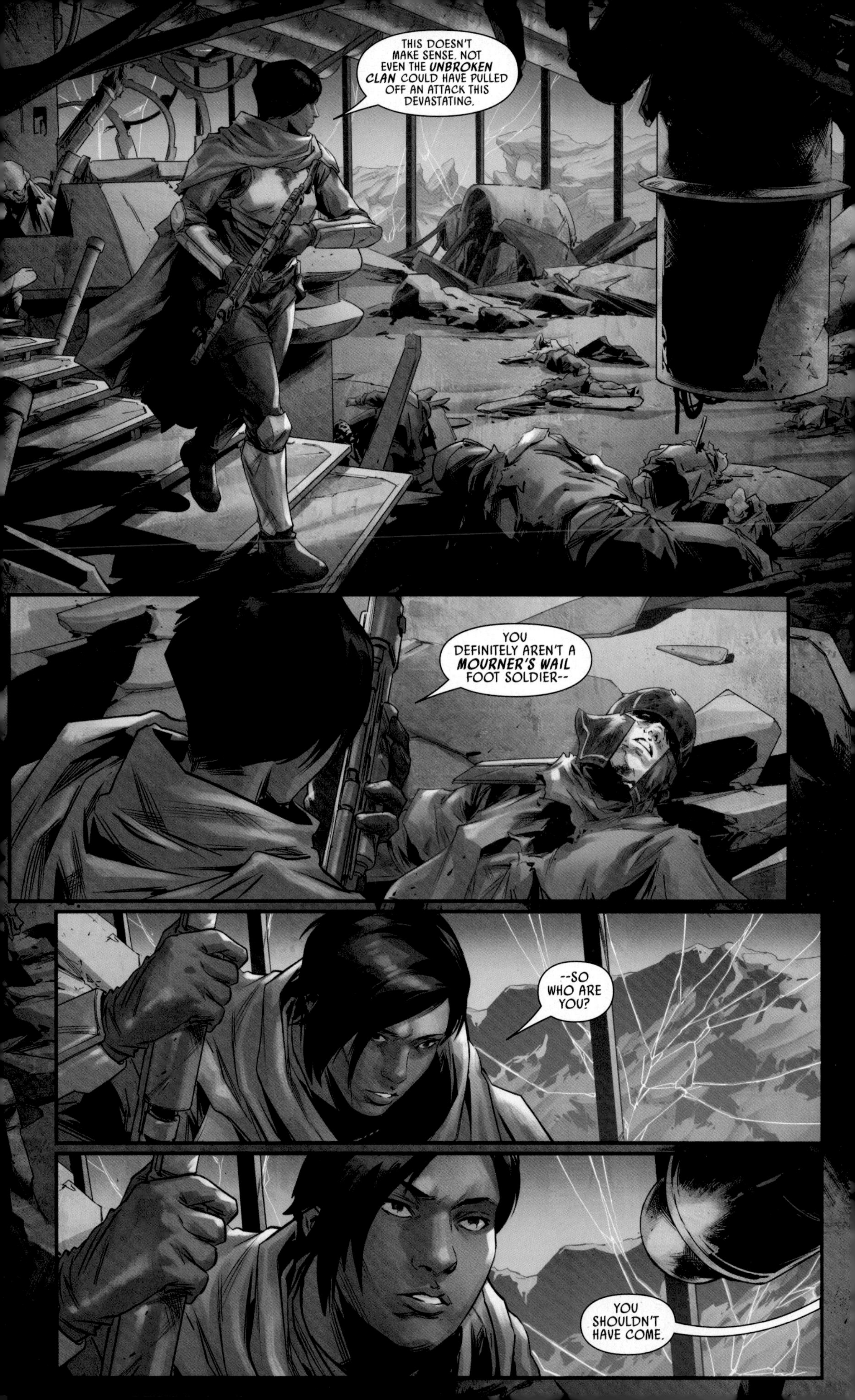
THIS DOESN'T MAKE SENSE. NOT EVEN THE UNBROKEN CLAN COULD HAVE PULLED OFF AN ATTACK THIS DEVASTATING.
YOU DEFINITELY AREN'T A MOURNER'S WAIL FOOT SOLDIER--
--SO WHO ARE YOU?
YOU SHOULDN'T HAVE COME.

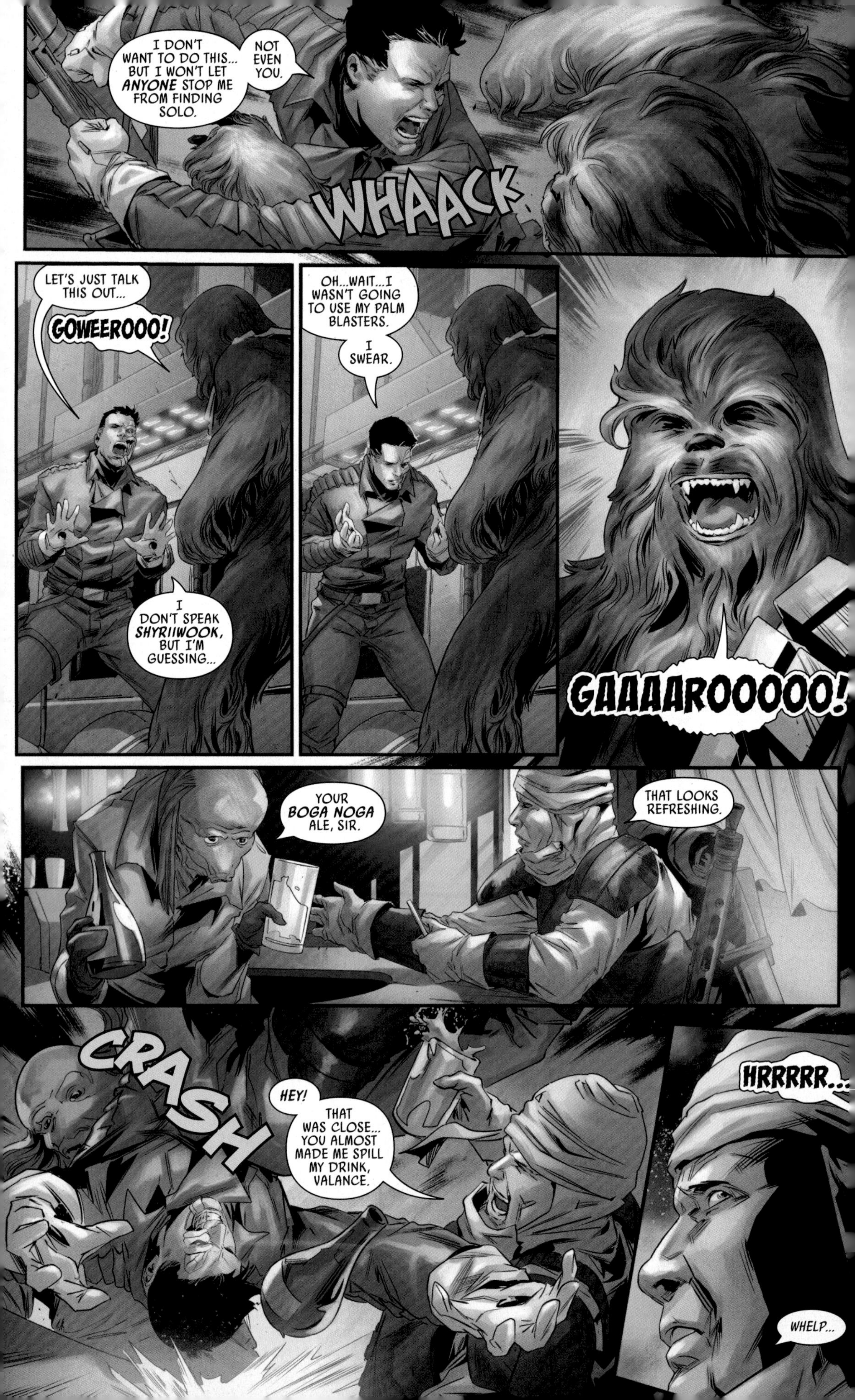
I DON'T WANT TO DO THIS... BUT I WON'T LET ANYONE STOP ME FROM FINDING SOLO.
NOT EVEN YOU.
WHAACK
LET'S JUST TALK THIS OUT...
GOWEEROOO!
I DON'T SPEAK SHYRIIWOOK, BUT I'M GUESSING...
OH...WAIT...I WASN'T GOING TO USE MY PALM BLASTERS.
I SWEAR.
GAAAAROOOOO!
YOUR BOGA NOGA ALE, SIR.
THAT LOOKS REFRESHING.
CRASH
HEY!
THAT WAS CLOSE... YOU ALMOST MADE ME SPILL MY DRINK, VALANCE.
HRRRRR...
WHELP...

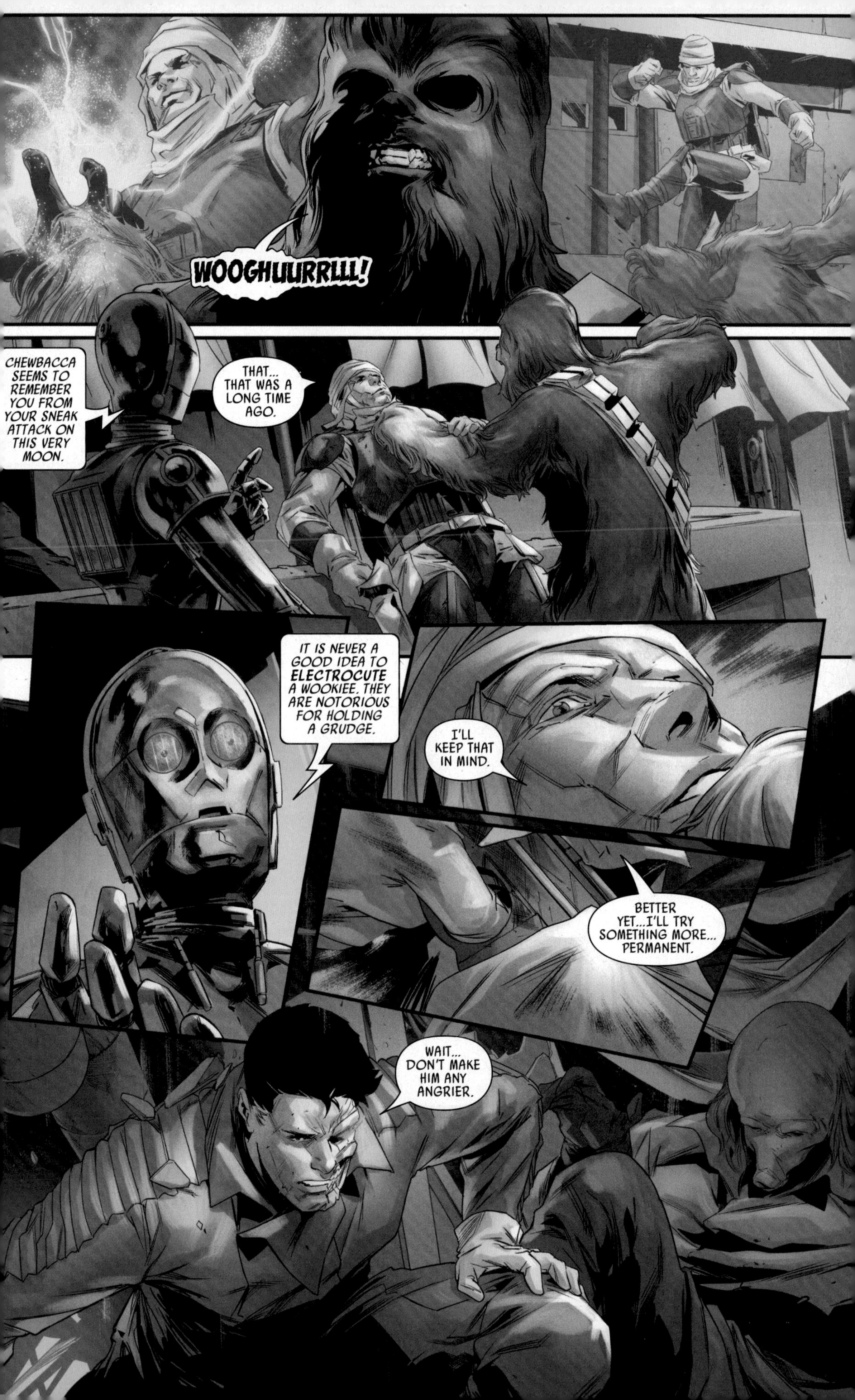
WOOGHUURRLLL!
CHEWBACCA SEEMS TO REMEMBER YOU FROM YOUR SNEAK ATTACK ON THIS VERY MOON.
THAT... THAT WAS A LONG TIME AGO.
IT IS NEVER A GOOD IDEA TO ELECTROCUTE A WOOKIEE. THEY ARE NOTORIOUS FOR HOLDING A GRUDGE.
I'LL KEEP THAT IN MIND.
BETTER YET...I'LL TRY SOMETHING MORE... PERMANENT.
WAIT... DON'T MAKE HIM ANY ANGRIER.

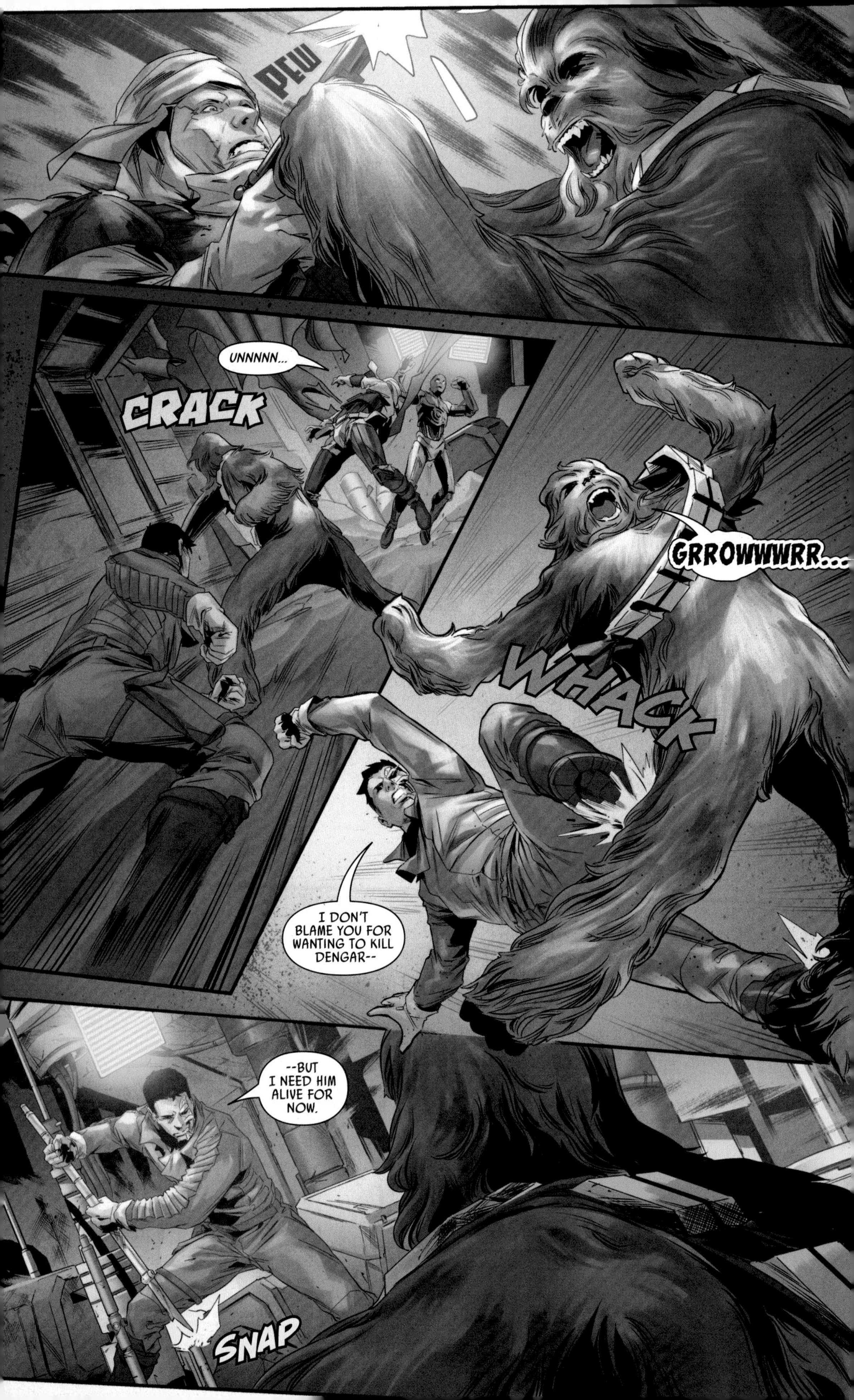
PEW
UNNNNN...
CRACK
GRROWWWRR...
WHACK
I DON'T BLAME YOU FOR WANTING TO KILL DENGAR--
--BUT I NEED HIM ALIVE FOR NOW.
SNAP

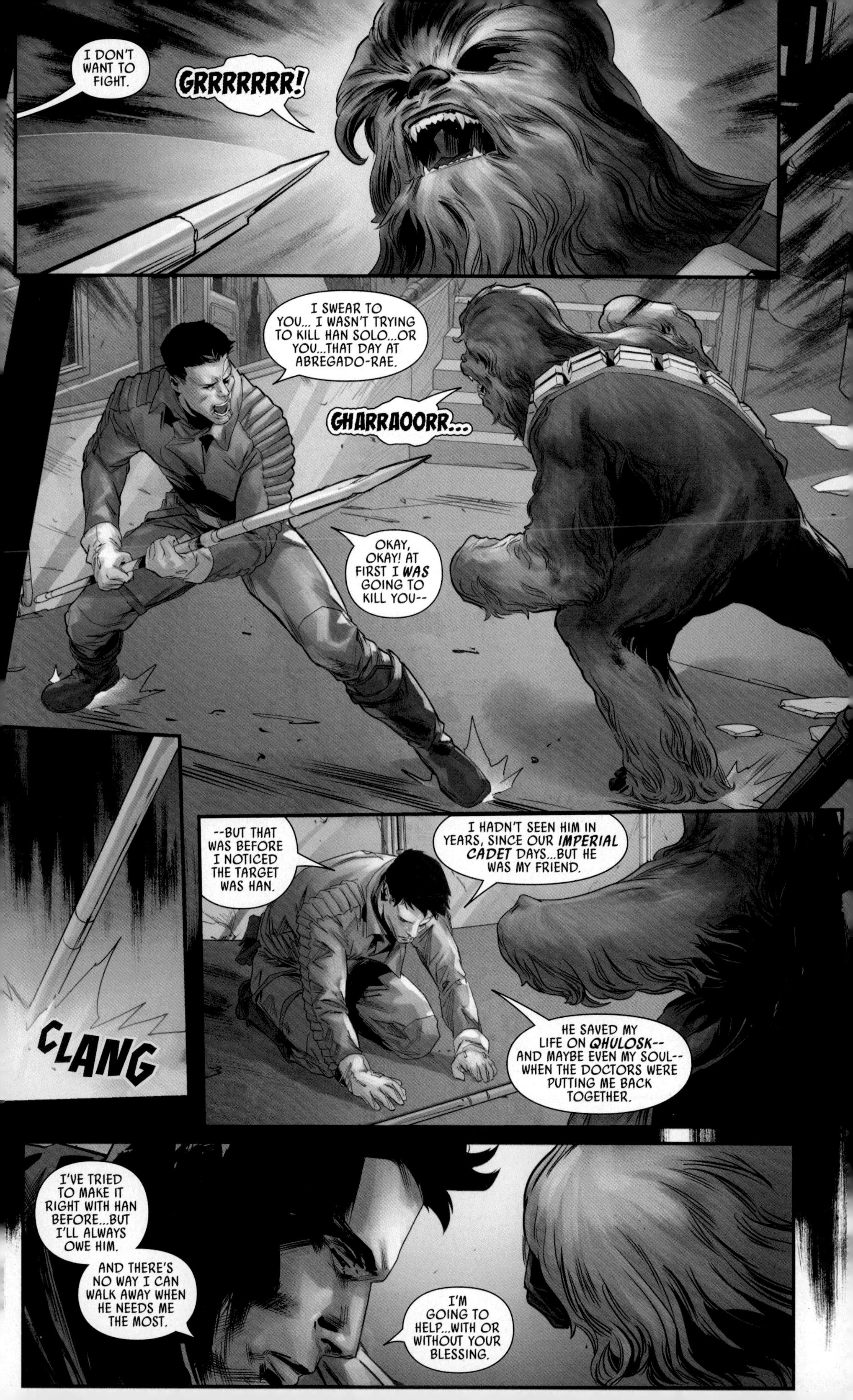
I DON'T WANT TO FIGHT.
GRRRRRRR!
I SWEAR TO YOU... I WASN'T TRYING TO KILL HAN SOLO...OR YOU...THAT DAY AT ABREGADO-RAE.
GHARRAOORR...
OKAY, OKAY! AT FIRST I WAS GOING TO KILL YOU--
CLANG
--BUT THAT WAS BEFORE I NOTICED THE TARGET WAS HAN.
I HADN'T SEEN HIM IN YEARS, SINCE OUR IMPERIAL CADET DAYS...BUT HE WAS MY FRIEND.
HE SAVED MY LIFE ON QHULOSK--AND MAYBE EVEN MY SOUL--WHEN THE DOCTORS WERE PUTTING ME BACK TOGETHER.
I'VE TRIED TO MAKE IT RIGHT WITH HAN BEFORE...BUT I'LL ALWAYS OWE HIM.
AND THERE'S NO WAY I CAN WALK AWAY WHEN HE NEEDS ME THE MOST.
I'M GOING TO HELP...WITH OR WITHOUT YOUR BLESSING.

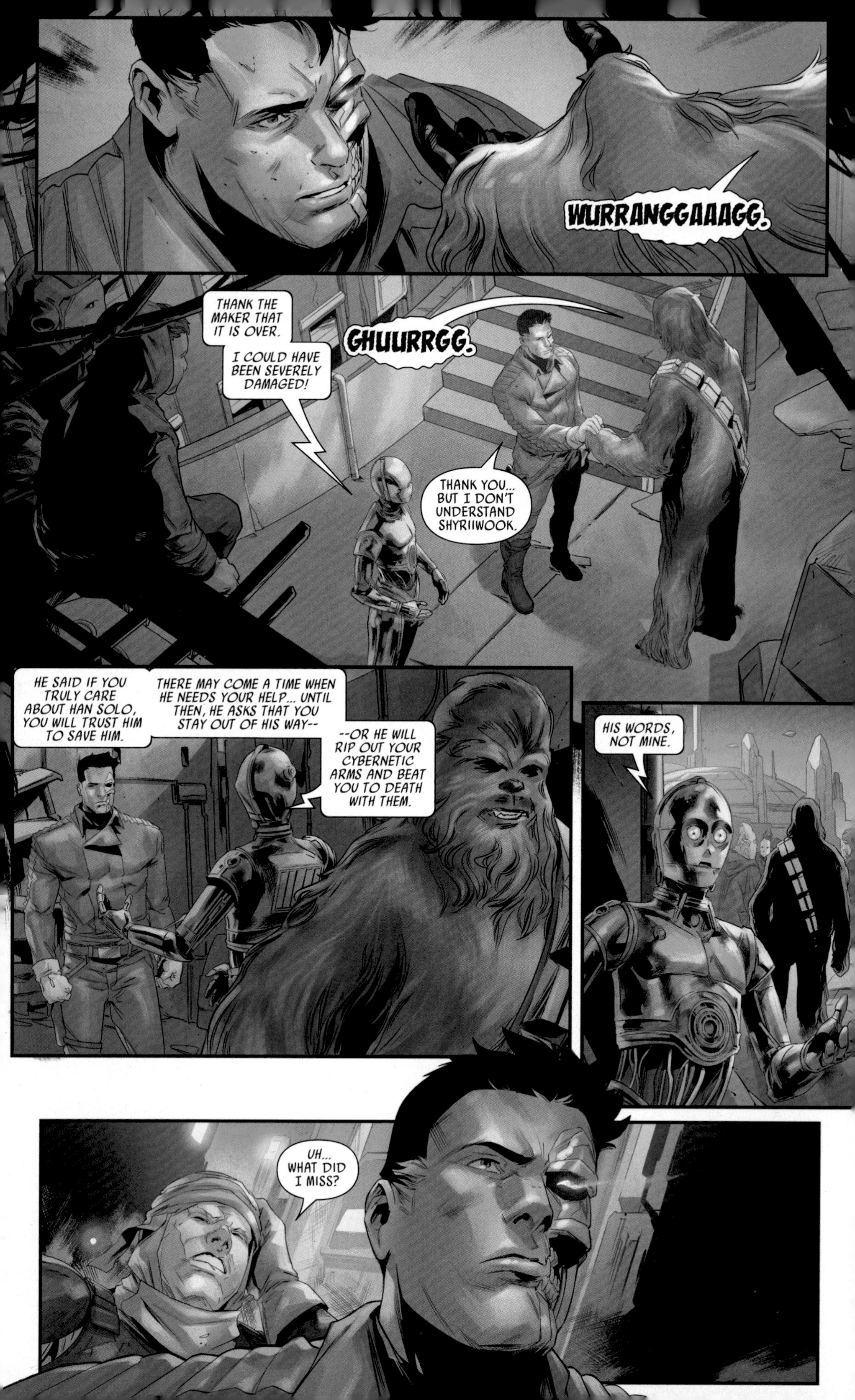
WURRANGGAAAGG.
THANK THE MAKER THAT IT IS OVER.
I COULD HAVE BEEN SEVERELY DAMAGED!
GHUURRGG.
THANK YOU... BUT I DON'T UNDERSTAND SHYRIIWOOK.
HE SAID IF YOU TRULY CARE ABOUT HAN SOLO, YOU WILL TRUST HIM TO SAVE HIM.
THERE MAY COME A TIME WHEN HE NEEDS YOUR HELP... UNTIL THEN, HE ASKS THAT YOU STAY OUT OF HIS WAY--
--OR HE WILL RIP OUT YOUR CYBERNETIC ARMS AND BEAT YOU TO DEATH WITH THEM.
HIS WORDS, NOT MINE.
UH... WHAT DID I MISS?

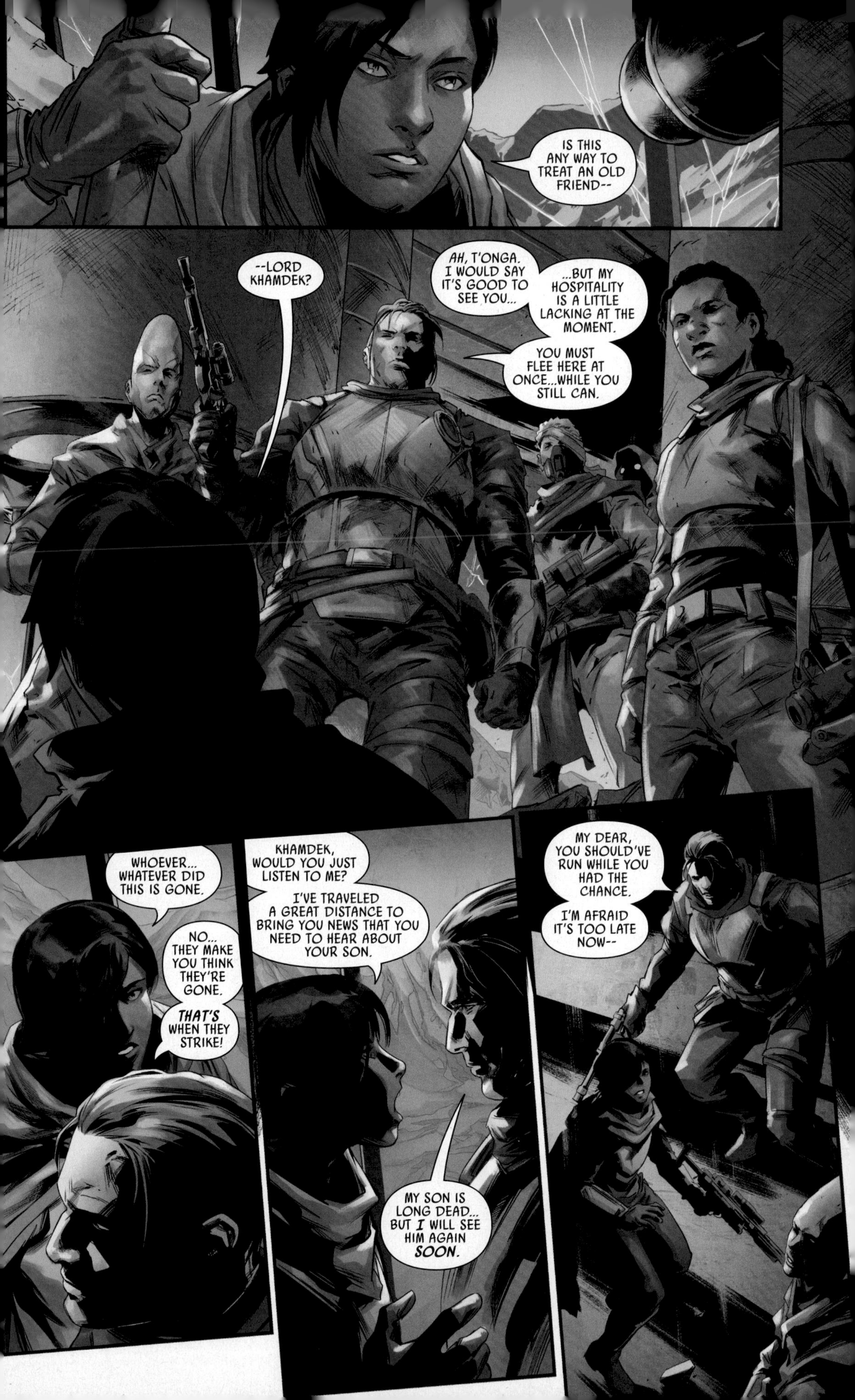

IS THIS ANY WAY TO TREAT AN OLD FRIEND--
--LORD KHAMDEK?
AH, T'ONGA. I WOULD SAY IT'S GOOD TO SEE YOU...
...BUT MY HOSPITALITY IS A LITTLE LACKING AT THE MOMENT.
YOU MUST FLEE HERE AT ONCE...WHILE YOU STILL CAN.
WHOEVER... WHATEVER DID THIS IS GONE.
NO... THEY MAKE YOU THINK THEY'RE GONE.
THAT'S WHEN THEY STRIKE!
KHAMDEK, WOULD YOU JUST LISTEN TO ME?
I'VE TRAVELED A GREAT DISTANCE TO BRING YOU NEWS THAT YOU NEED TO HEAR ABOUT YOUR SON.
MY SON IS LONG DEAD... BUT I WILL SEE HIM AGAIN SOON.
MY DEAR, YOU SHOULD'VE RUN WHILE YOU HAD THE CHANCE.
I'M AFRAID IT'S TOO LATE NOW--

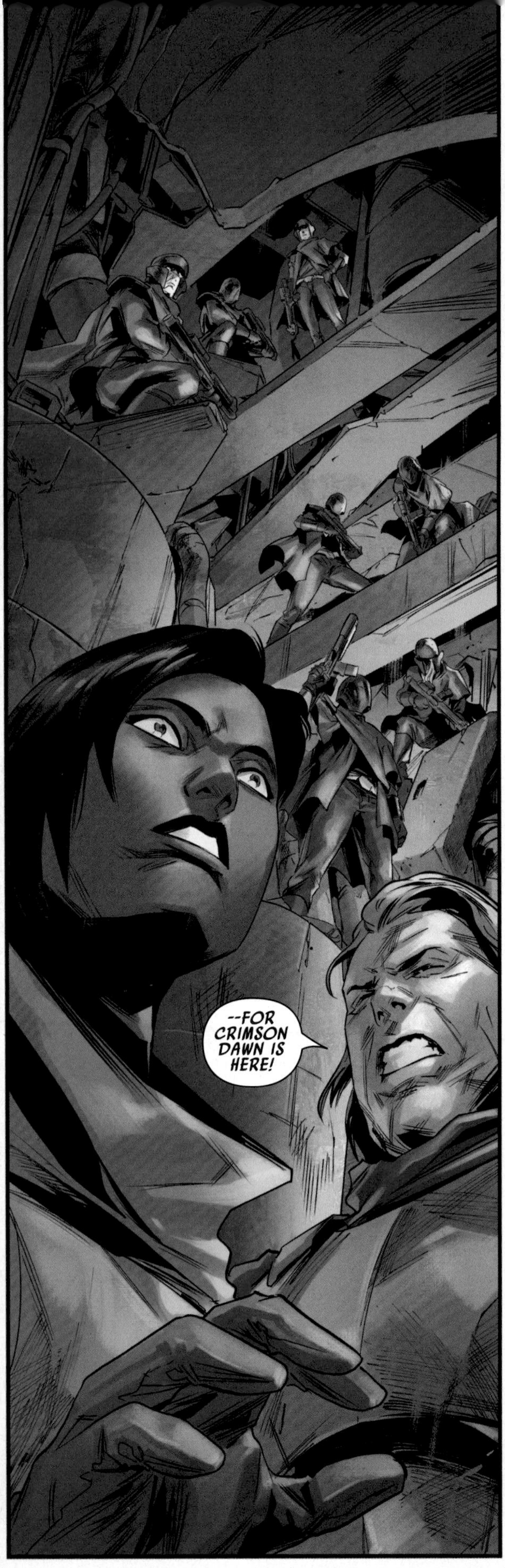
--FOR CRIMSON DAWN IS HERE!
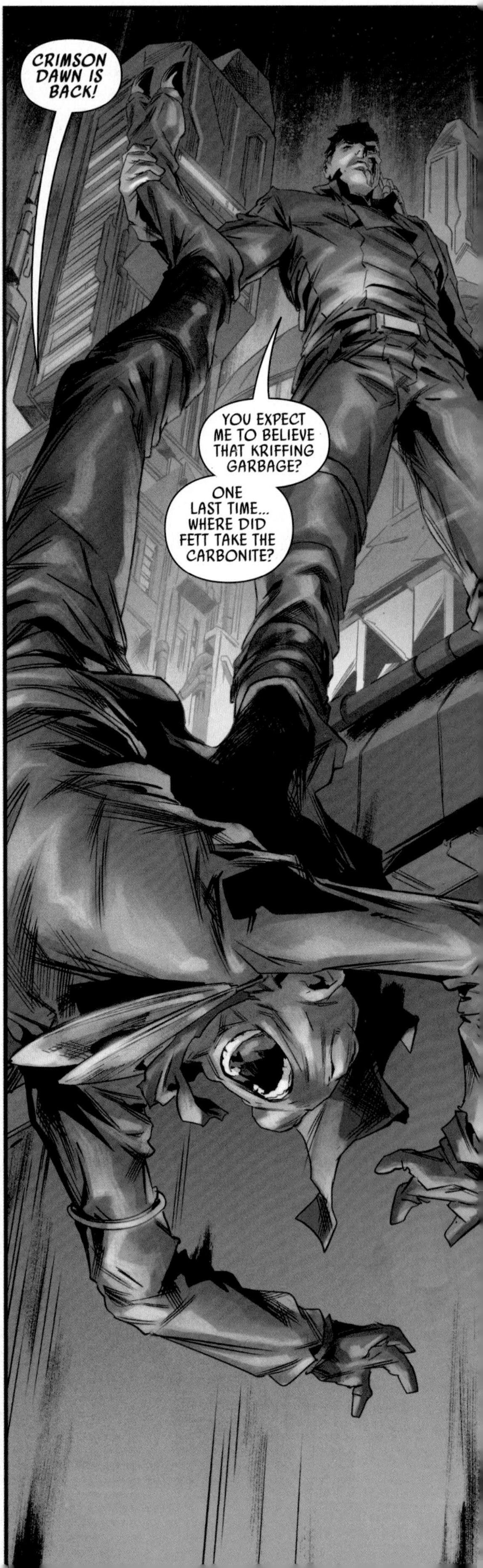
CRIMSON DAWN IS BACK!
YOU EXPECT ME TO BELIEVE THAT KRIFFING GARBAGE?
ONE LAST TIME... WHERE DID FETT TAKE THE CARBONITE?

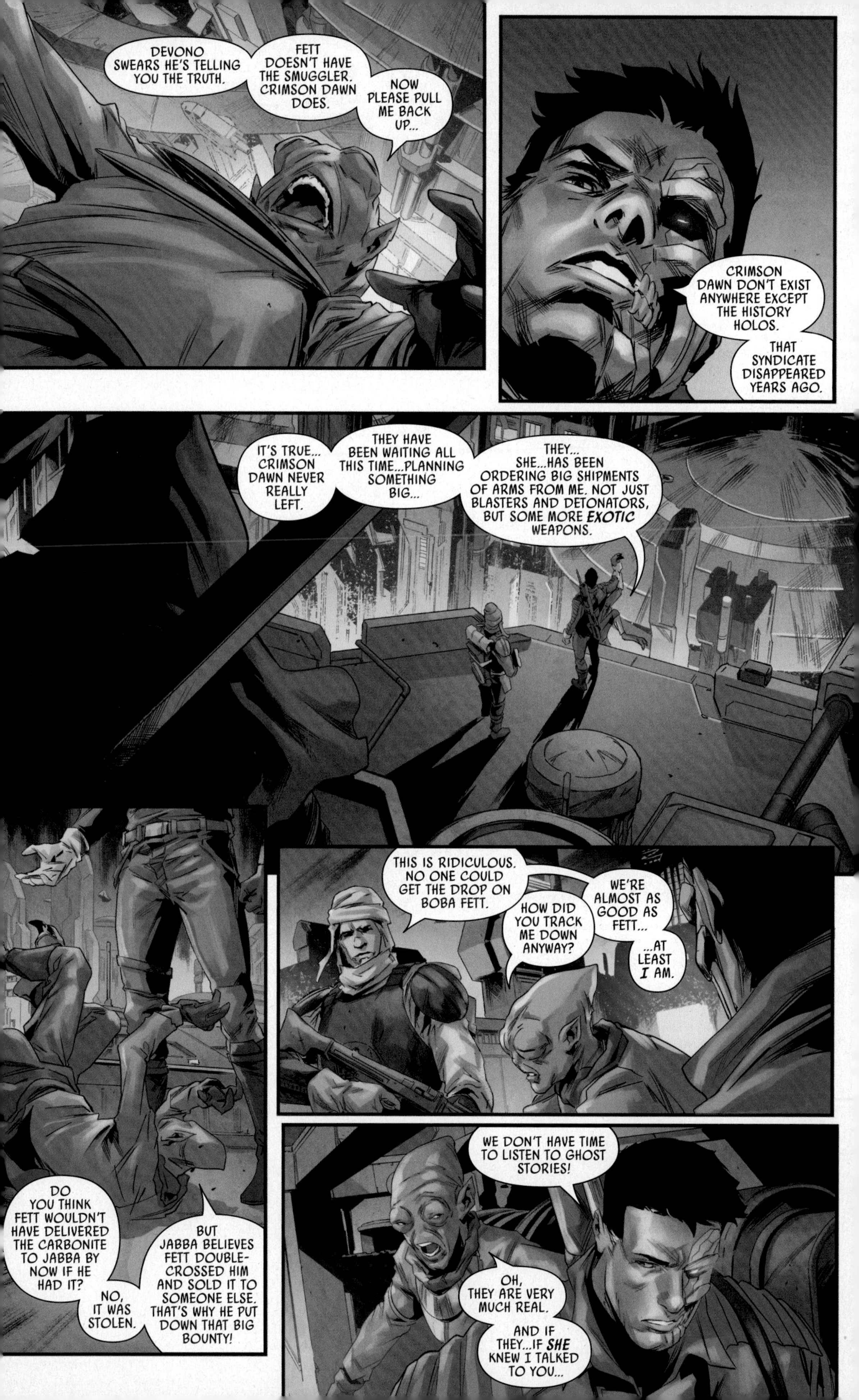

DEVONO SWEARS HE'S TELLING YOU THE TRUTH.
FETT DOESN'T HAVE THE SMUGGLER. CRIMSON DAWN DOES.
NOW PLEASE PULL ME BACK UP...
CRIMSON DAWN DON'T EXIST ANYWHERE EXCEPT THE HISTORY HOLOS.
THAT SYNDICATE DISAPPEARED YEARS AGO.
IT'S TRUE... CRIMSON DAWN NEVER REALLY LEFT.
THEY HAVE BEEN WAITING ALL THIS TIME...PLANNING SOMETHING BIG...
THEY... SHE...HAS BEEN ORDERING BIG SHIPMENTS OF ARMS FROM ME. NOT JUST BLASTERS AND DETONATORS, BUT SOME MORE EXOTIC WEAPONS.
DO YOU THINK FETT WOULDN'T HAVE DELIVERED THE CARBONITE TO JABBA BY NOW IF HE HAD IT?
NO, IT WAS STOLEN.
BUT JABBA BELIEVES FETT DOUBLE-CROSSED HIM AND SOLD IT TO SOMEONE ELSE. THAT'S WHY HE PUT DOWN THAT BIG BOUNTY!
THIS IS RIDICULOUS. NO ONE COULD GET THE DROP ON BOBA FETT.
HOW DID YOU TRACK ME DOWN ANYWAY?
WE'RE ALMOST AS GOOD AS FETT...
...AT LEAST I AM.
WE DON'T HAVE TIME TO LISTEN TO GHOST STORIES!
OH, THEY ARE VERY MUCH REAL.
AND IF THEY...IF SHE KNEW I TALKED TO YOU...

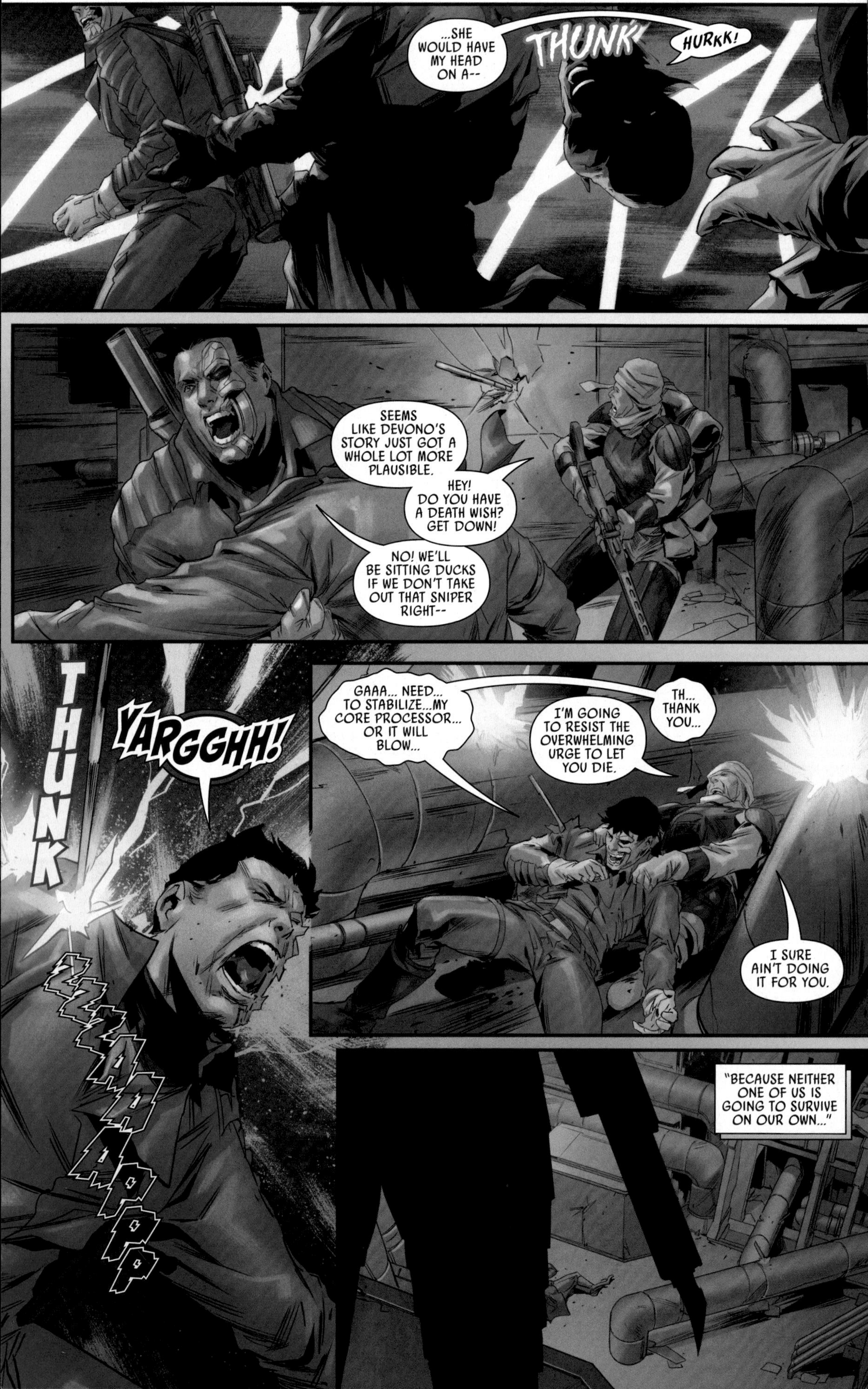
...SHE WOULD HAVE MY HEAD ON A--
THUNK
HURKK!
SEEMS LIKE DEVONO'S STORY JUST GOT A WHOLE LOT MORE PLAUSIBLE.
HEY! DO YOU HAVE A DEATH WISH? GET DOWN!
NO! WE'LL BE SITTING DUCKS IF WE DON'T TAKE OUT THAT SNIPER RIGHT--
THUNK
YARGGHH!
ZZZAAAPPPP
GAAA... NEED... TO STABILIZE...MY CORE PROCESSOR... OR IT WILL BLOW...
I'M GOING TO RESIST THE OVERWHELMING URGE TO LET YOU DIE.
TH... THANK YOU...
I SURE AIN'T DOING IT FOR YOU.
"BECAUSE NEITHER ONE OF US IS GOING TO SURVIVE ON OUR OWN..."

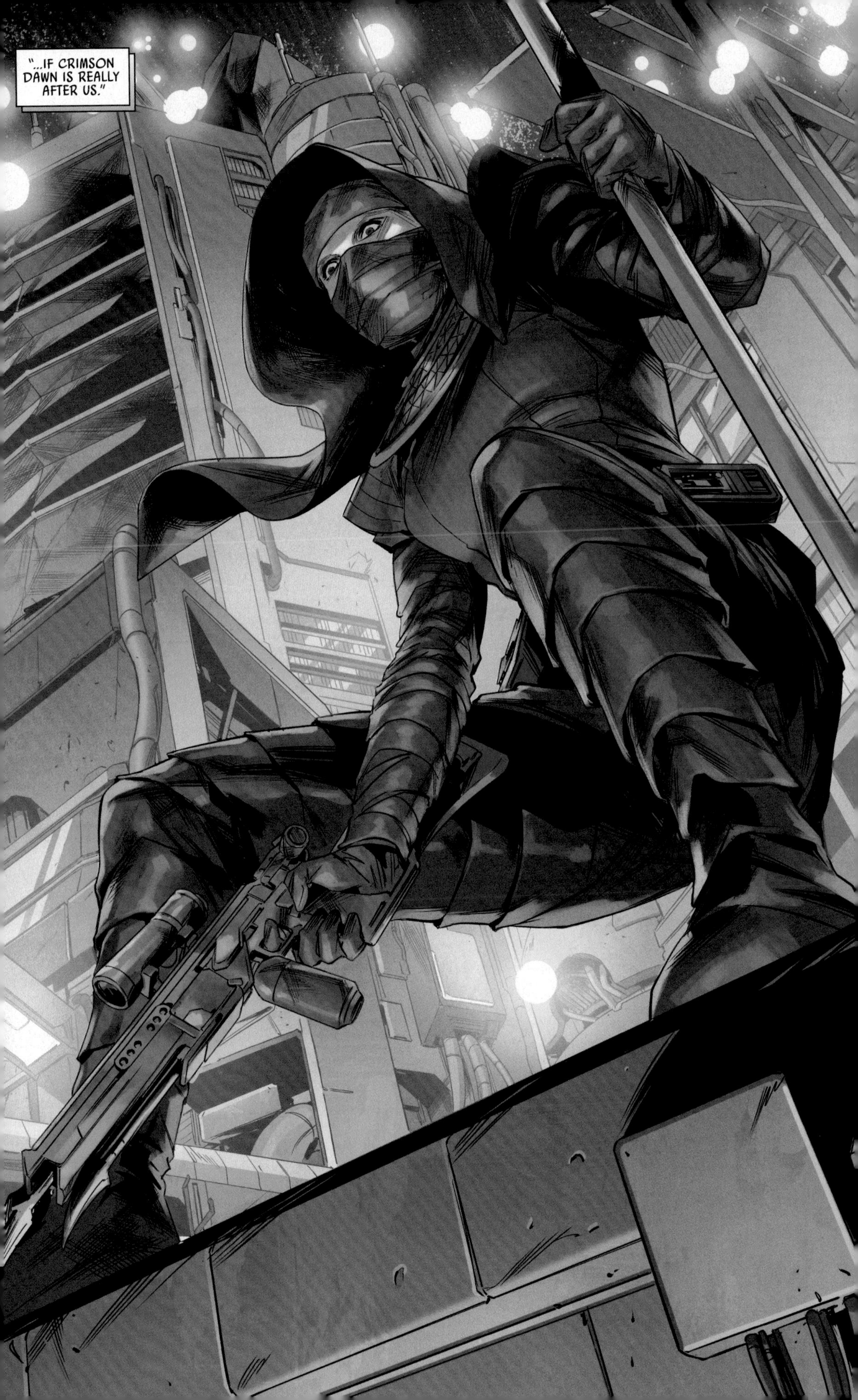
"...IF CRIMSON DAWN IS REALLY AFTER US."

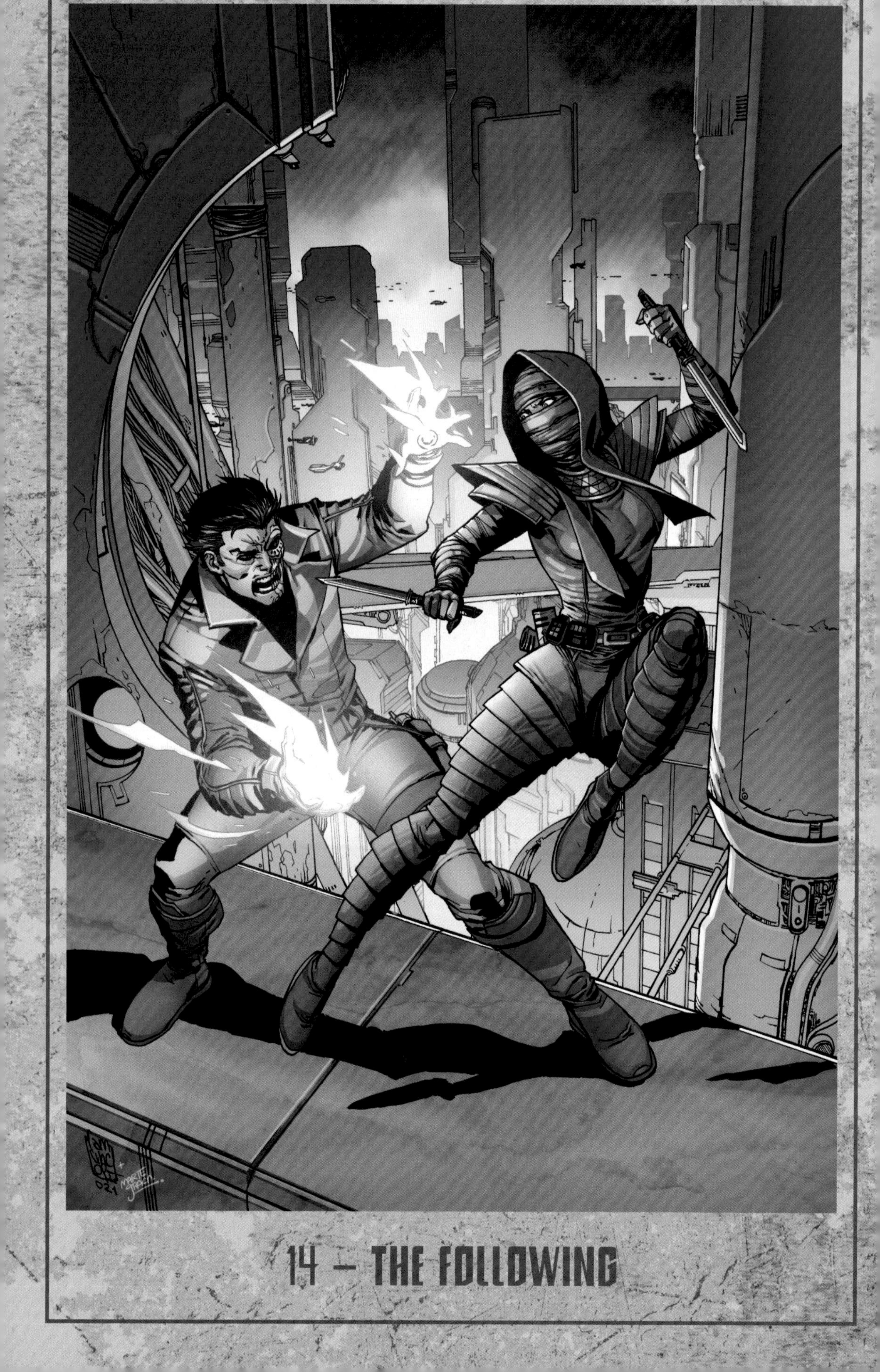

14 – THE FOLLOWING

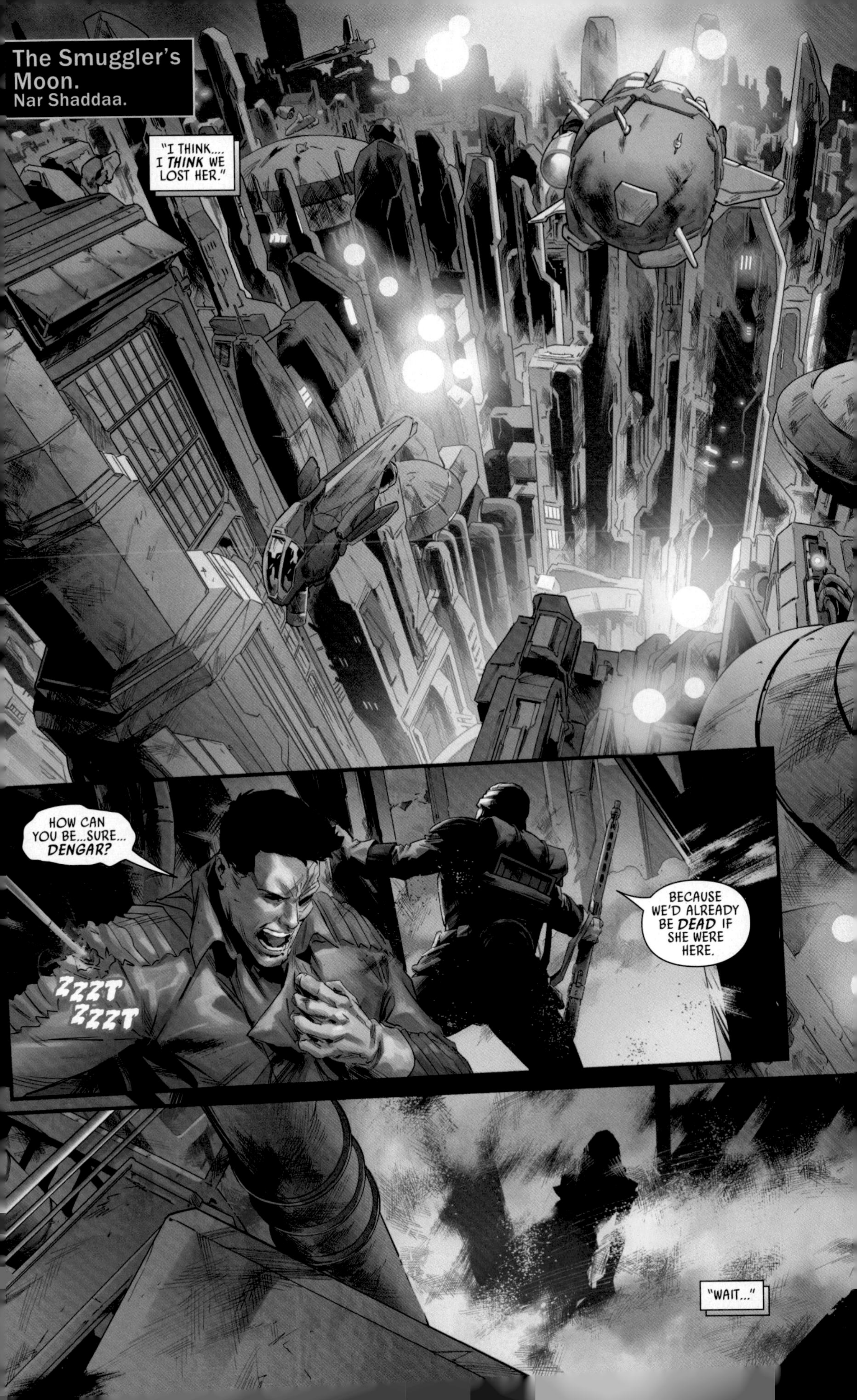
The Smuggler's Moon.
Nar Shaddaa.
"I THINK.... I THINK WE LOST HER."
HOW CAN YOU BE...SURE... DENGAR?
BECAUSE WE'D ALREADY BE DEAD IF SHE WERE HERE.
ZZZT
ZZZT
"WAIT..."

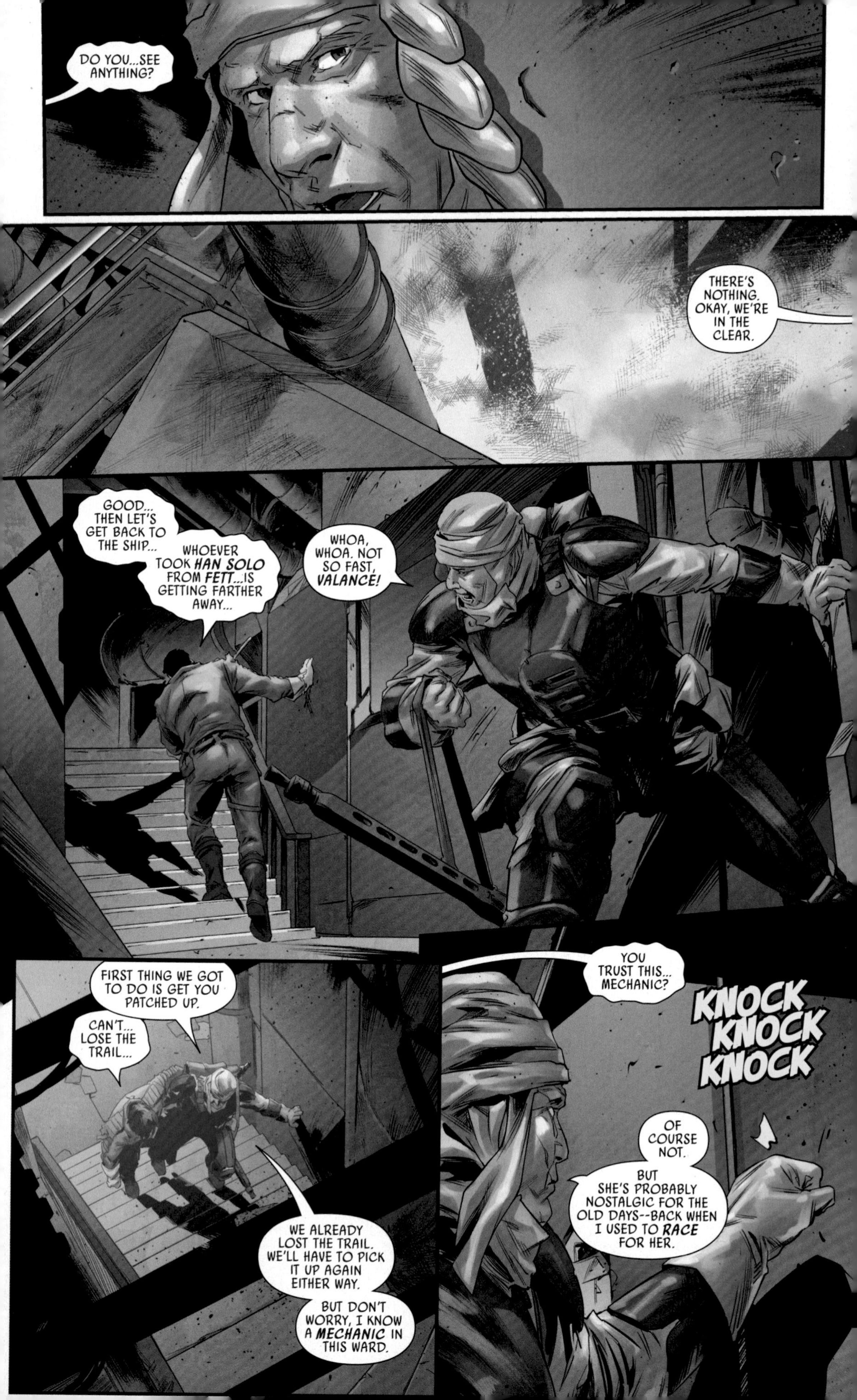
DO YOU...SEE ANYTHING?
THERE'S NOTHING. OKAY, WE'RE IN THE CLEAR.
GOOD... THEN LET'S GET BACK TO THE SHIP...
WHOEVER TOOK HAN SOLO FROM FETT...IS GETTING FARTHER AWAY...
WHOA, WHOA. NOT SO FAST, VALANCE!
FIRST THING WE GOT TO DO IS GET YOU PATCHED UP.
CAN'T... LOSE THE TRAIL...
WE ALREADY LOST THE TRAIL. WE'LL HAVE TO PICK IT UP AGAIN EITHER WAY.
BUT DON'T WORRY, I KNOW A MECHANIC IN THIS WARD.
YOU TRUST THIS... MECHANIC?
KNOCK KNOCK KNOCK
OF COURSE NOT.
BUT SHE'S PROBABLY NOSTALGIC FOR THE OLD DAYS--BACK WHEN I USED TO RACE FOR HER.

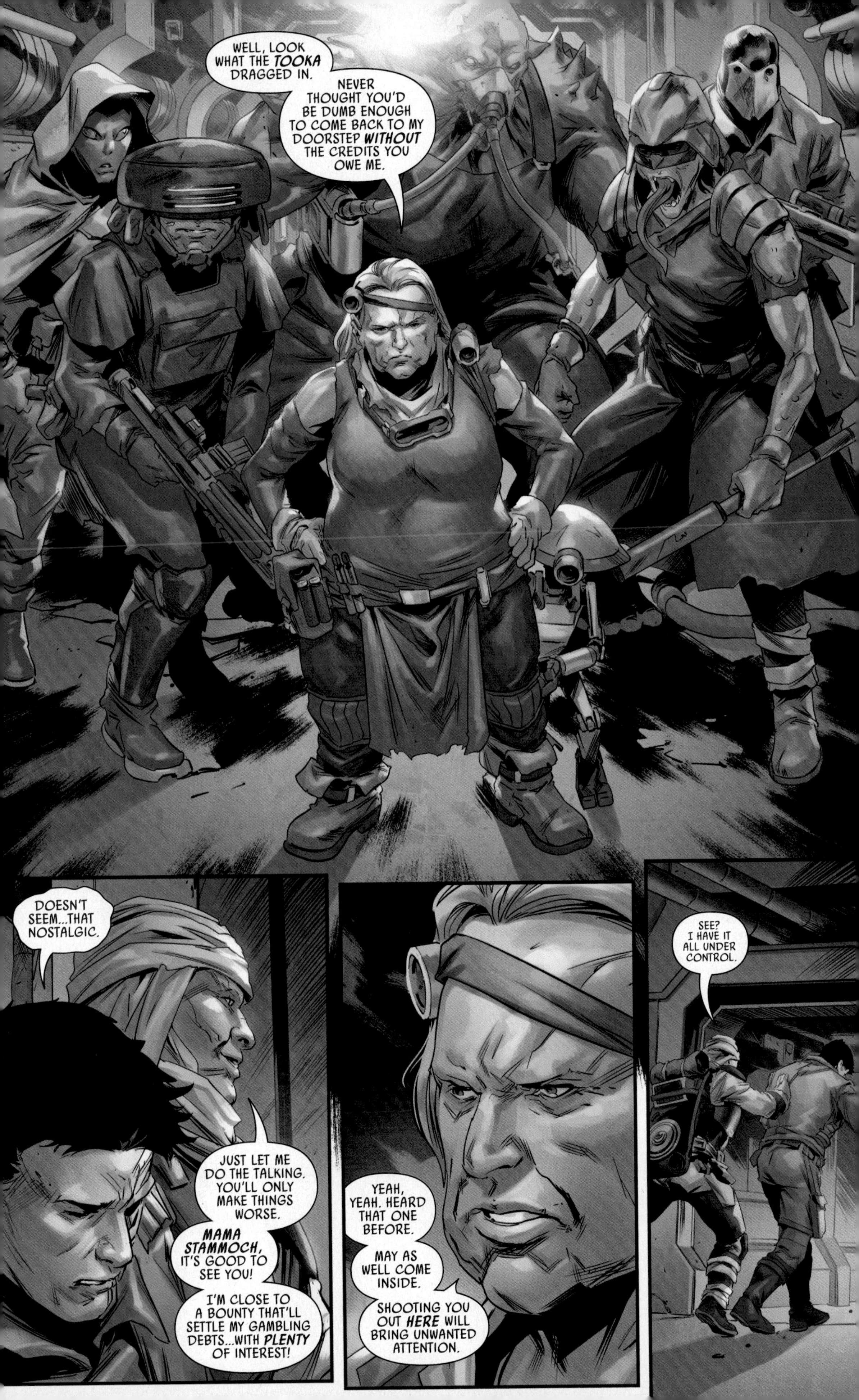
WELL, LOOK WHAT THE *TOOKA* DRAGGED IN.
NEVER THOUGHT YOU'D BE DUMB ENOUGH TO COME BACK TO MY DOORSTEP *WITHOUT* THE CREDITS YOU OWE ME.
DOESN'T SEEM...THAT NOSTALGIC.
JUST LET ME DO THE TALKING. YOU'LL ONLY MAKE THINGS WORSE.
MAMA STAMMOCH, IT'S GOOD TO SEE YOU!
I'M CLOSE TO A BOUNTY THAT'LL SETTLE MY GAMBLING DEBTS...WITH *PLENTY* OF INTEREST!
YEAH, YEAH. HEARD THAT ONE BEFORE.
MAY AS WELL COME INSIDE.
SHOOTING YOU OUT *HERE* WILL BRING UNWANTED ATTENTION.
SEE? I HAVE IT ALL UNDER CONTROL.

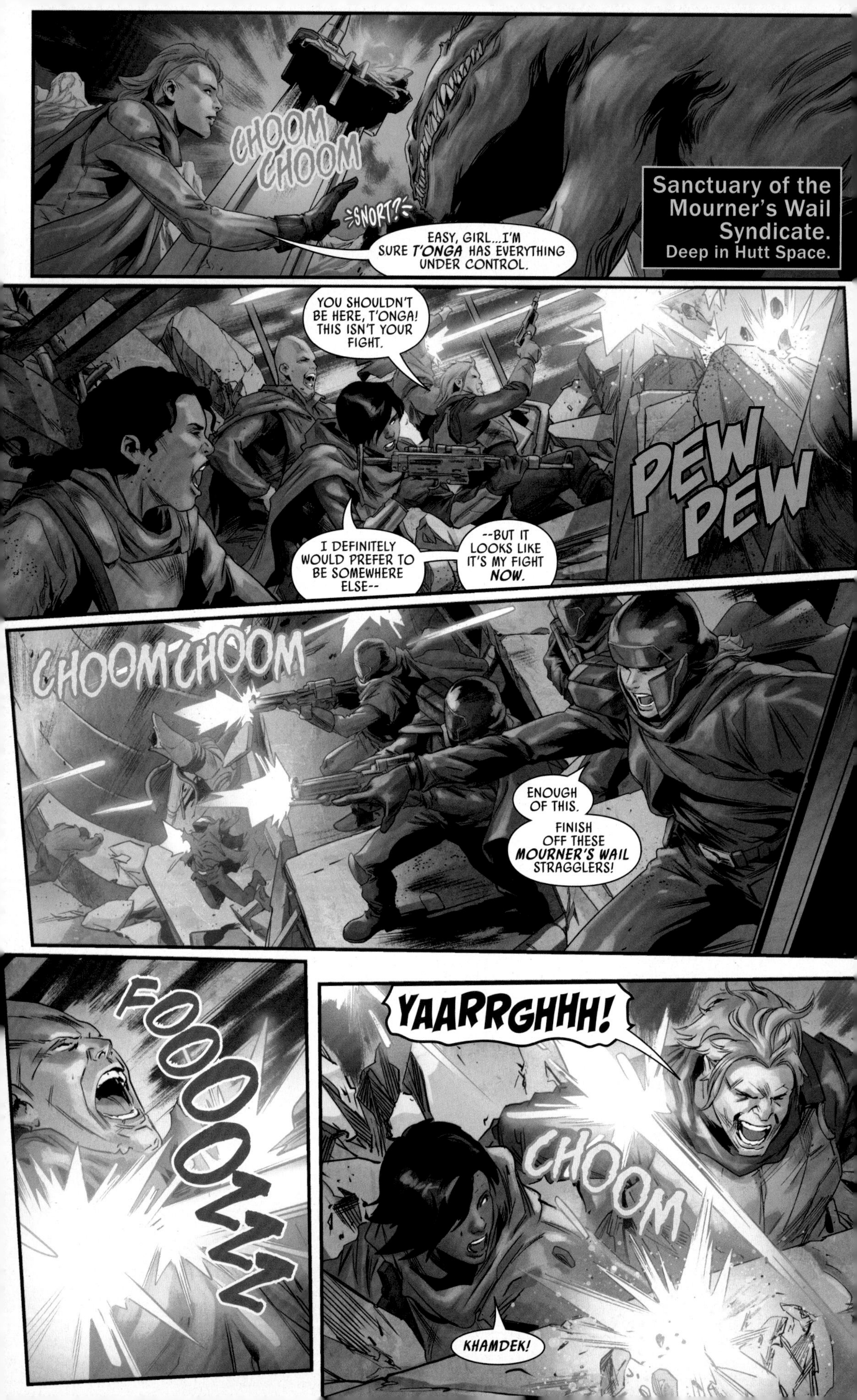
CHOOM CHOOM
Sanctuary of the Mourner's Wail Syndicate. Deep in Hutt Space.
SNORT?
EASY, GIRL...I'M SURE T'ONGA HAS EVERYTHING UNDER CONTROL.
YOU SHOULDN'T BE HERE, T'ONGA! THIS ISN'T YOUR FIGHT.
PEW PEW
I DEFINITELY WOULD PREFER TO BE SOMEWHERE ELSE--
--BUT IT LOOKS LIKE IT'S MY FIGHT NOW.
CHOOM CHOOM
ENOUGH OF THIS.
FINISH OFF THESE MOURNER'S WAIL STRAGGLERS!
FOOOOMM
YAARRGHHH!
CHOOM
KHAMDEK!

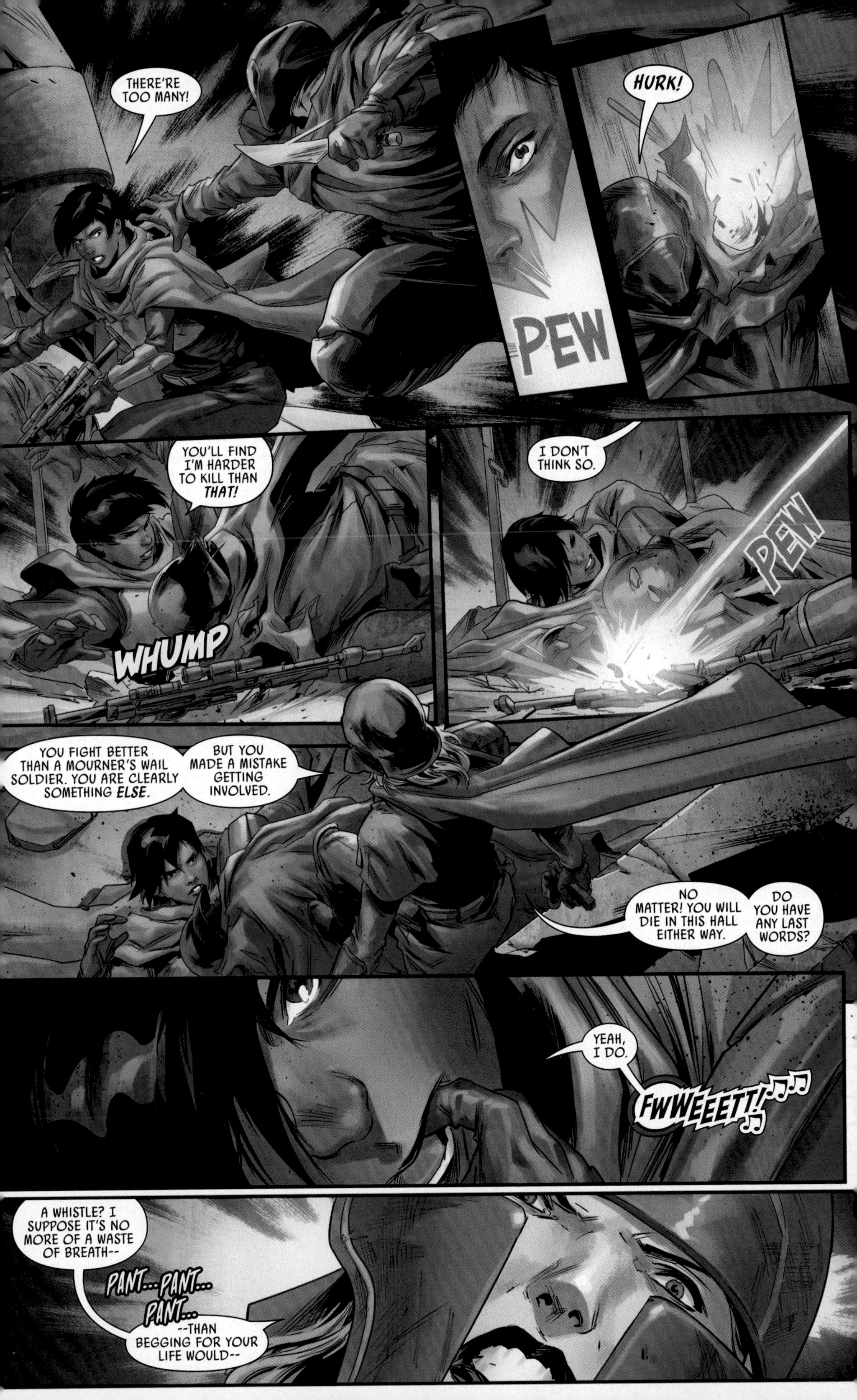
THERE'RE TOO MANY!
HURK!
PEW
YOU'LL FIND I'M HARDER TO KILL THAN THAT!
WHUMP
I DON'T THINK SO.
PEW
YOU FIGHT BETTER THAN A MOURNER'S WAIL SOLDIER. YOU ARE CLEARLY SOMETHING ELSE.
BUT YOU MADE A MISTAKE GETTING INVOLVED.
NO MATTER! YOU WILL DIE IN THIS HALL EITHER WAY.
DO YOU HAVE ANY LAST WORDS?
YEAH, I DO.
FWWEEETT!
A WHISTLE? I SUPPOSE IT'S NO MORE OF A WASTE OF BREATH--
PANT... PANT... PANT...
--THAN BEGGING FOR YOUR LIFE WOULD--

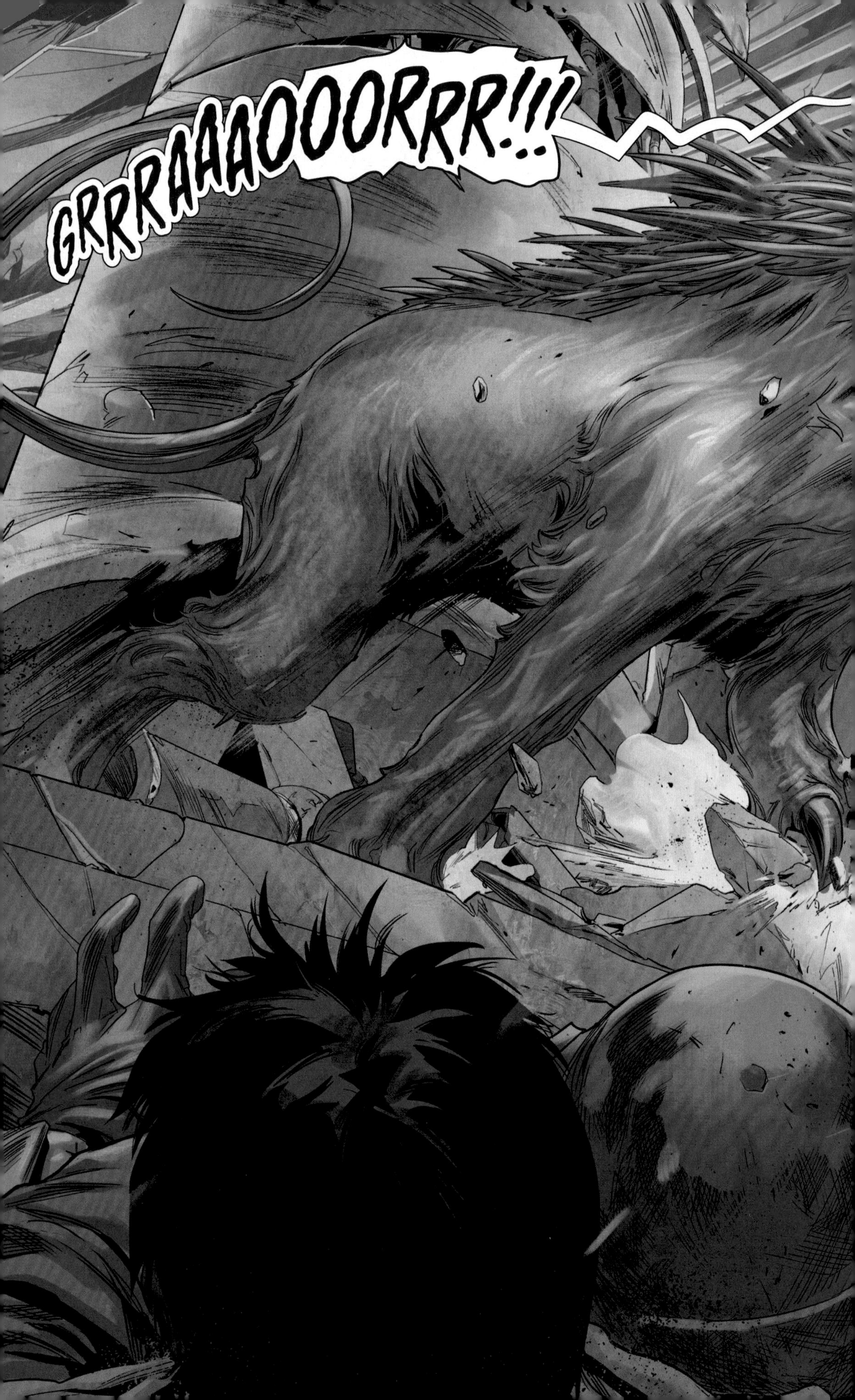
GRRRAAAOOORRRR!!!

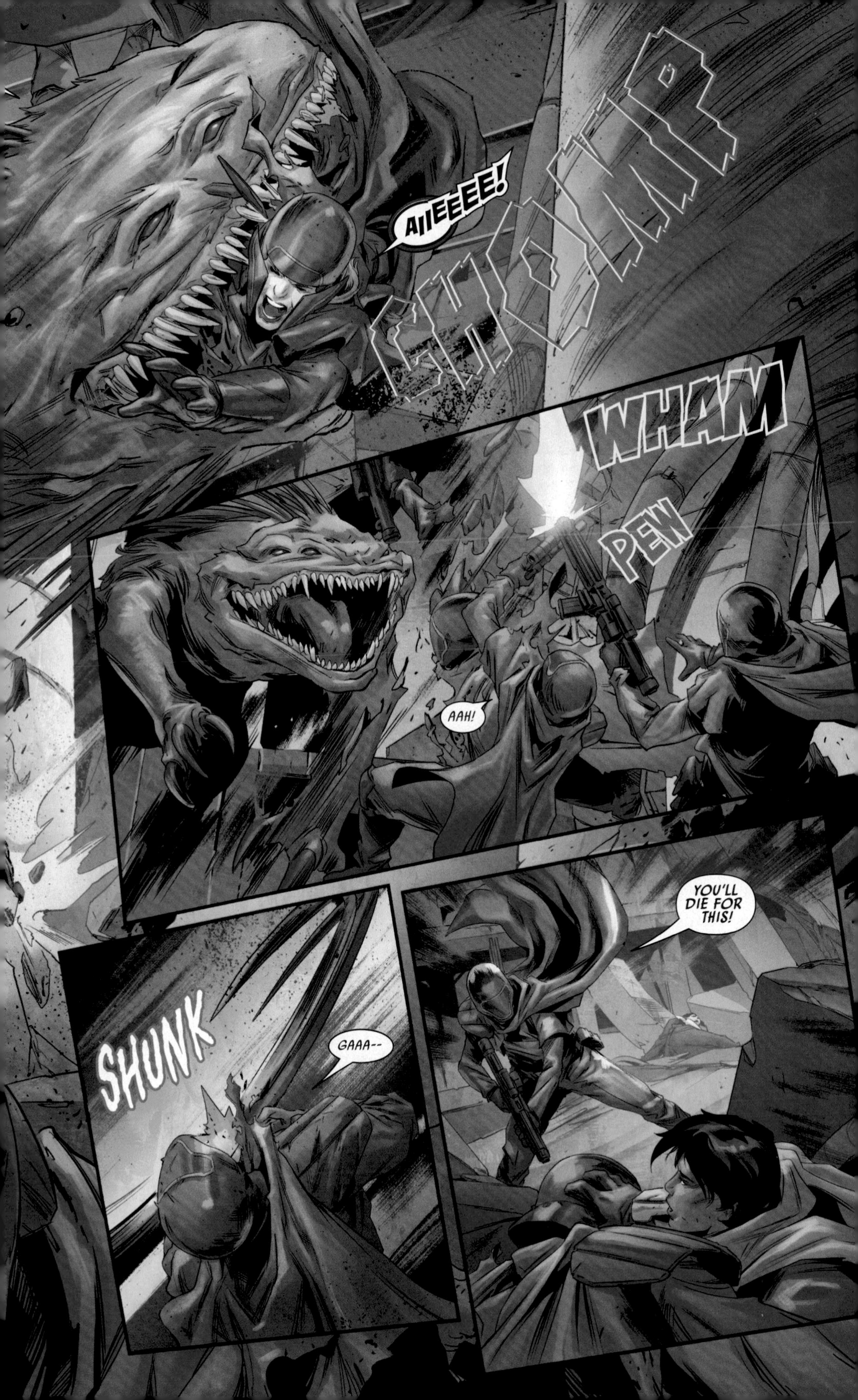
AIIEEEE!
CHOMP
WHAM
PEW
AAH!
YOU'LL DIE FOR THIS!
SHUNK
GAAA--

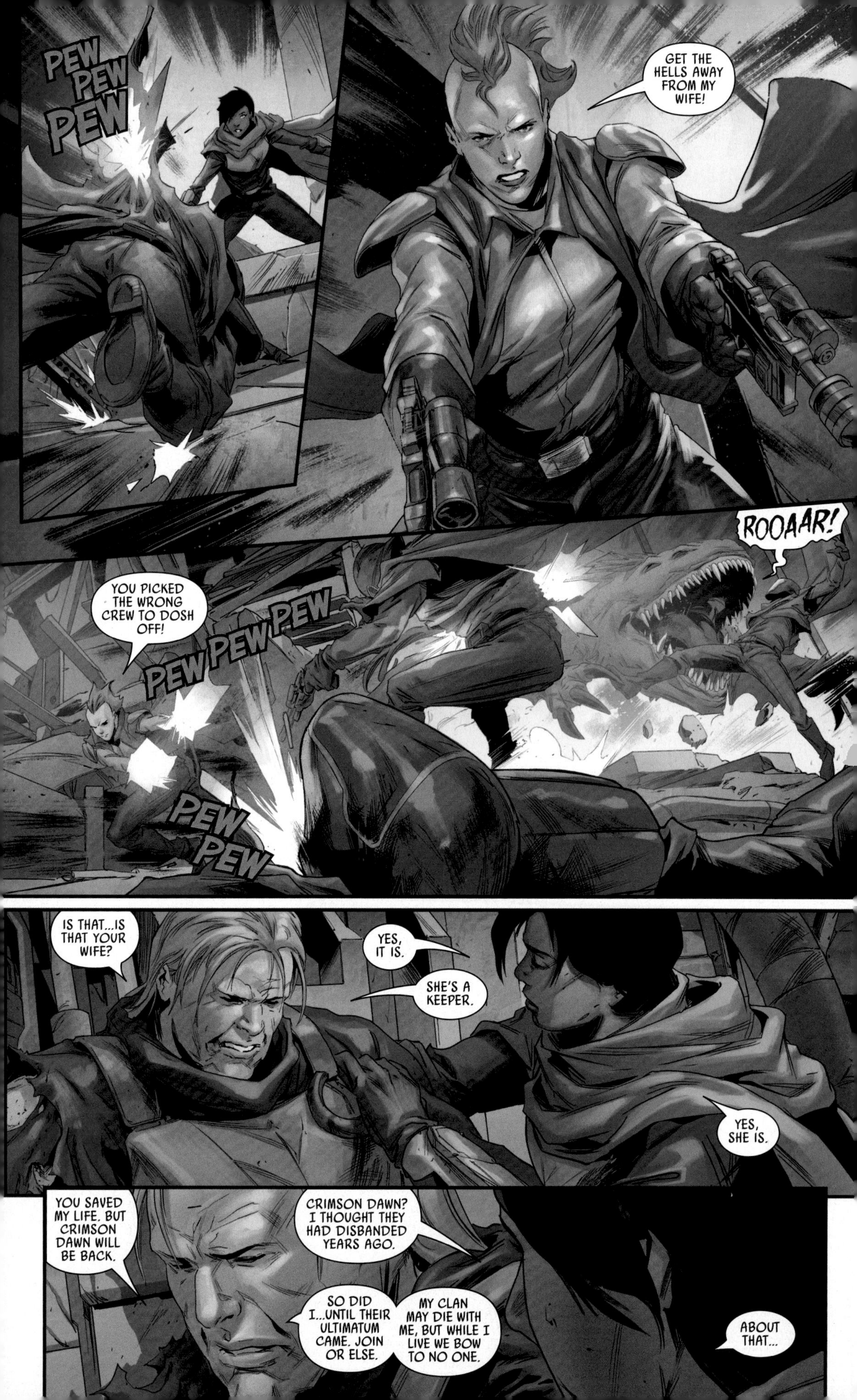
PEW PEW PEW
GET THE HELLS AWAY FROM MY WIFE!
ROOAAR!
YOU PICKED THE WRONG CREW TO DOSH OFF!
PEW PEW PEW
PEW PEW
IS THAT...IS THAT YOUR WIFE?
YES, IT IS.
SHE'S A KEEPER.
YES, SHE IS.
YOU SAVED MY LIFE. BUT CRIMSON DAWN WILL BE BACK.
CRIMSON DAWN? I THOUGHT THEY HAD DISBANDED YEARS AGO.
SO DID I...UNTIL THEIR ULTIMATUM CAME. JOIN OR ELSE.
MY CLAN MAY DIE WITH ME, BUT WHILE I LIVE WE BOW TO NO ONE.
ABOUT THAT...

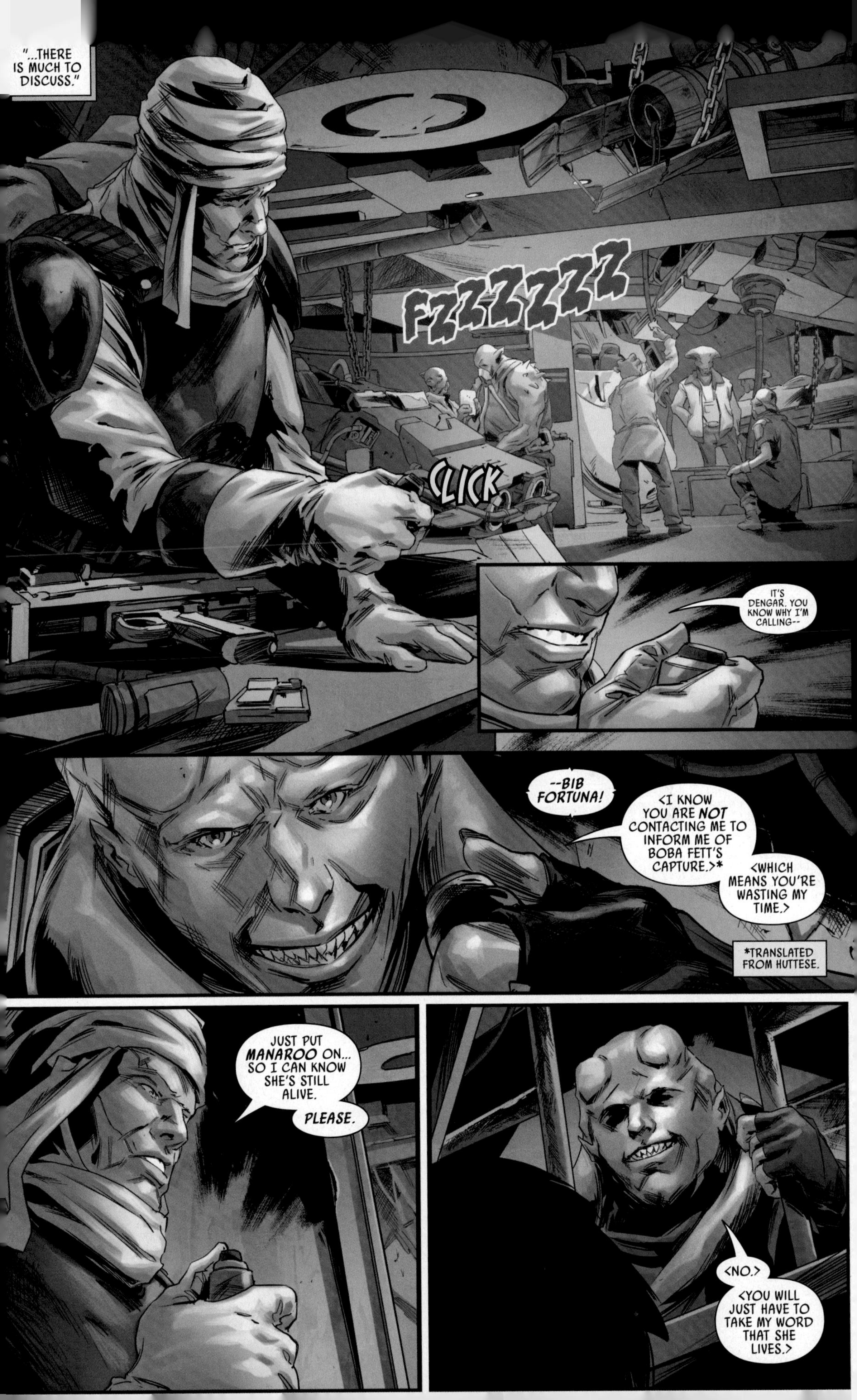
"...THERE IS MUCH TO DISCUSS."
FZZZZZZZ
CLICK
IT'S DENGAR. YOU KNOW WHY I'M CALLING--
--BIB FORTUNA!
<I KNOW YOU ARE NOT CONTACTING ME TO INFORM ME OF BOBA FETT'S CAPTURE.>*
<WHICH MEANS YOU'RE WASTING MY TIME.>
*TRANSLATED FROM HUTTESE.
JUST PUT MANAROO ON... SO I CAN KNOW SHE'S STILL ALIVE.
PLEASE.
<NO.>
<YOU WILL JUST HAVE TO TAKE MY WORD THAT SHE LIVES.>

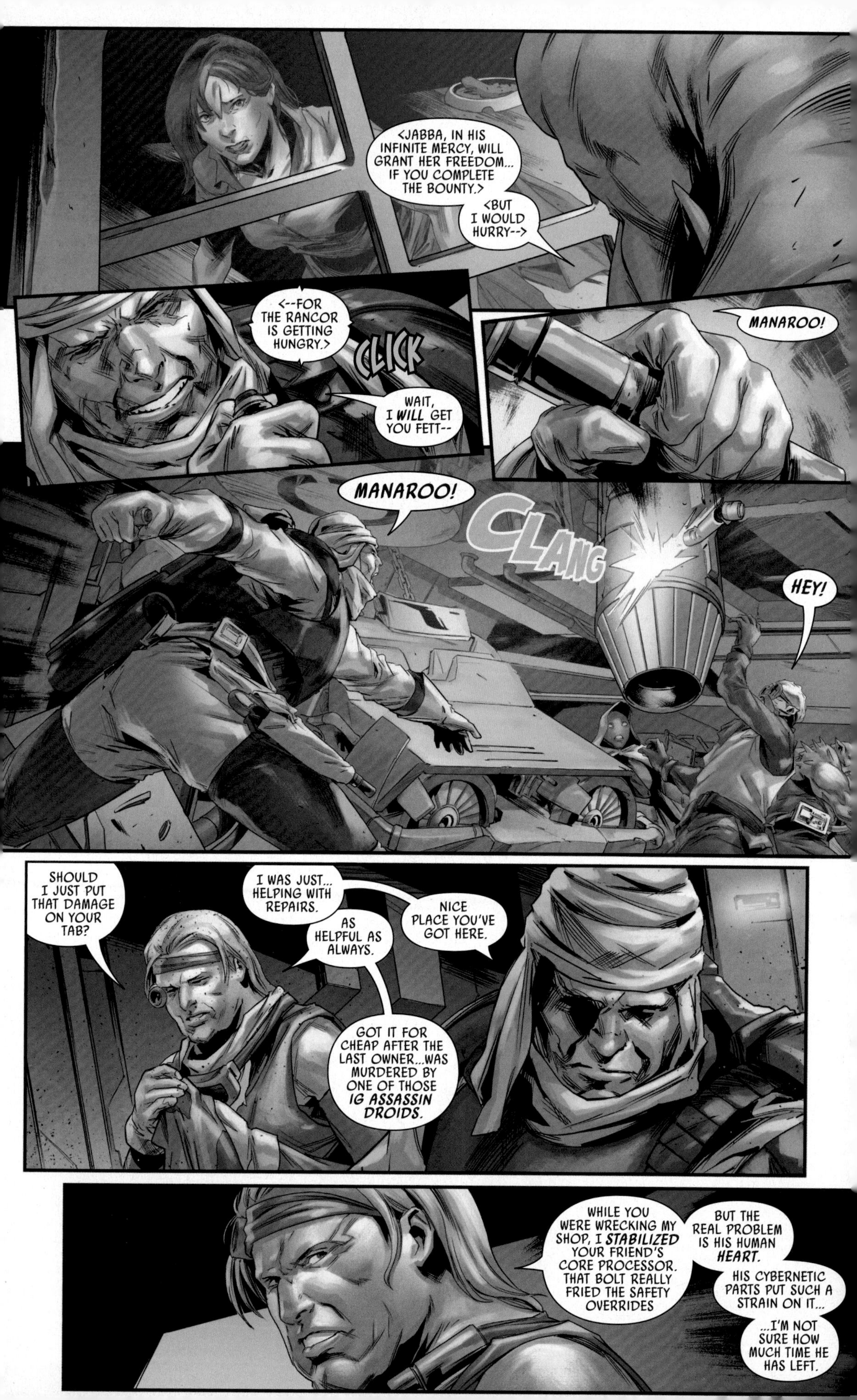

<JABBA, IN HIS INFINITE MERCY, WILL GRANT HER FREEDOM... IF YOU COMPLETE THE BOUNTY.>
<BUT I WOULD HURRY-->
<--FOR THE RANCOR IS GETTING HUNGRY.>
CLICK
WAIT, I WILL GET YOU FETT--
MANAROO!
MANAROO!
CLANG
HEY!
SHOULD I JUST PUT THAT DAMAGE ON YOUR TAB?
I WAS JUST... HELPING WITH REPAIRS.
AS HELPFUL AS ALWAYS.
NICE PLACE YOU'VE GOT HERE.
GOT IT FOR CHEAP AFTER THE LAST OWNER...WAS MURDERED BY ONE OF THOSE IG ASSASSIN DROIDS.
WHILE YOU WERE WRECKING MY SHOP, I STABILIZED YOUR FRIEND'S CORE PROCESSOR. THAT BOLT REALLY FRIED THE SAFETY OVERRIDES
BUT THE REAL PROBLEM IS HIS HUMAN HEART.
HIS CYBERNETIC PARTS PUT SUCH A STRAIN ON IT...
...I'M NOT SURE HOW MUCH TIME HE HAS LEFT.

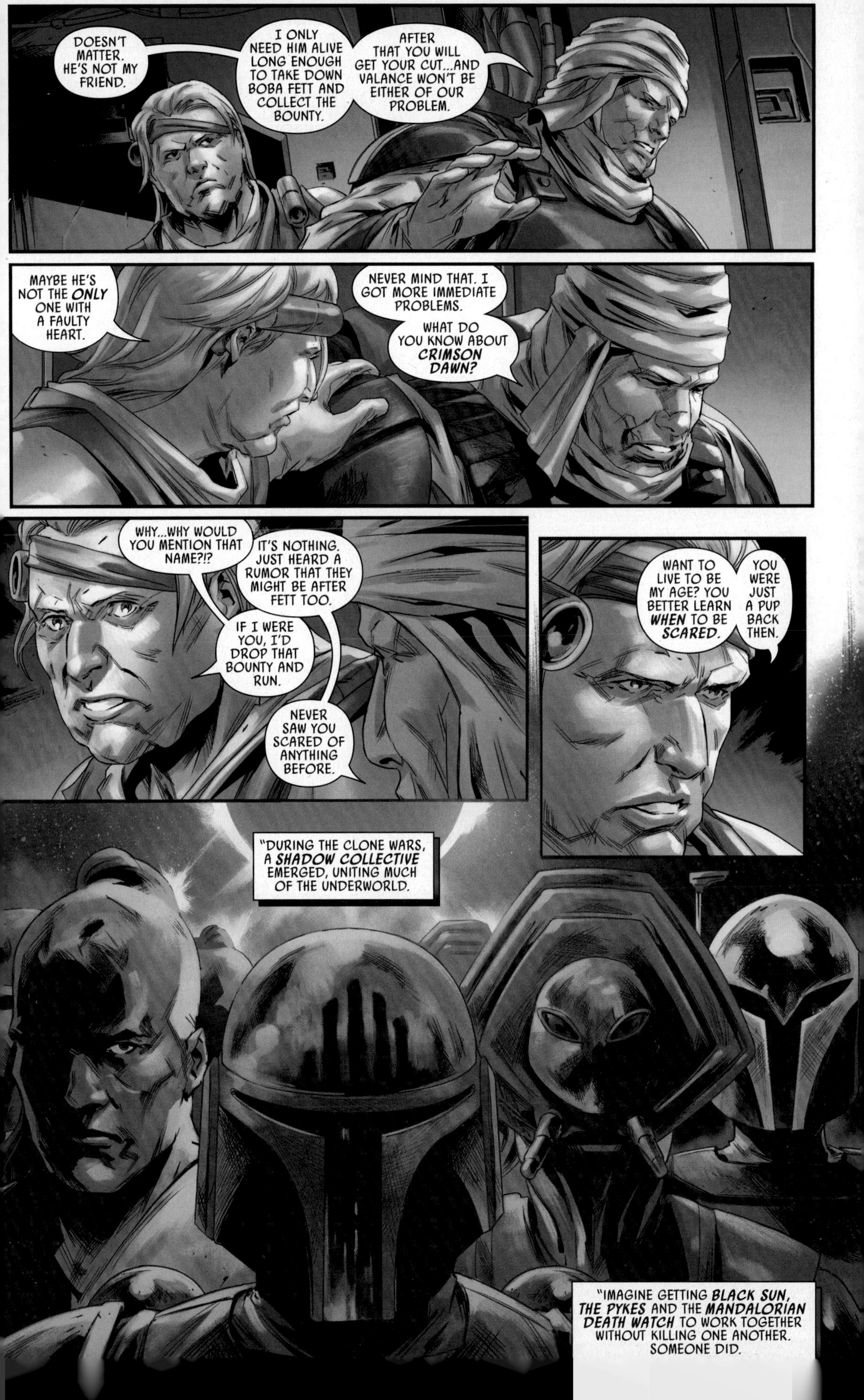
DOESN'T MATTER. HE'S NOT MY FRIEND.
I ONLY NEED HIM ALIVE LONG ENOUGH TO TAKE DOWN BOBA FETT AND COLLECT THE BOUNTY.
AFTER THAT YOU WILL GET YOUR CUT...AND VALANCE WON'T BE EITHER OF OUR PROBLEM.
MAYBE HE'S NOT THE ONLY ONE WITH A FAULTY HEART.
NEVER MIND THAT. I GOT MORE IMMEDIATE PROBLEMS.
WHAT DO YOU KNOW ABOUT CRIMSON DAWN?
WHY...WHY WOULD YOU MENTION THAT NAME?!?
IT'S NOTHING. JUST HEARD A RUMOR THAT THEY MIGHT BE AFTER FETT TOO.
IF I WERE YOU, I'D DROP THAT BOUNTY AND RUN.
NEVER SAW YOU SCARED OF ANYTHING BEFORE.
YOU WERE JUST A PUP BACK THEN.
WANT TO LIVE TO BE MY AGE? YOU BETTER LEARN WHEN TO BE SCARED.
"DURING THE CLONE WARS, A SHADOW COLLECTIVE EMERGED, UNITING MUCH OF THE UNDERWORLD.
"IMAGINE GETTING BLACK SUN, THE PYKES AND THE MANDALORIAN DEATH WATCH TO WORK TOGETHER WITHOUT KILLING ONE ANOTHER. SOMEONE DID.

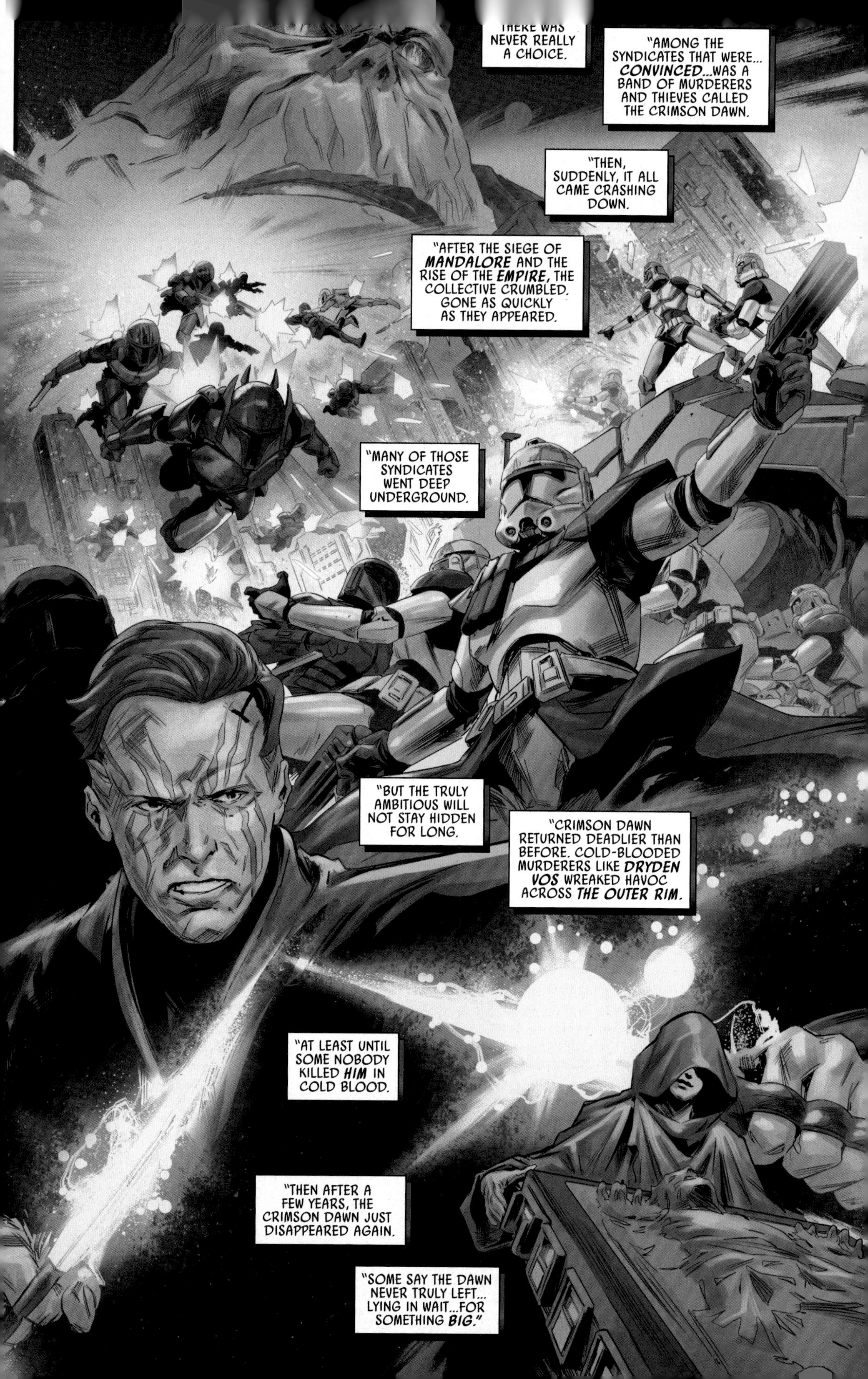
THERE WAS NEVER REALLY A CHOICE.
"AMONG THE SYNDICATES THAT WERE... CONVINCED...WAS A BAND OF MURDERERS AND THIEVES CALLED THE CRIMSON DAWN.
"THEN, SUDDENLY, IT ALL CAME CRASHING DOWN.
"AFTER THE SIEGE OF MANDALORE AND THE RISE OF THE EMPIRE, THE COLLECTIVE CRUMBLED. GONE AS QUICKLY AS THEY APPEARED.
"MANY OF THOSE SYNDICATES WENT DEEP UNDERGROUND.
"BUT THE TRULY AMBITIOUS WILL NOT STAY HIDDEN FOR LONG.
"CRIMSON DAWN RETURNED DEADLIER THAN BEFORE. COLD-BLOODED MURDERERS LIKE DRYDEN VOS WREAKED HAVOC ACROSS THE OUTER RIM.
"AT LEAST UNTIL SOME NOBODY KILLED HIM IN COLD BLOOD.
"THEN AFTER A FEW YEARS, THE CRIMSON DAWN JUST DISAPPEARED AGAIN.
"SOME SAY THE DAWN NEVER TRULY LEFT... LYING IN WAIT...FOR SOMETHING BIG."

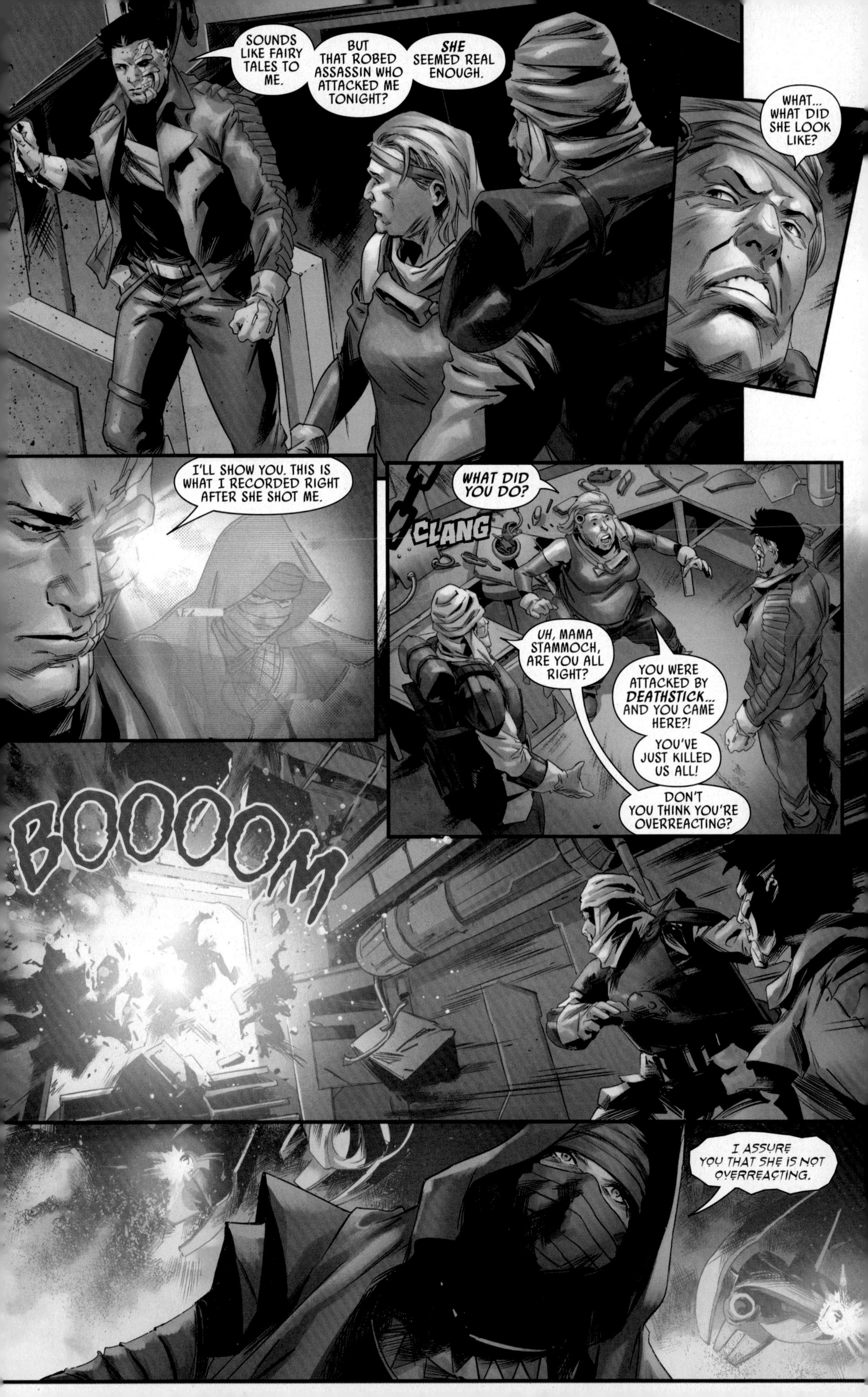
SOUNDS LIKE FAIRY TALES TO ME.
BUT THAT ROBED ASSASSIN WHO ATTACKED ME TONIGHT?
SHE SEEMED REAL ENOUGH.
WHAT... WHAT DID SHE LOOK LIKE?
I'LL SHOW YOU. THIS IS WHAT I RECORDED RIGHT AFTER SHE SHOT ME.
WHAT DID YOU DO?
CLANG
UH, MAMA STAMMOCH, ARE YOU ALL RIGHT?
YOU WERE ATTACKED BY DEATHSTICK... AND YOU CAME HERE?!
YOU'VE JUST KILLED US ALL!
DON'T YOU THINK YOU'RE OVERREACTING?
BOOOOM
I ASSURE YOU THAT SHE IS NOT OVERREACTING.

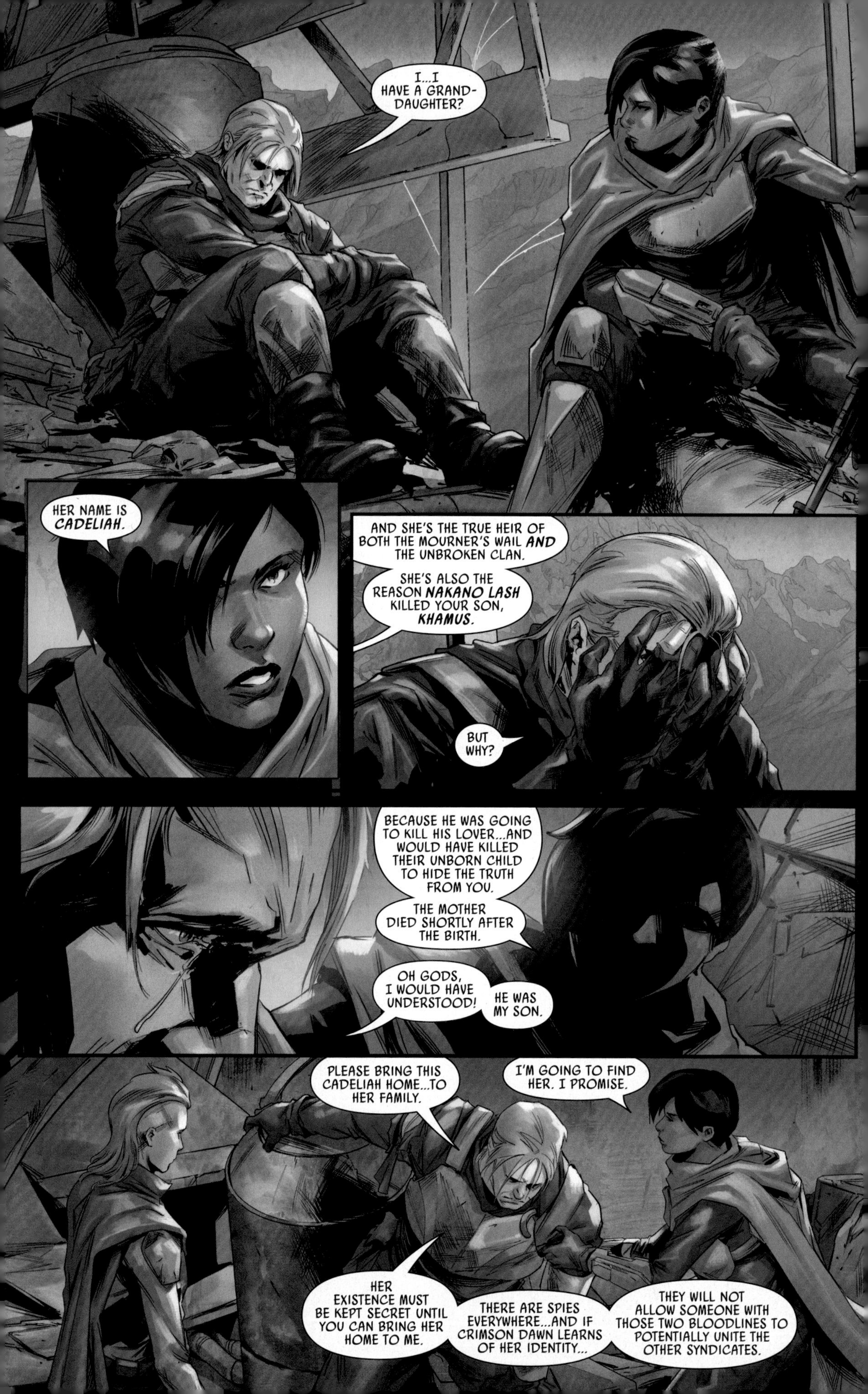
I...I HAVE A GRAND-DAUGHTER?
HER NAME IS CADELIAH.
AND SHE'S THE TRUE HEIR OF BOTH THE MOURNER'S WAIL AND THE UNBROKEN CLAN.
SHE'S ALSO THE REASON NAKANO LASH KILLED YOUR SON, KHAMUS.
BUT WHY?
BECAUSE HE WAS GOING TO KILL HIS LOVER...AND WOULD HAVE KILLED THEIR UNBORN CHILD TO HIDE THE TRUTH FROM YOU.
THE MOTHER DIED SHORTLY AFTER THE BIRTH.
OH GODS, I WOULD HAVE UNDERSTOOD!
HE WAS MY SON.
PLEASE BRING THIS CADELIAH HOME...TO HER FAMILY.
I'M GOING TO FIND HER. I PROMISE.
HER EXISTENCE MUST BE KEPT SECRET UNTIL YOU CAN BRING HER HOME TO ME.
THERE ARE SPIES EVERYWHERE...AND IF CRIMSON DAWN LEARNS OF HER IDENTITY...
THEY WILL NOT ALLOW SOMEONE WITH THOSE TWO BLOODLINES TO POTENTIALLY UNITE THE OTHER SYNDICATES.

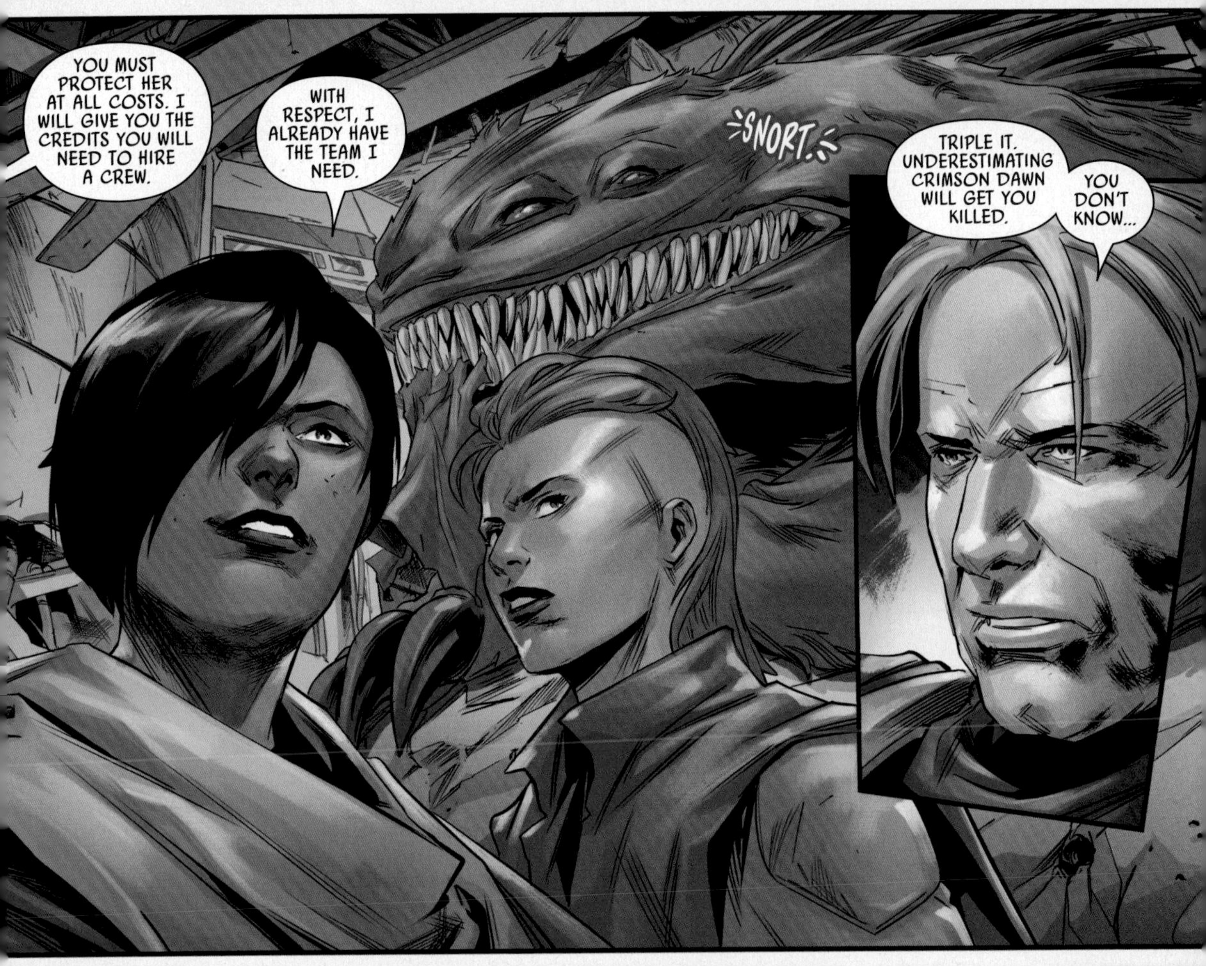
YOU MUST PROTECT HER AT ALL COSTS. I WILL GIVE YOU THE CREDITS YOU WILL NEED TO HIRE A CREW.
WITH RESPECT, I ALREADY HAVE THE TEAM I NEED.
SNORT.
TRIPLE IT. UNDERESTIMATING CRIMSON DAWN WILL GET YOU KILLED.
YOU DON'T KNOW...

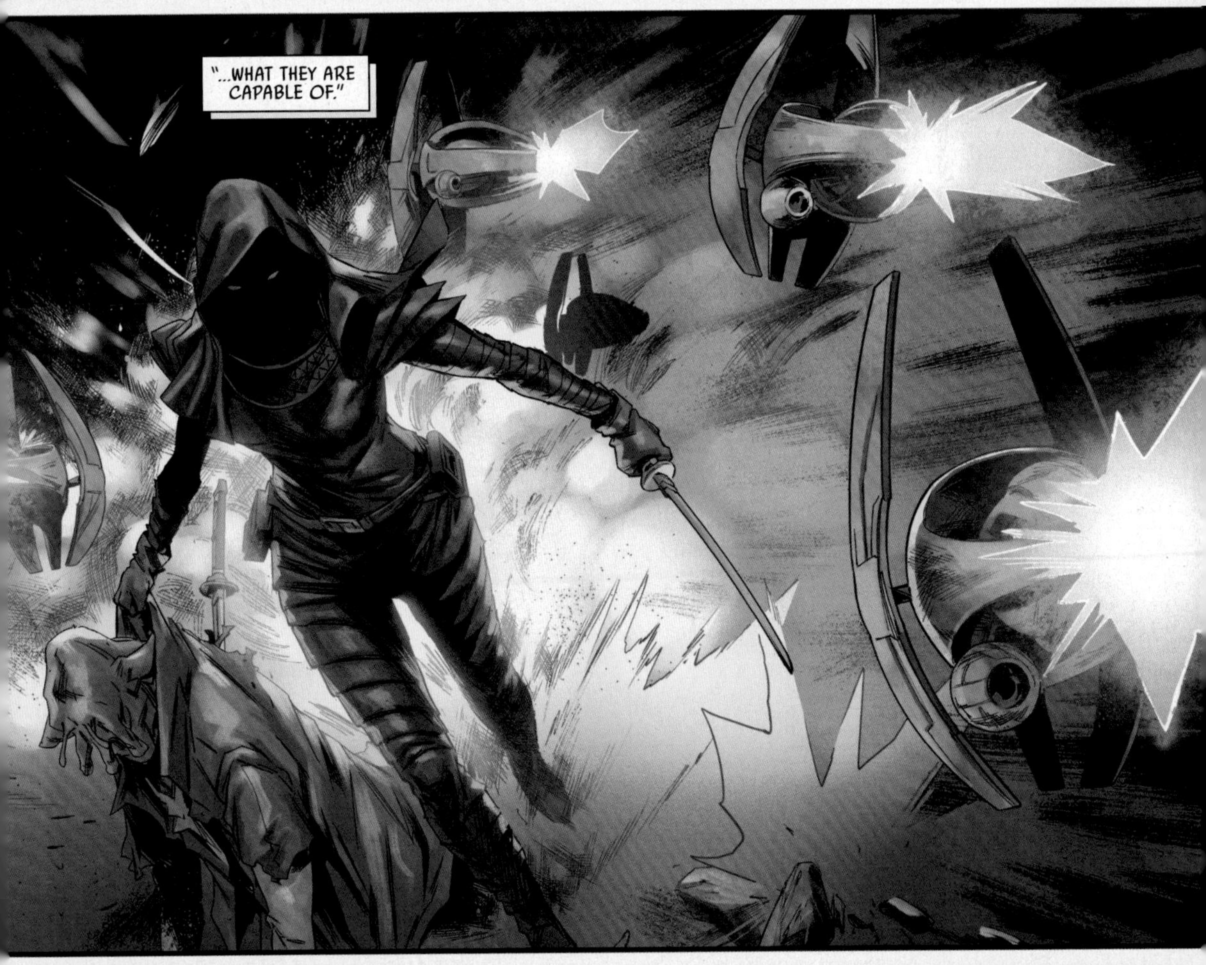
"...WHAT THEY ARE CAPABLE OF."

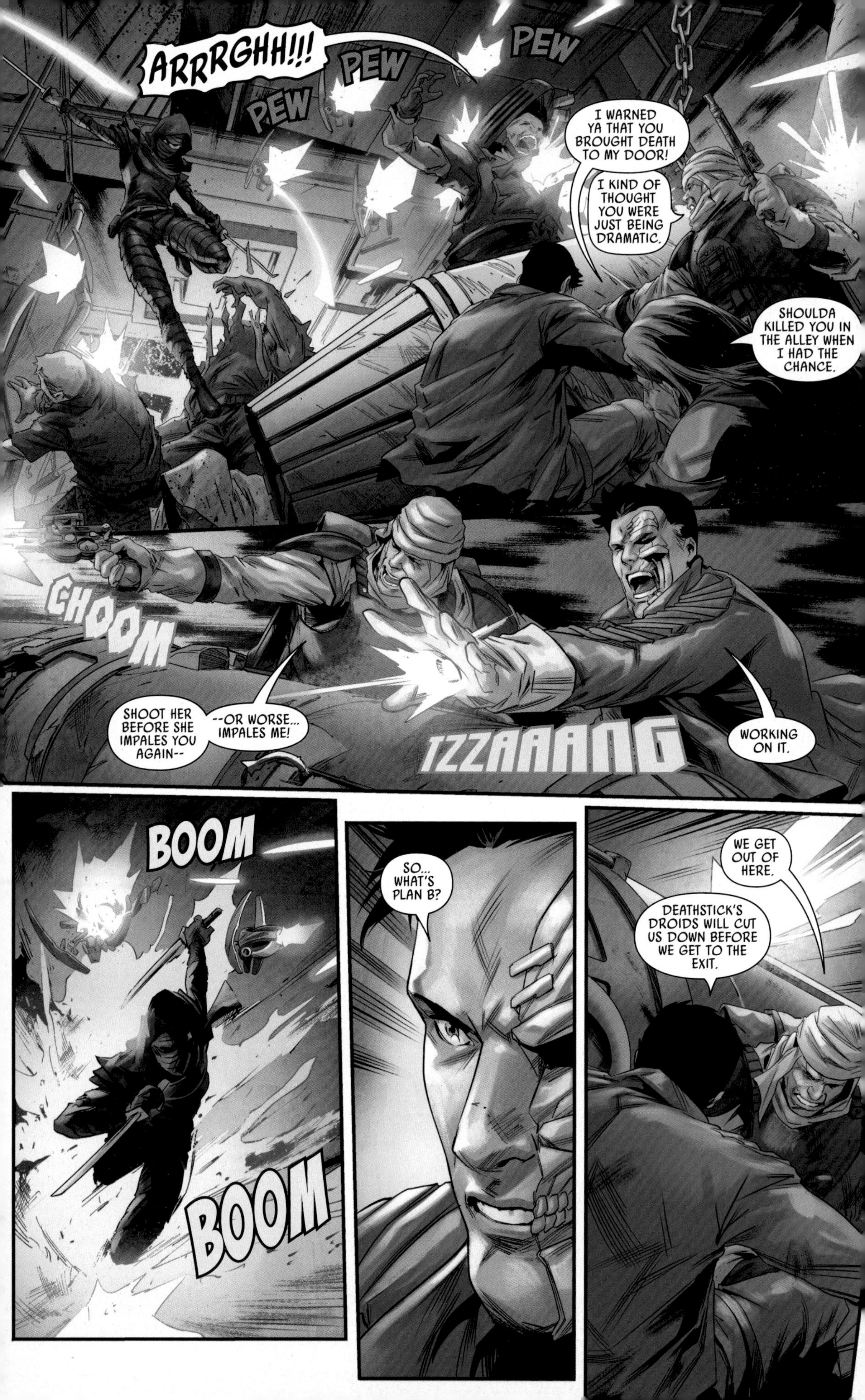
ARRRGHH!!!
PEW
PEW
PEW
I WARNED YA THAT YOU BROUGHT DEATH TO MY DOOR!
I KIND OF THOUGHT YOU WERE JUST BEING DRAMATIC.
SHOULDA KILLED YOU IN THE ALLEY WHEN I HAD THE CHANCE.
CHOOM
SHOOT HER BEFORE SHE IMPALES YOU AGAIN--
--OR WORSE... IMPALES ME!
TZZAAANG
WORKING ON IT.
BOOM
BOOM
SO... WHAT'S PLAN B?
WE GET OUT OF HERE.
DEATHSTICK'S DROIDS WILL CUT US DOWN BEFORE WE GET TO THE EXIT.

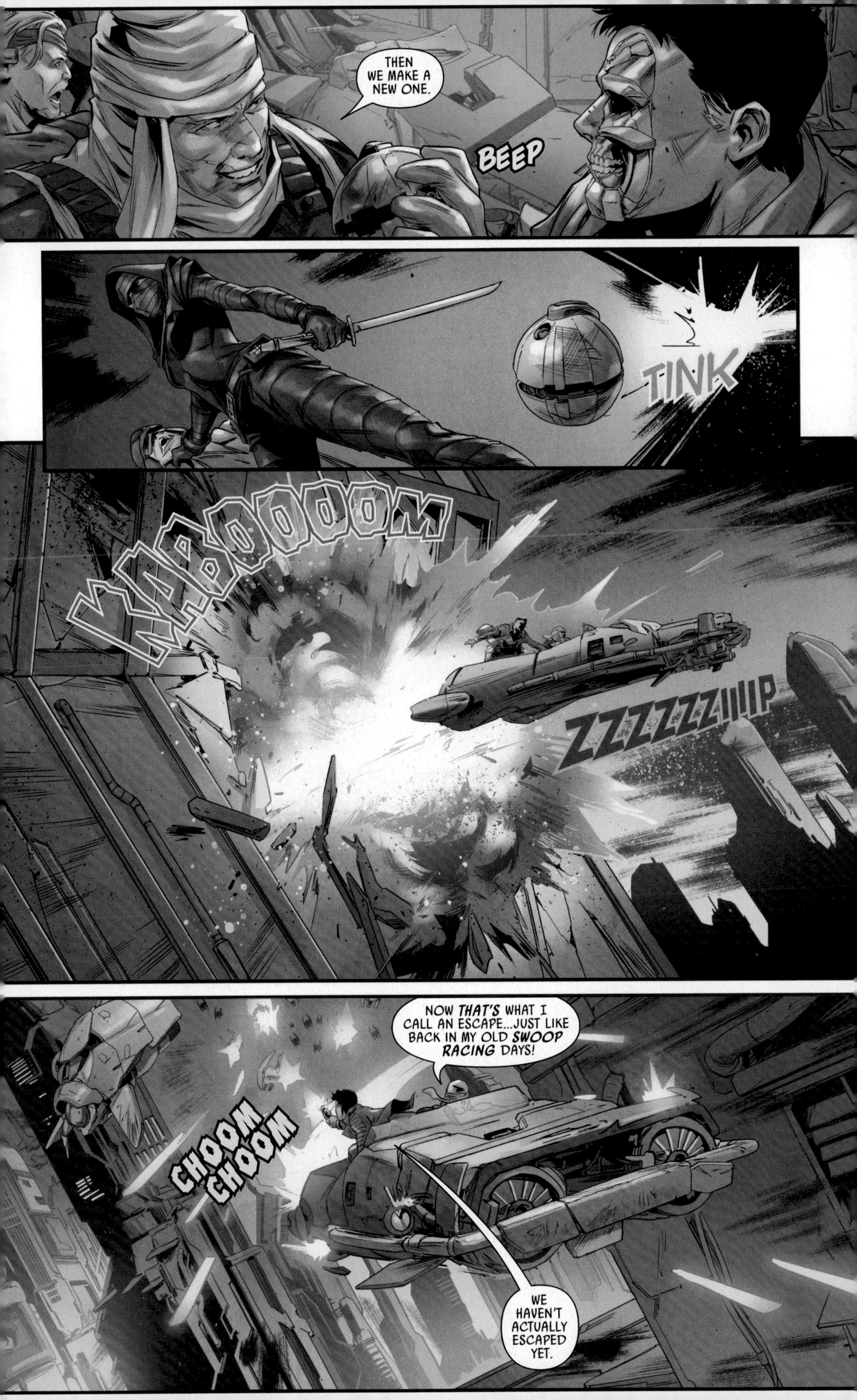
THEN WE MAKE A NEW ONE.
BEEP
TINK
WHOOOOOOM
ZZZZZZIIIIP
NOW THAT'S WHAT I CALL AN ESCAPE...JUST LIKE BACK IN MY OLD SWOOP RACING DAYS!
CHOOM CHOOM
WE HAVEN'T ACTUALLY ESCAPED YET.

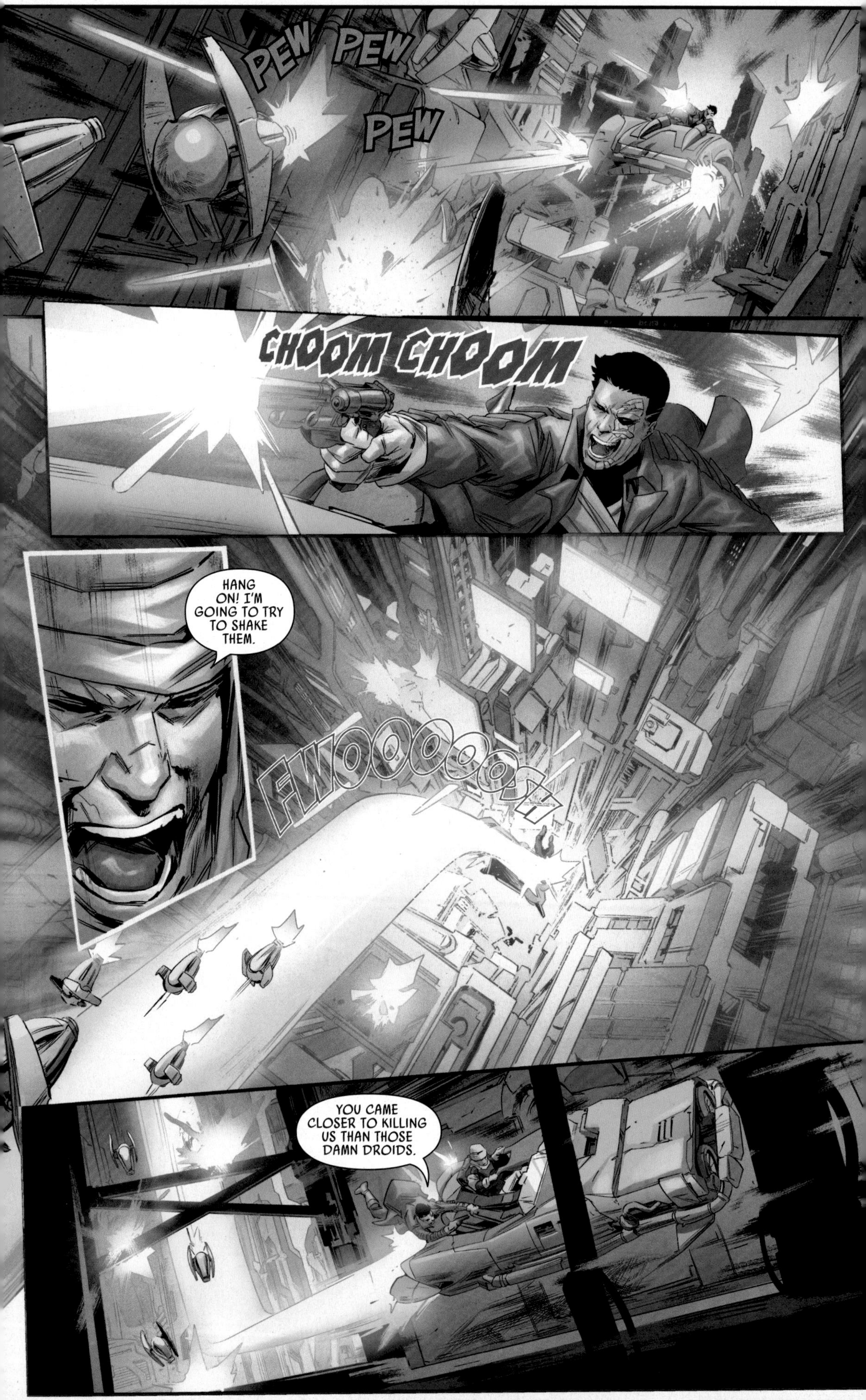
PEW PEW
PEW
CHOOM CHOOM
HANG ON! I'M GOING TO TRY TO SHAKE THEM.
FWOOOOOSH
YOU CAME CLOSER TO KILLING US THAN THOSE DAMN DROIDS.

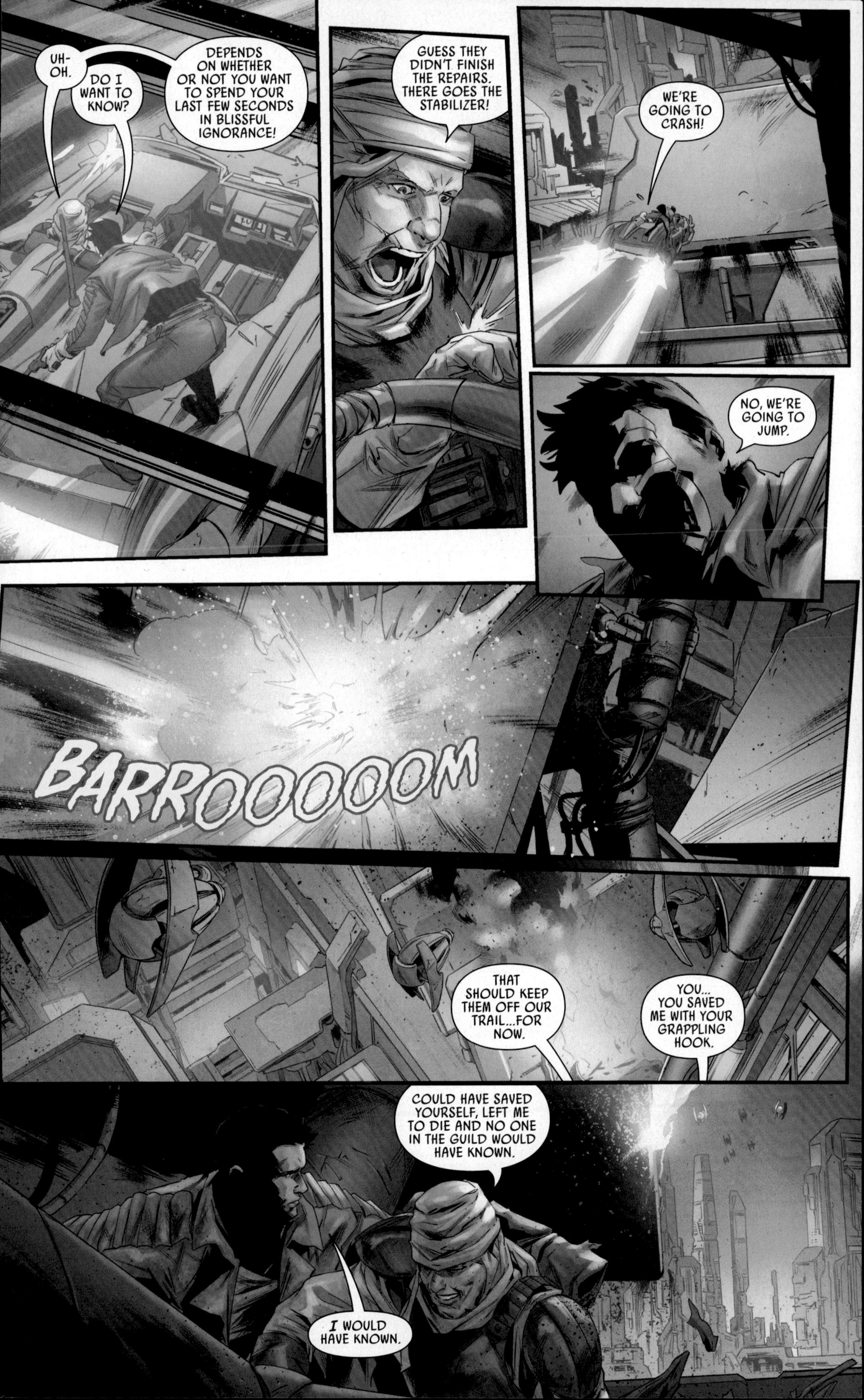
UH-OH.
DO I WANT TO KNOW?
DEPENDS ON WHETHER OR NOT YOU WANT TO SPEND YOUR LAST FEW SECONDS IN BLISSFUL IGNORANCE!
GUESS THEY DIDN'T FINISH THE REPAIRS. THERE GOES THE STABILIZER!
WE'RE GOING TO CRASH!
NO, WE'RE GOING TO JUMP.
BARROOOOOOM
THAT SHOULD KEEP THEM OFF OUR TRAIL...FOR NOW.
YOU... YOU SAVED ME WITH YOUR GRAPPLING HOOK.
COULD HAVE SAVED YOURSELF, LEFT ME TO DIE AND NO ONE IN THE GUILD WOULD HAVE KNOWN.
I WOULD HAVE KNOWN.

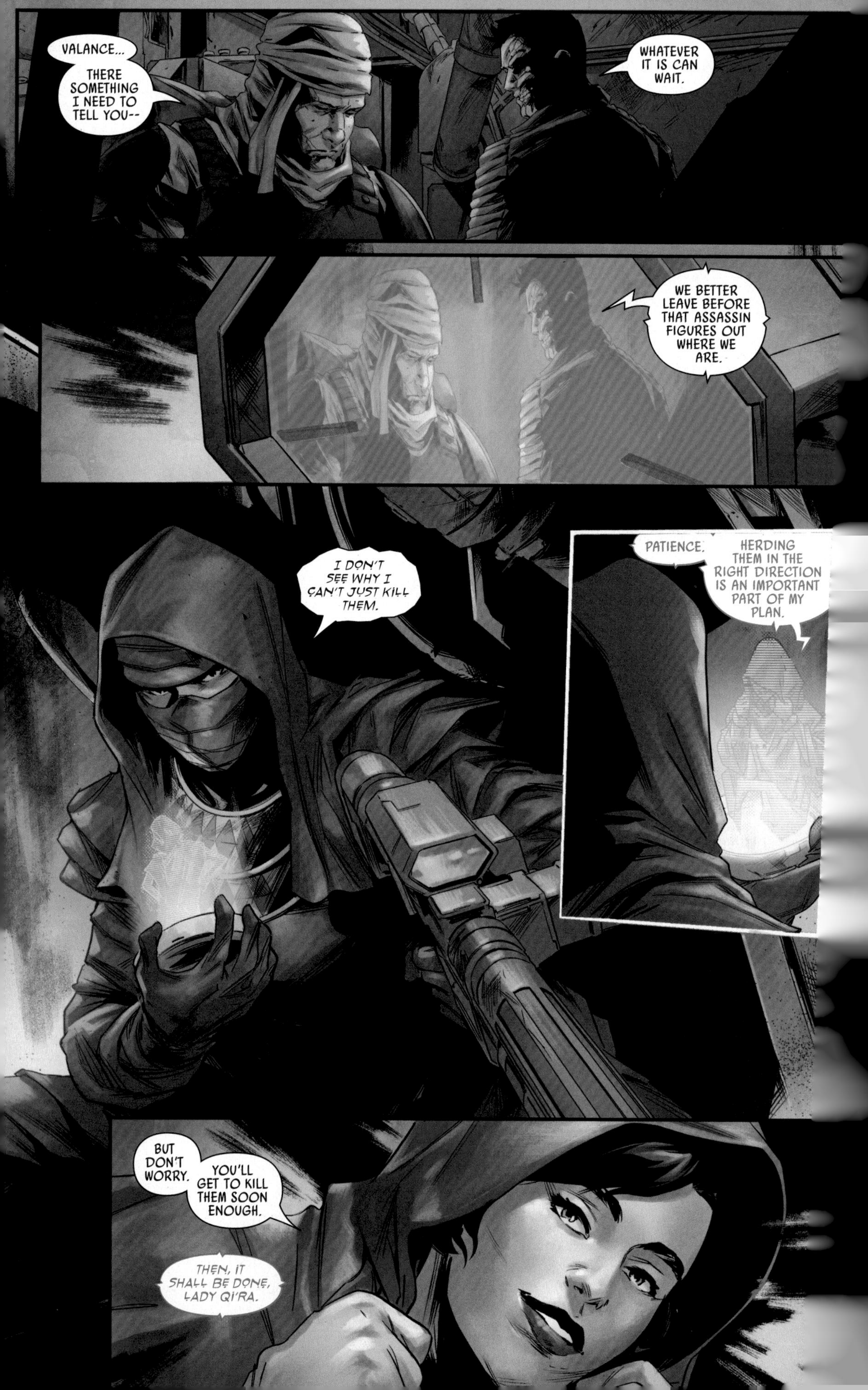
VALANCE...
THERE SOMETHING I NEED TO TELL YOU--
WHATEVER IT IS CAN WAIT.
WE BETTER LEAVE BEFORE THAT ASSASSIN FIGURES OUT WHERE WE ARE.
I DON'T SEE WHY I CAN'T JUST KILL THEM.
PATIENCE.
HERDING THEM IN THE RIGHT DIRECTION IS AN IMPORTANT PART OF MY PLAN.
BUT DON'T WORRY.
YOU'LL GET TO KILL THEM SOON ENOUGH.
THEN, IT SHALL BE DONE, LADY QI'RA.

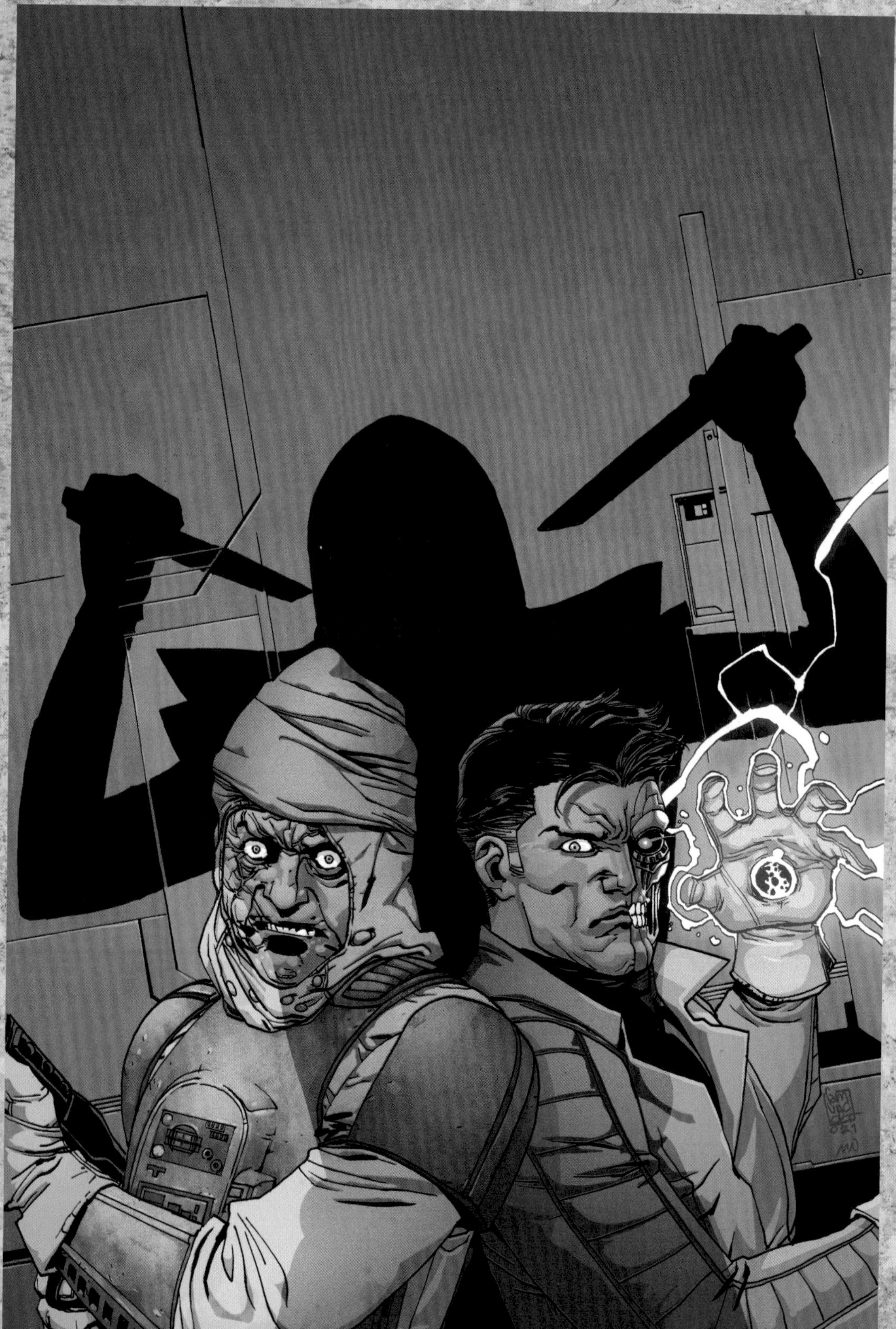

15 – THE GATHERING

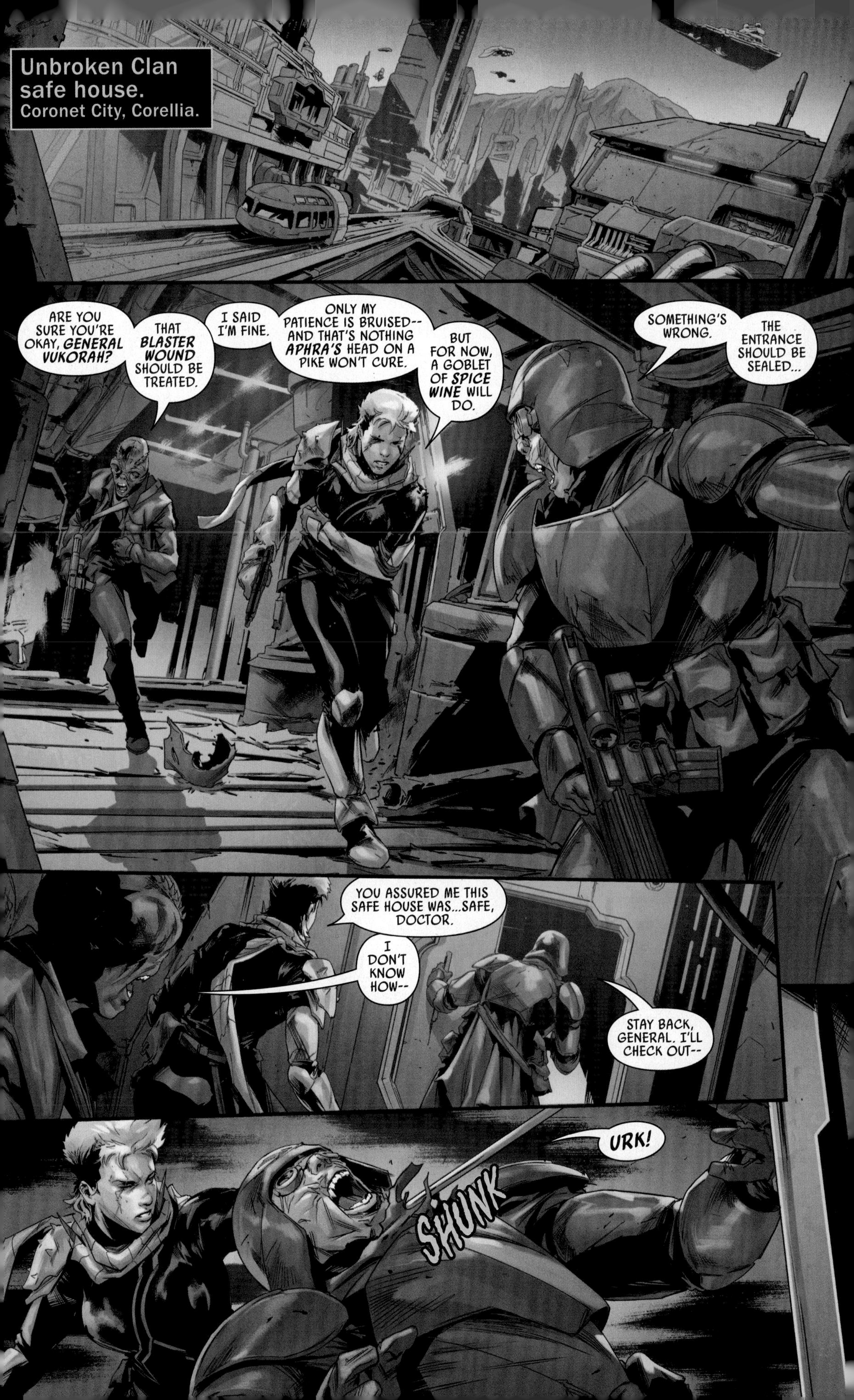
Unbroken Clan safe house.
Coronet City, Corellia.
ARE YOU SURE YOU'RE OKAY, GENERAL VUKORAH?
THAT BLASTER WOUND SHOULD BE TREATED.
I SAID I'M FINE.
ONLY MY PATIENCE IS BRUISED-- AND THAT'S NOTHING APHRA'S HEAD ON A PIKE WON'T CURE.
BUT FOR NOW, A GOBLET OF SPICE WINE WILL DO.
SOMETHING'S WRONG.
THE ENTRANCE SHOULD BE SEALED...
YOU ASSURED ME THIS SAFE HOUSE WAS...SAFE, DOCTOR.
I DON'T KNOW HOW--
STAY BACK, GENERAL. I'LL CHECK OUT--
URK!
SHUNK

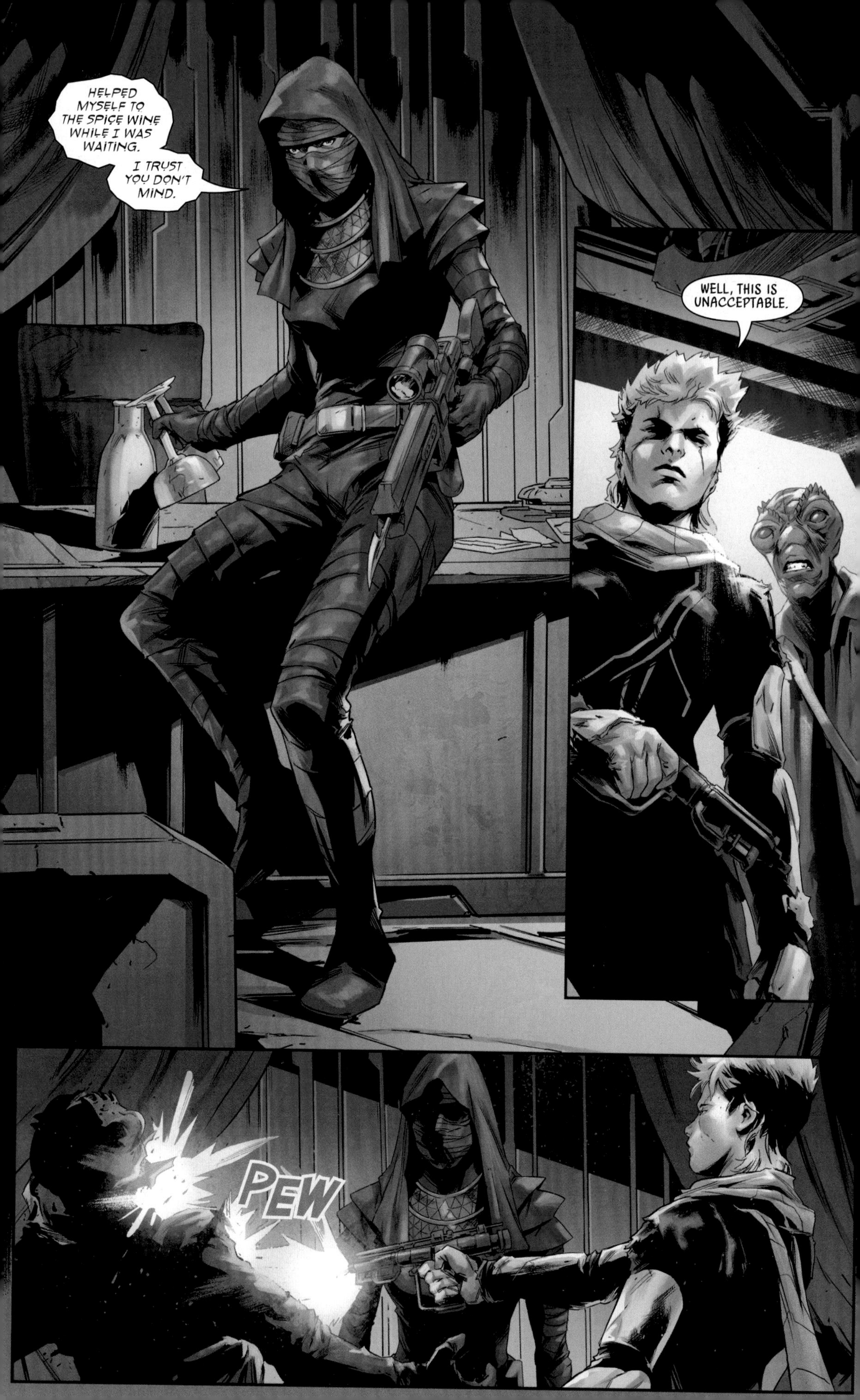
HELPED MYSELF TO THE SPICE WINE WHILE I WAS WAITING.
I TRUST YOU DON'T MIND.
WELL, THIS IS UNACCEPTABLE.
PEW

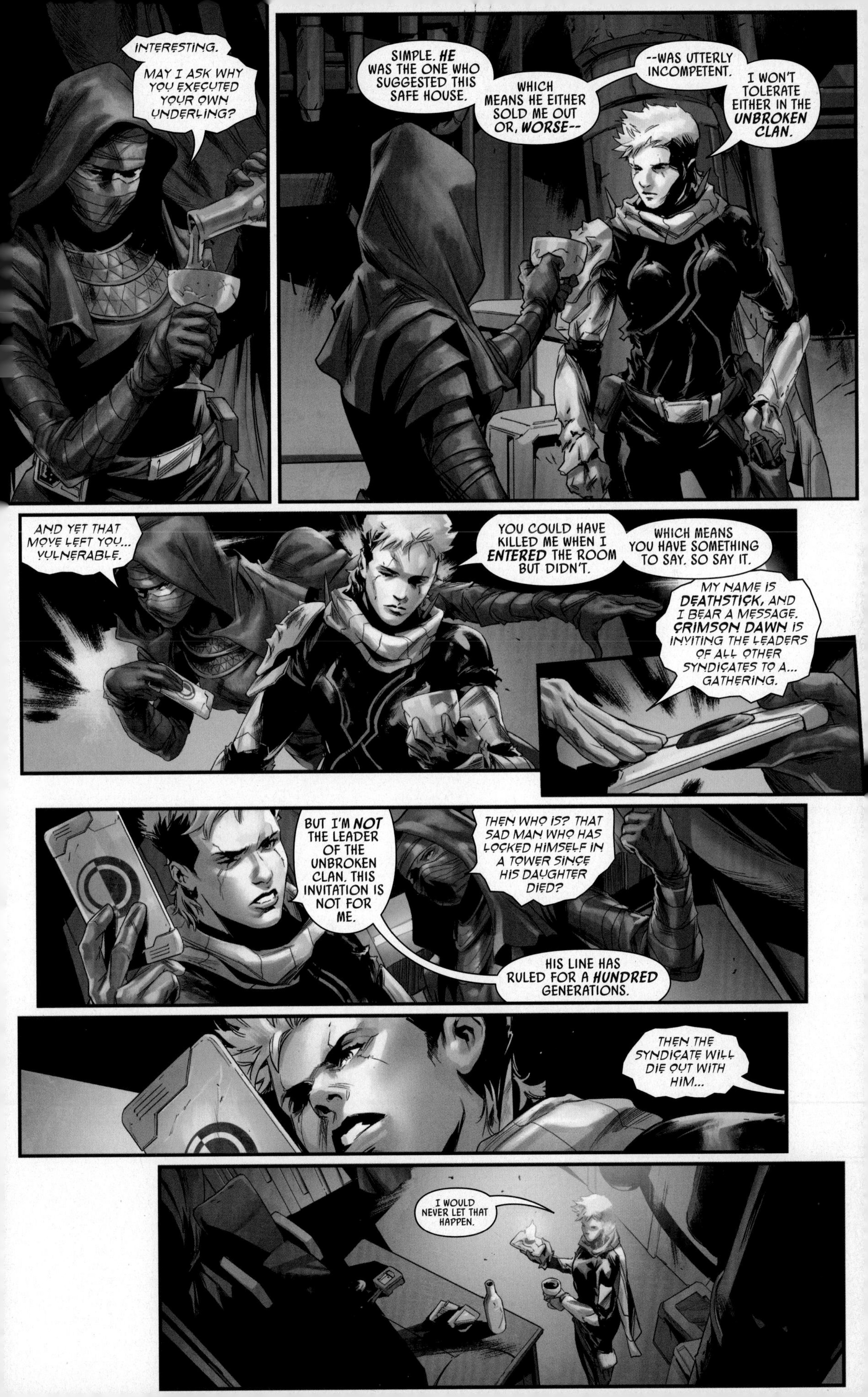
INTERESTING.
MAY I ASK WHY YOU EXECUTED YOUR OWN UNDERLING?
SIMPLE. HE WAS THE ONE WHO SUGGESTED THIS SAFE HOUSE.
WHICH MEANS HE EITHER SOLD ME OUT OR, WORSE--
--WAS UTTERLY INCOMPETENT.
I WON'T TOLERATE EITHER IN THE UNBROKEN CLAN.
AND YET THAT MOVE LEFT YOU... VULNERABLE.
YOU COULD HAVE KILLED ME WHEN I ENTERED THE ROOM BUT DIDN'T.
WHICH MEANS YOU HAVE SOMETHING TO SAY. SO SAY IT.
MY NAME IS DEATHSTICK, AND I BEAR A MESSAGE. CRIMSON DAWN IS INVITING THE LEADERS OF ALL OTHER SYNDICATES TO A... GATHERING.
BUT I'M NOT THE LEADER OF THE UNBROKEN CLAN. THIS INVITATION IS NOT FOR ME.
THEN WHO IS? THAT SAD MAN WHO HAS LOCKED HIMSELF IN A TOWER SINCE HIS DAUGHTER DIED?
HIS LINE HAS RULED FOR A HUNDRED GENERATIONS.
THEN THE SYNDICATE WILL DIE OUT WITH HIM...
I WOULD NEVER LET THAT HAPPEN.

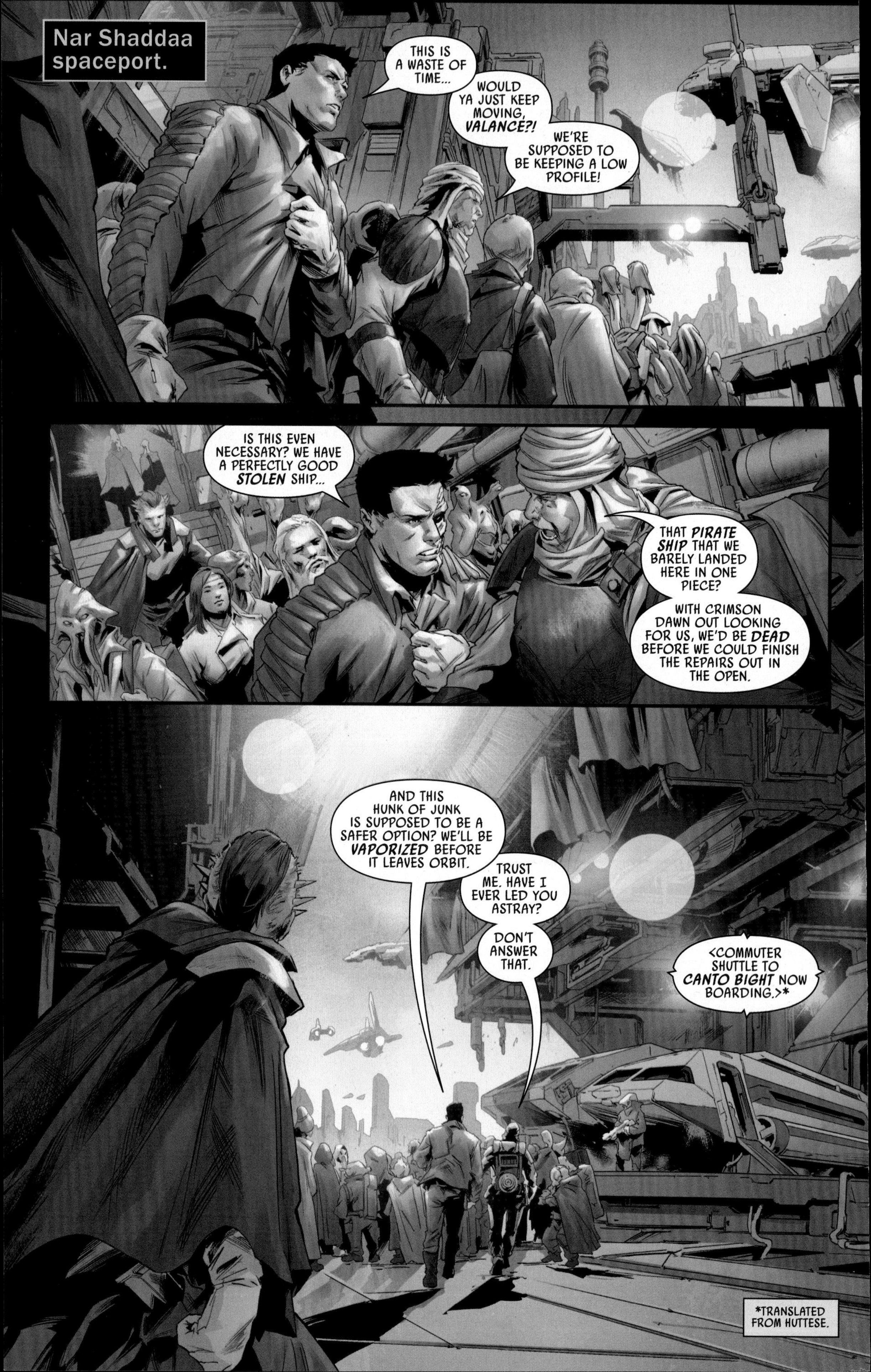
Nar Shaddaa spaceport.
THIS IS A WASTE OF TIME...
WOULD YA JUST KEEP MOVING, VALANCE?!
WE'RE SUPPOSED TO BE KEEPING A LOW PROFILE!
IS THIS EVEN NECESSARY? WE HAVE A PERFECTLY GOOD STOLEN SHIP...
THAT PIRATE SHIP THAT WE BARELY LANDED HERE IN ONE PIECE?
WITH CRIMSON DAWN OUT LOOKING FOR US, WE'D BE DEAD BEFORE WE COULD FINISH THE REPAIRS OUT IN THE OPEN.
AND THIS HUNK OF JUNK IS SUPPOSED TO BE A SAFER OPTION? WE'LL BE VAPORIZED BEFORE IT LEAVES ORBIT.
TRUST ME. HAVE I EVER LED YOU ASTRAY?
DON'T ANSWER THAT.
<COMMUTER SHUTTLE TO CANTO BIGHT NOW BOARDING.>*
*TRANSLATED FROM HUTTESE.

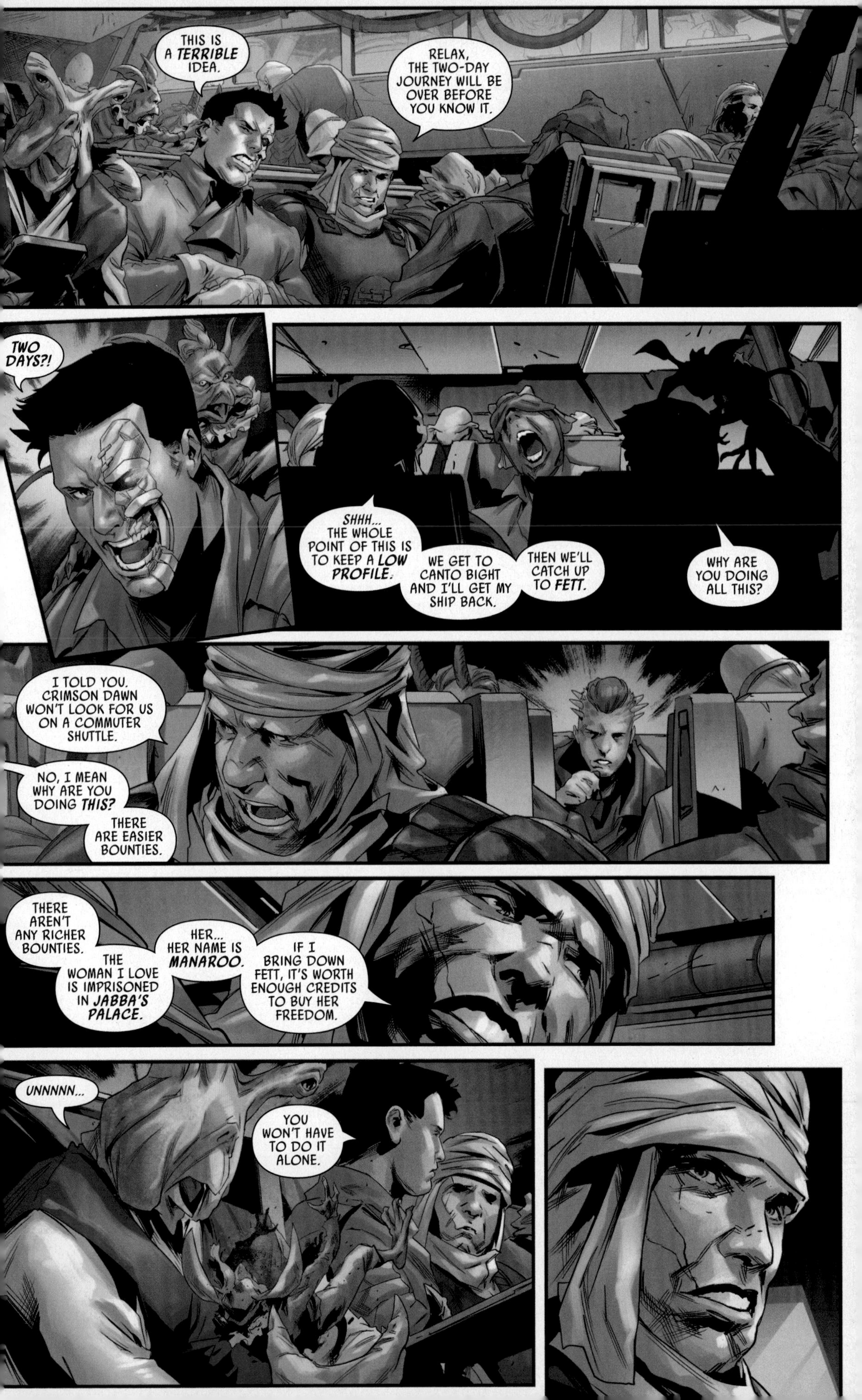
THIS IS A *TERRIBLE* IDEA.
RELAX, THE TWO-DAY JOURNEY WILL BE OVER BEFORE YOU KNOW IT.
TWO DAYS?!
SHHH... THE WHOLE POINT OF THIS IS TO KEEP A *LOW PROFILE.*
WE GET TO CANTO BIGHT AND I'LL GET MY SHIP BACK.
THEN WE'LL CATCH UP TO *FETT.*
WHY ARE YOU DOING ALL THIS?
I TOLD YOU. CRIMSON DAWN WON'T LOOK FOR US ON A COMMUTER SHUTTLE.
NO, I MEAN WHY ARE YOU DOING *THIS?*
THERE ARE EASIER BOUNTIES.
THERE AREN'T ANY RICHER BOUNTIES.
THE WOMAN I LOVE IS IMPRISONED IN *JABBA'S PALACE.*
HER... HER NAME IS *MANAROO.*
IF I BRING DOWN FETT, IT'S WORTH ENOUGH CREDITS TO BUY HER FREEDOM.
UNNNNN...
YOU WON'T HAVE TO DO IT ALONE.

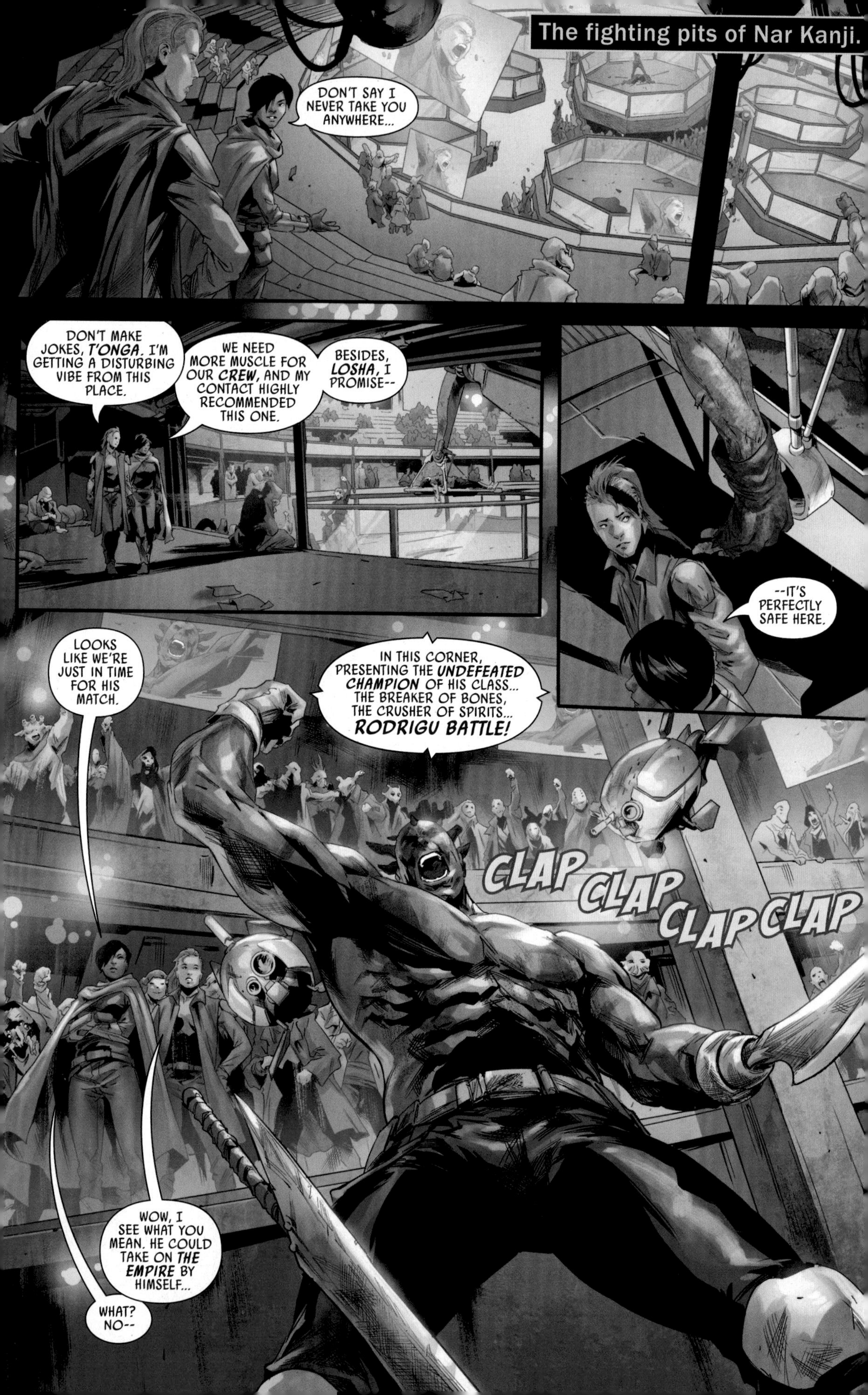
The fighting pits of Nar Kanji.
DON'T SAY I NEVER TAKE YOU ANYWHERE...
DON'T MAKE JOKES, T'ONGA. I'M GETTING A DISTURBING VIBE FROM THIS PLACE.
WE NEED MORE MUSCLE FOR OUR CREW, AND MY CONTACT HIGHLY RECOMMENDED THIS ONE.
BESIDES, LOSHA, I PROMISE--
--IT'S PERFECTLY SAFE HERE.
LOOKS LIKE WE'RE JUST IN TIME FOR HIS MATCH.
IN THIS CORNER, PRESENTING THE UNDEFEATED CHAMPION OF HIS CLASS... THE BREAKER OF BONES, THE CRUSHER OF SPIRITS... RODRIGU BATTLE!
CLAP CLAP CLAP CLAP
WOW, I SEE WHAT YOU MEAN. HE COULD TAKE ON THE EMPIRE BY HIMSELF...
WHAT? NO--

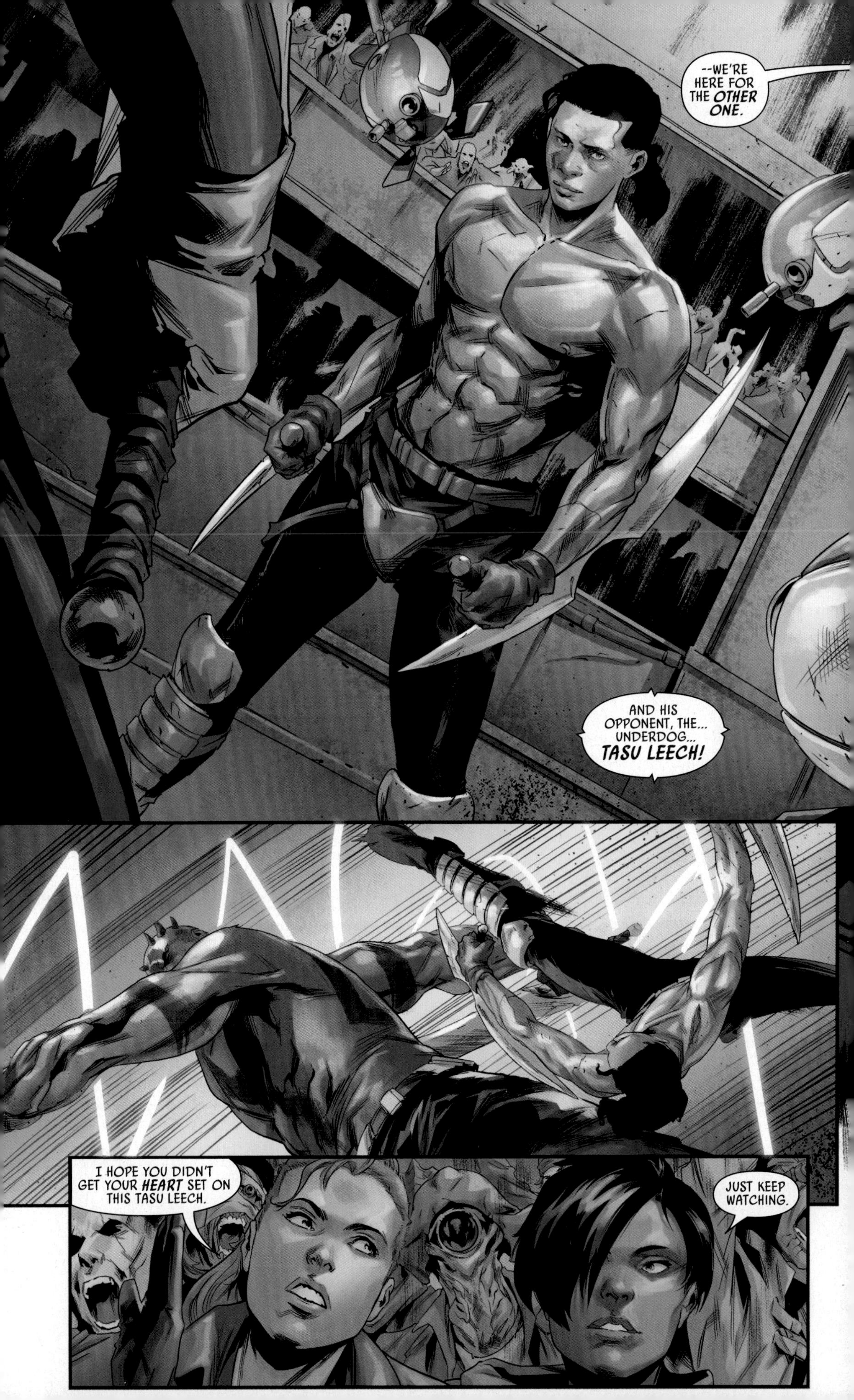
--WE'RE HERE FOR THE OTHER ONE.
AND HIS OPPONENT, THE... UNDERDOG... TASU LEECH!
I HOPE YOU DIDN'T GET YOUR HEART SET ON THIS TASU LEECH.
JUST KEEP WATCHING.

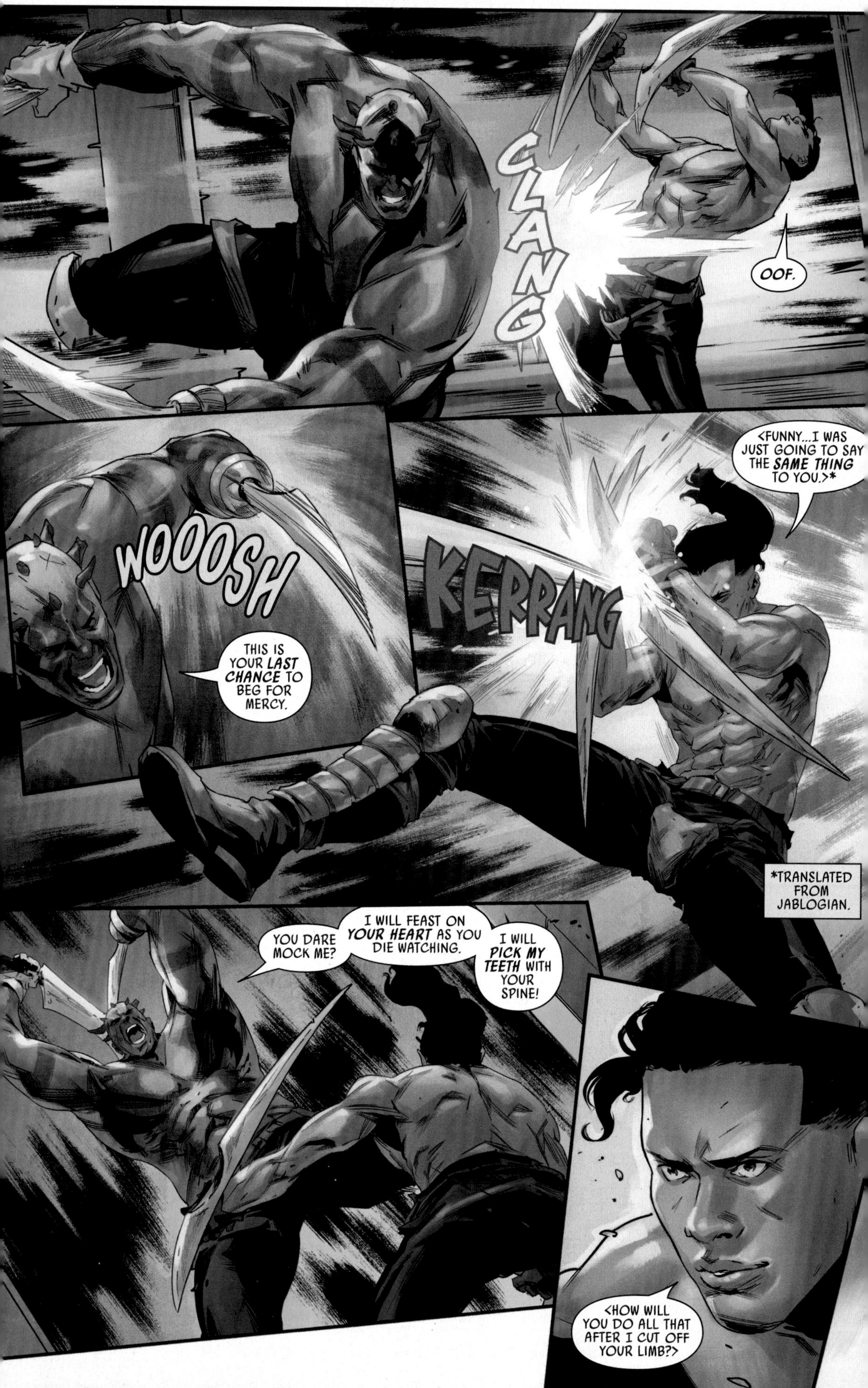
CLANG
OOF.
WOOOSH
THIS IS YOUR LAST CHANCE TO BEG FOR MERCY.
KERRANG
<FUNNY...I WAS JUST GOING TO SAY THE SAME THING TO YOU.>*
*TRANSLATED FROM JABLOGIAN.
YOU DARE MOCK ME?
I WILL FEAST ON YOUR HEART AS YOU DIE WATCHING.
I WILL PICK MY TEETH WITH YOUR SPINE!
<HOW WILL YOU DO ALL THAT AFTER I CUT OFF YOUR LIMB?>

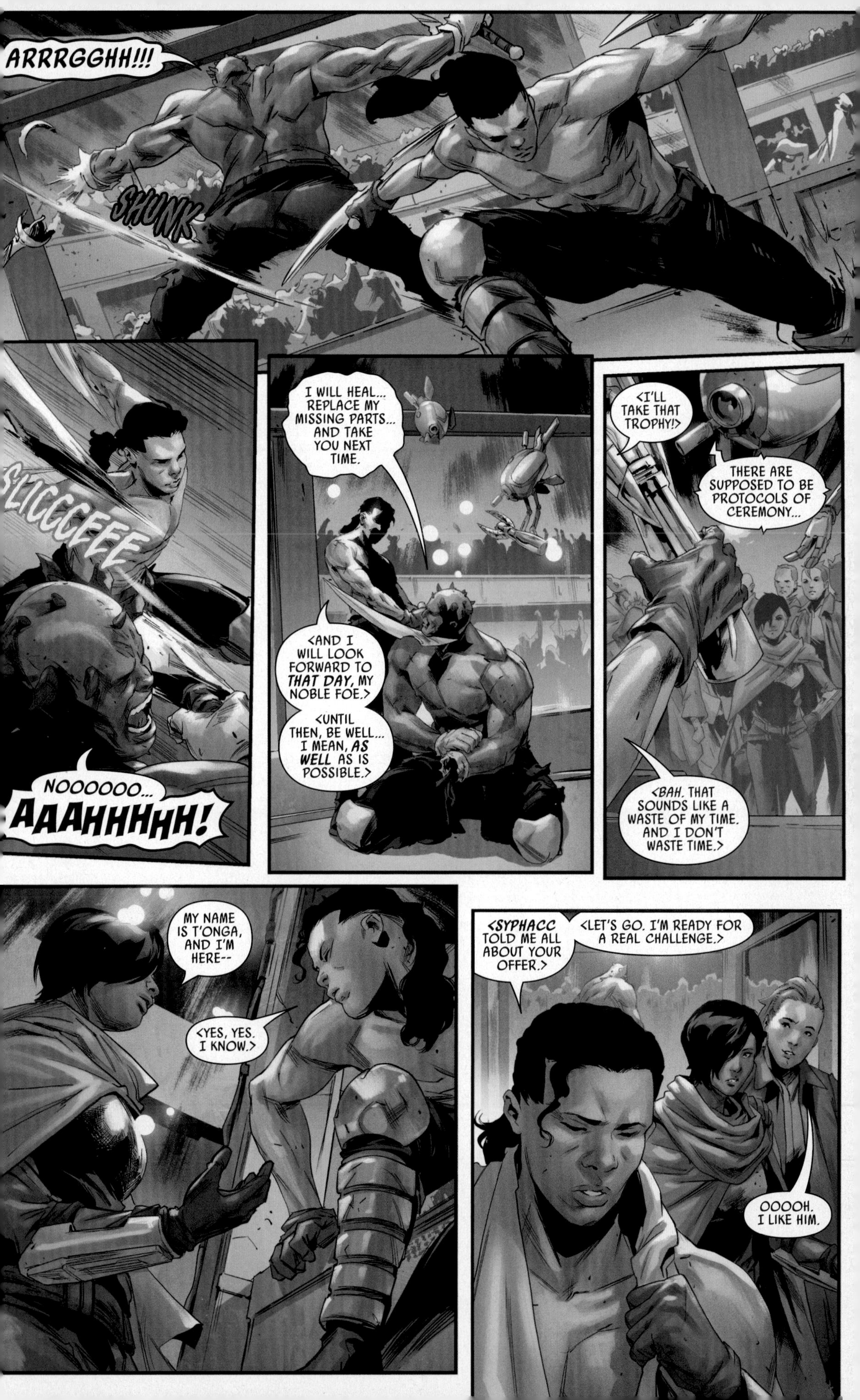
ARRRGGHH!!!
SHUNK
SLICCCEEEE
NOOOOOO...
AAAHHHHH!
I WILL HEAL... REPLACE MY MISSING PARTS... AND TAKE YOU NEXT TIME.
<AND I WILL LOOK FORWARD TO THAT DAY, MY NOBLE FOE.>
<UNTIL THEN, BE WELL... I MEAN, AS WELL AS IS POSSIBLE.>
<I'LL TAKE THAT TROPHY!>
THERE ARE SUPPOSED TO BE PROTOCOLS OF CEREMONY...
<BAH. THAT SOUNDS LIKE A WASTE OF MY TIME. AND I DON'T WASTE TIME.>
MY NAME IS T'ONGA, AND I'M HERE--
<YES, YES. I KNOW.>
<SYPHACC TOLD ME ALL ABOUT YOUR OFFER.>
<LET'S GO. I'M READY FOR A REAL CHALLENGE.>
OOOOH. I LIKE HIM.

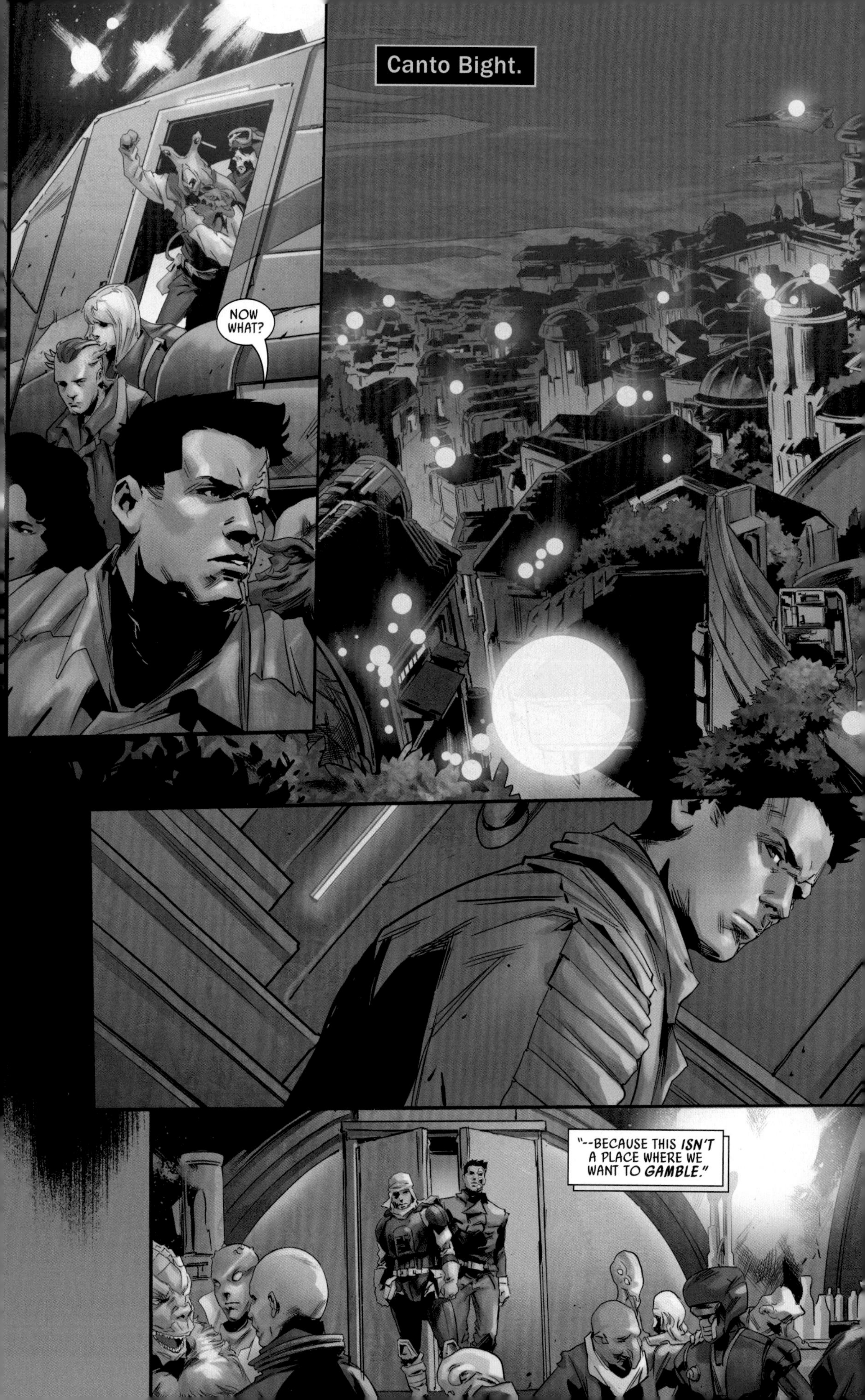
Canto Bight.
NOW WHAT?
"--BECAUSE THIS ISN'T A PLACE WHERE WE WANT TO GAMBLE."

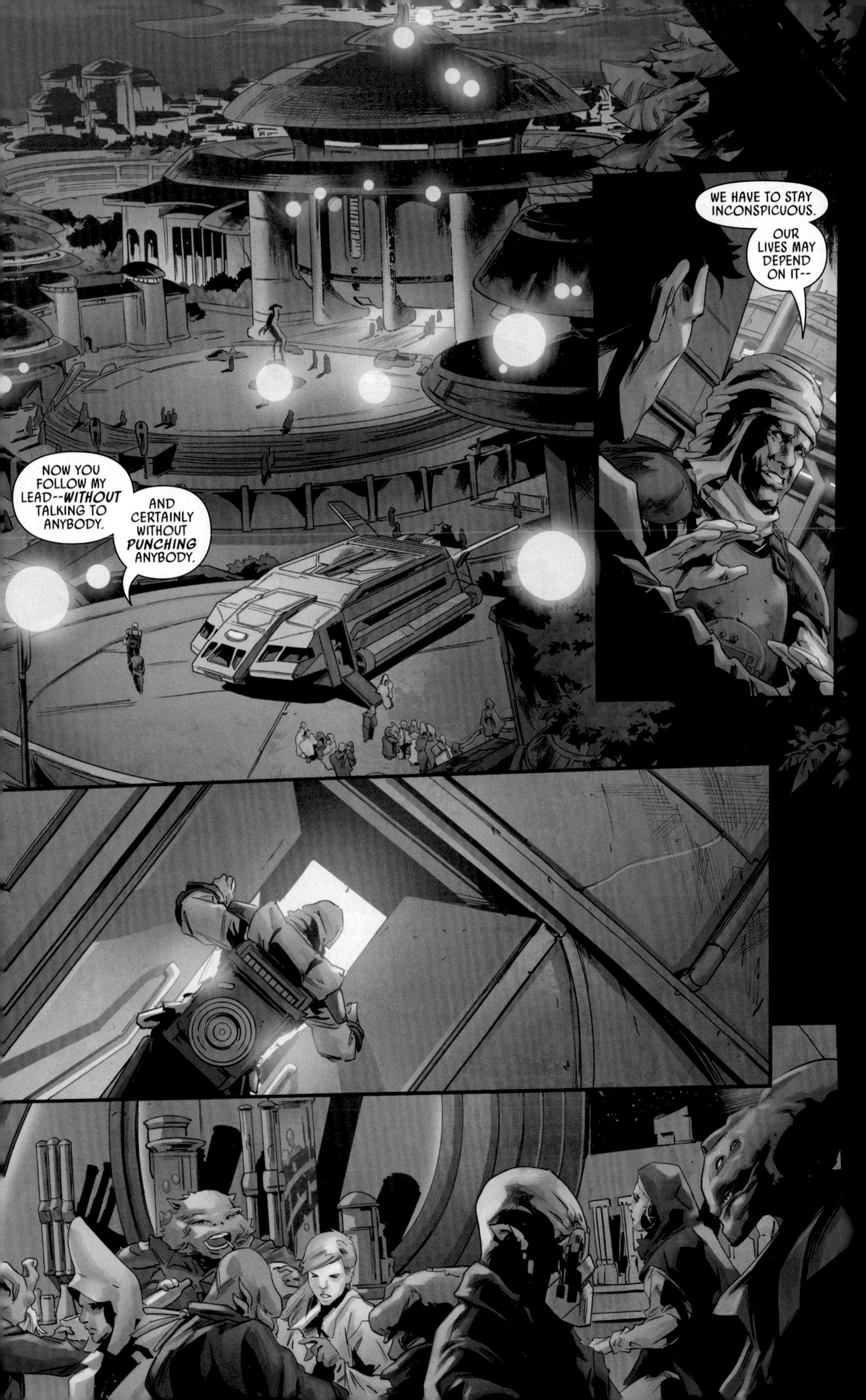
NOW YOU FOLLOW MY LEAD--*WITHOUT* TALKING TO ANYBODY.
AND CERTAINLY WITHOUT *PUNCHING* ANYBODY.
WE HAVE TO STAY INCONSPICUOUS.
OUR LIVES MAY DEPEND ON IT--

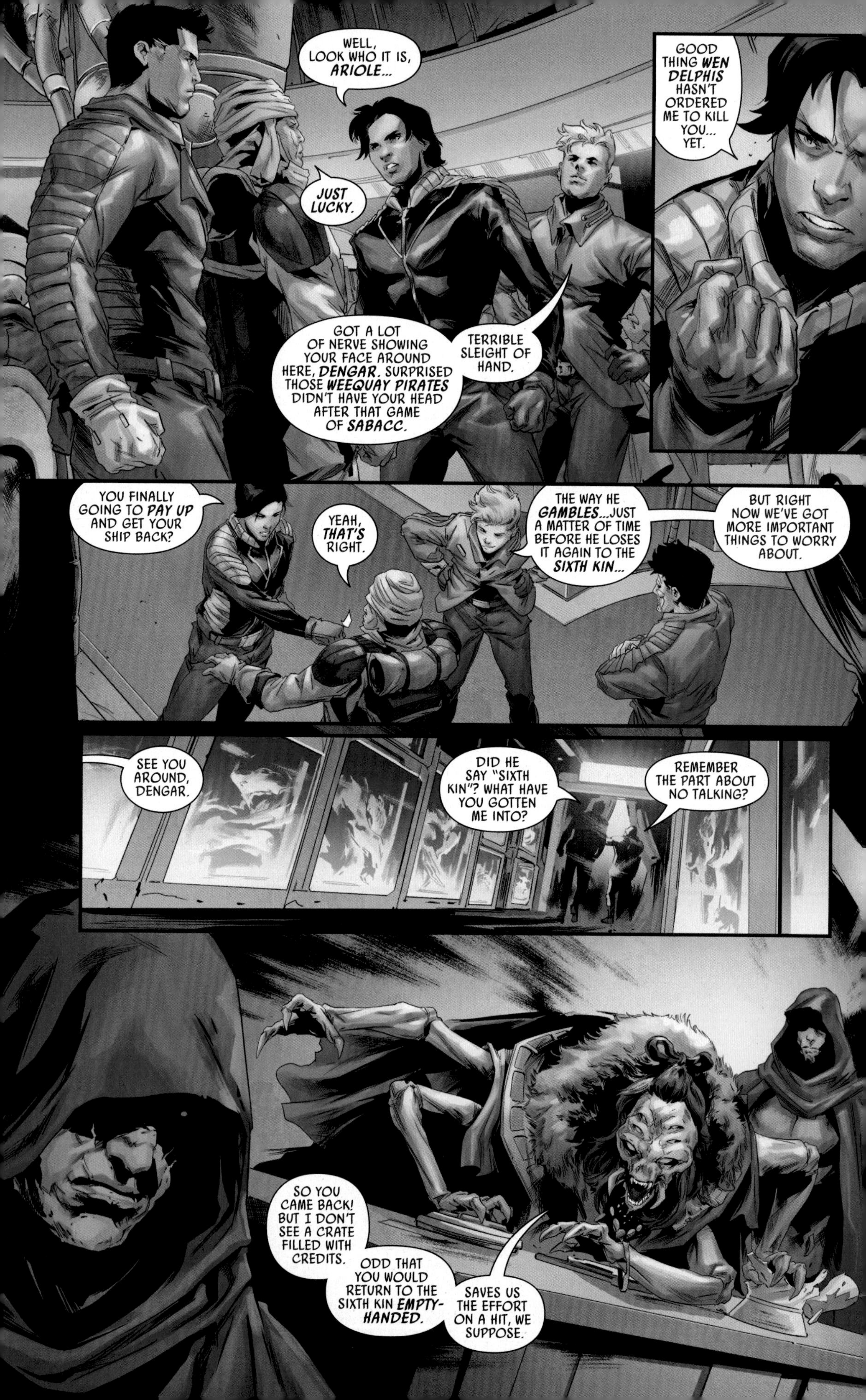
WELL, LOOK WHO IT IS, ARIOLE...
JUST LUCKY.
GOOD THING WEN DELPHIS HASN'T ORDERED ME TO KILL YOU... YET.
GOT A LOT OF NERVE SHOWING YOUR FACE AROUND HERE, DENGAR. SURPRISED THOSE WEEQUAY PIRATES DIDN'T HAVE YOUR HEAD AFTER THAT GAME OF SABACC.
TERRIBLE SLEIGHT OF HAND.
YOU FINALLY GOING TO PAY UP AND GET YOUR SHIP BACK?
YEAH, THAT'S RIGHT.
THE WAY HE GAMBLES...JUST A MATTER OF TIME BEFORE HE LOSES IT AGAIN TO THE SIXTH KIN...
BUT RIGHT NOW WE'VE GOT MORE IMPORTANT THINGS TO WORRY ABOUT.
SEE YOU AROUND, DENGAR.
DID HE SAY "SIXTH KIN"? WHAT HAVE YOU GOTTEN ME INTO?
REMEMBER THE PART ABOUT NO TALKING?
SO YOU CAME BACK! BUT I DON'T SEE A CRATE FILLED WITH CREDITS.
ODD THAT YOU WOULD RETURN TO THE SIXTH KIN EMPTY-HANDED.
SAVES US THE EFFORT ON A HIT, WE SUPPOSE.

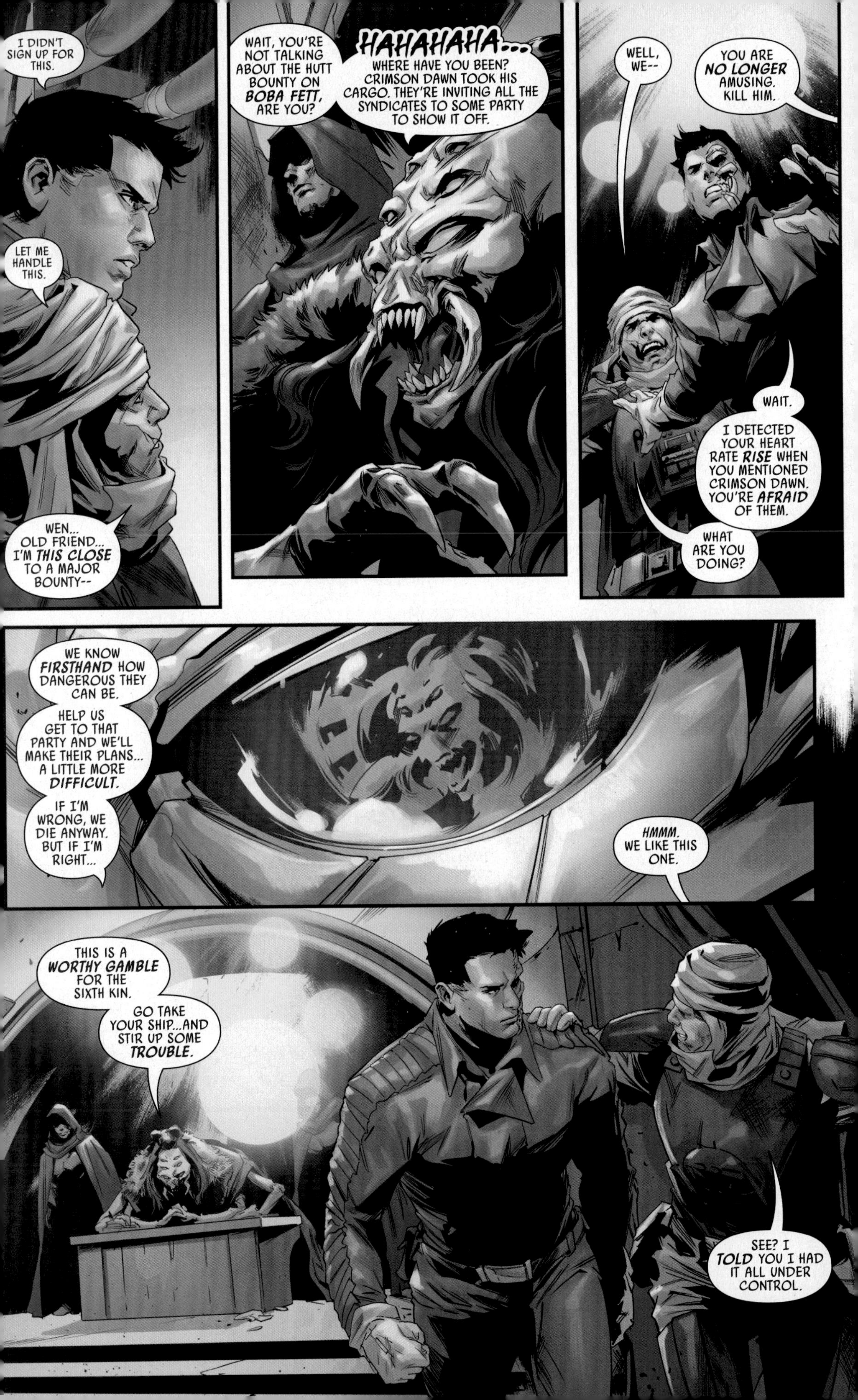
I DIDN'T SIGN UP FOR THIS.
LET ME HANDLE THIS.
WEN... OLD FRIEND... I'M **THIS CLOSE** TO A MAJOR BOUNTY--
WAIT, YOU'RE NOT TALKING ABOUT THE HUTT BOUNTY ON **BOBA FETT**, ARE YOU?
HAHAHAHA...
WHERE HAVE YOU BEEN? CRIMSON DAWN TOOK HIS CARGO. THEY'RE INVITING ALL THE SYNDICATES TO SOME PARTY TO SHOW IT OFF.
WELL, WE--
YOU ARE **NO LONGER** AMUSING. KILL HIM.
WAIT.
I DETECTED YOUR HEART RATE **RISE** WHEN YOU MENTIONED CRIMSON DAWN. YOU'RE **AFRAID** OF THEM.
WHAT ARE YOU DOING?
WE KNOW **FIRSTHAND** HOW DANGEROUS THEY CAN BE.
HELP US GET TO THAT PARTY AND WE'LL MAKE THEIR PLANS... A LITTLE MORE **DIFFICULT**.
IF I'M WRONG, WE DIE ANYWAY. BUT IF I'M RIGHT...
HMMM. WE LIKE THIS ONE.
THIS IS A **WORTHY GAMBLE** FOR THE SIXTH KIN.
GO TAKE YOUR SHIP...AND STIR UP SOME **TROUBLE**.
SEE? I **TOLD** YOU I HAD IT ALL UNDER CONTROL.

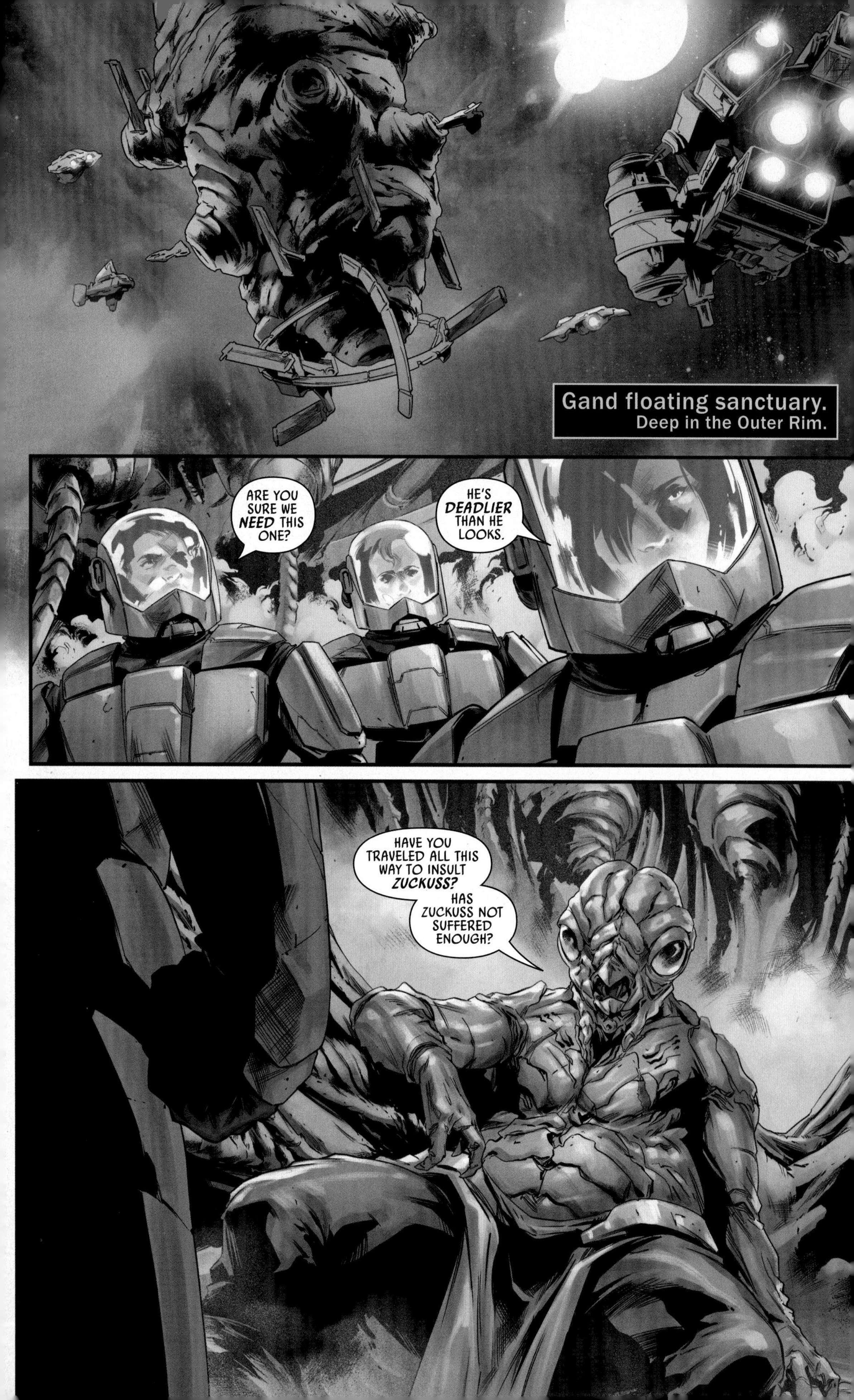
Gand floating sanctuary.
Deep in the Outer Rim.
ARE YOU SURE WE NEED THIS ONE?
HE'S DEADLIER THAN HE LOOKS.
HAVE YOU TRAVELED ALL THIS WAY TO INSULT ZUCKUSS?
HAS ZUCKUSS NOT SUFFERED ENOUGH?

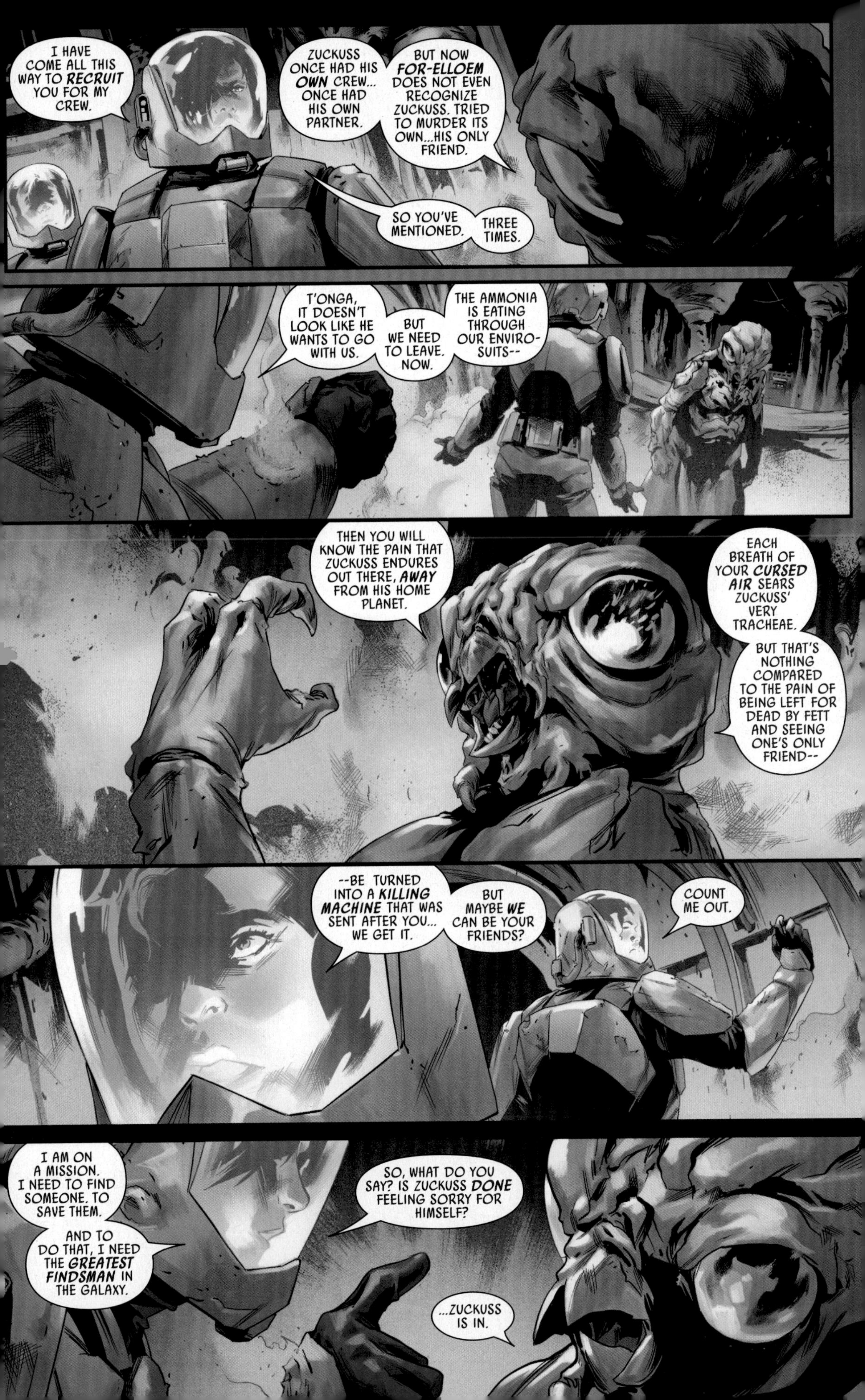
I HAVE COME ALL THIS WAY TO RECRUIT YOU FOR MY CREW.
ZUCKUSS ONCE HAD HIS OWN CREW... ONCE HAD HIS OWN PARTNER.
BUT NOW FOR-ELLOEM DOES NOT EVEN RECOGNIZE ZUCKUSS. TRIED TO MURDER ITS OWN...HIS ONLY FRIEND.
SO YOU'VE MENTIONED.
THREE TIMES.
T'ONGA, IT DOESN'T LOOK LIKE HE WANTS TO GO WITH US.
BUT WE NEED TO LEAVE. NOW.
THE AMMONIA IS EATING THROUGH OUR ENVIRO-SUITS--
THEN YOU WILL KNOW THE PAIN THAT ZUCKUSS ENDURES OUT THERE, AWAY FROM HIS HOME PLANET.
EACH BREATH OF YOUR CURSED AIR SEARS ZUCKUSS' VERY TRACHEAE.
BUT THAT'S NOTHING COMPARED TO THE PAIN OF BEING LEFT FOR DEAD BY FETT AND SEEING ONE'S ONLY FRIEND--
--BE TURNED INTO A KILLING MACHINE THAT WAS SENT AFTER YOU... WE GET IT.
BUT MAYBE WE CAN BE YOUR FRIENDS?
COUNT ME OUT.
I AM ON A MISSION. I NEED TO FIND SOMEONE. TO SAVE THEM.
AND TO DO THAT, I NEED THE GREATEST FINDSMAN IN THE GALAXY.
SO, WHAT DO YOU SAY? IS ZUCKUSS DONE FEELING SORRY FOR HIMSELF?
...ZUCKUSS IS IN.

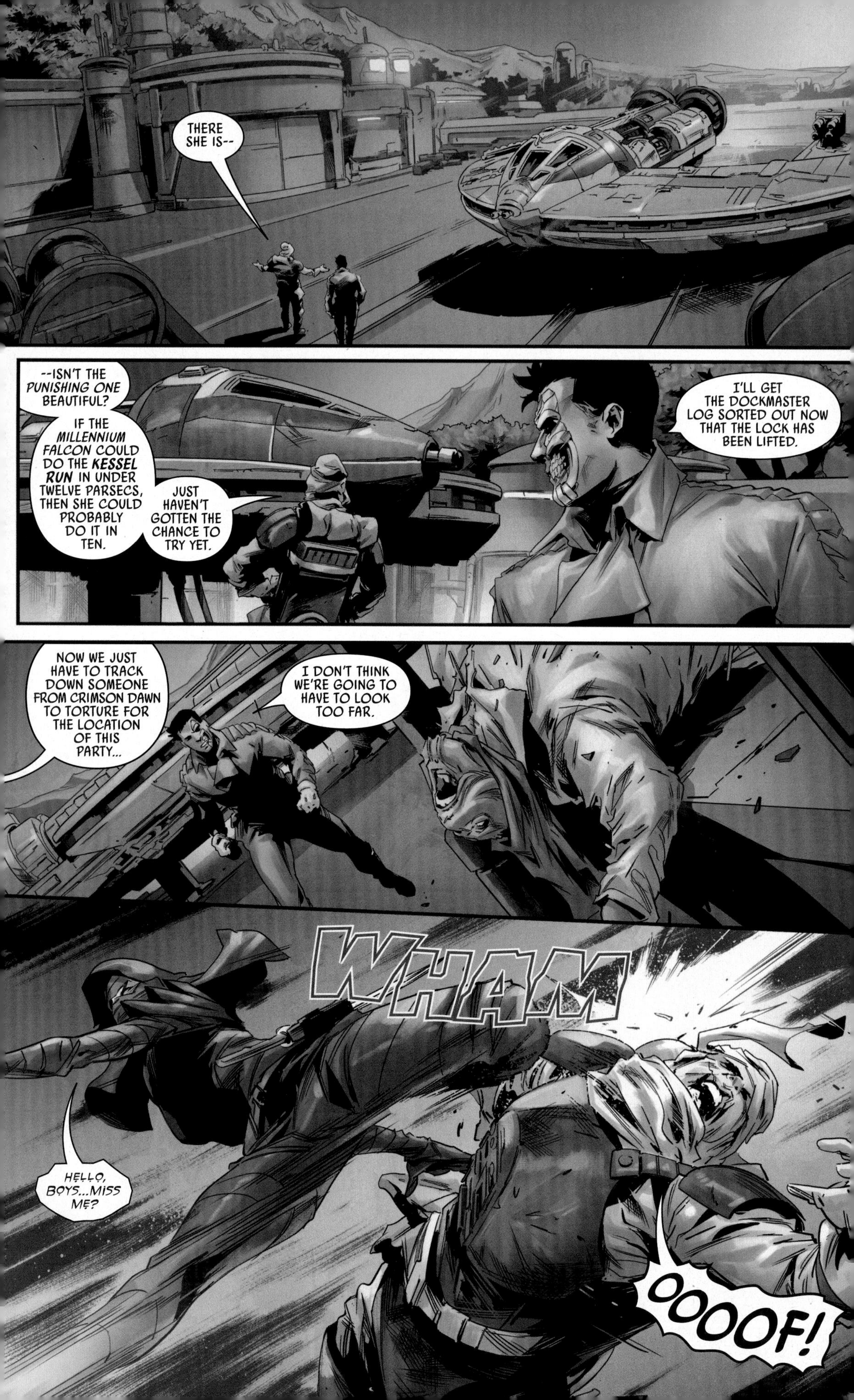
THERE SHE IS--
--ISN'T THE *PUNISHING ONE* BEAUTIFUL?
IF THE *MILLENNIUM FALCON* COULD DO THE **KESSEL RUN** IN UNDER TWELVE PARSECS, THEN SHE COULD PROBABLY DO IT IN TEN.
JUST HAVEN'T GOTTEN THE CHANCE TO TRY YET.
I'LL GET THE DOCKMASTER LOG SORTED OUT NOW THAT THE LOCK HAS BEEN LIFTED.
NOW WE JUST HAVE TO TRACK DOWN SOMEONE FROM CRIMSON DAWN TO TORTURE FOR THE LOCATION OF THIS PARTY...
I DON'T THINK WE'RE GOING TO HAVE TO LOOK TOO FAR.
WHAM
HELLO, BOYS...MISS ME?
OOOOF!

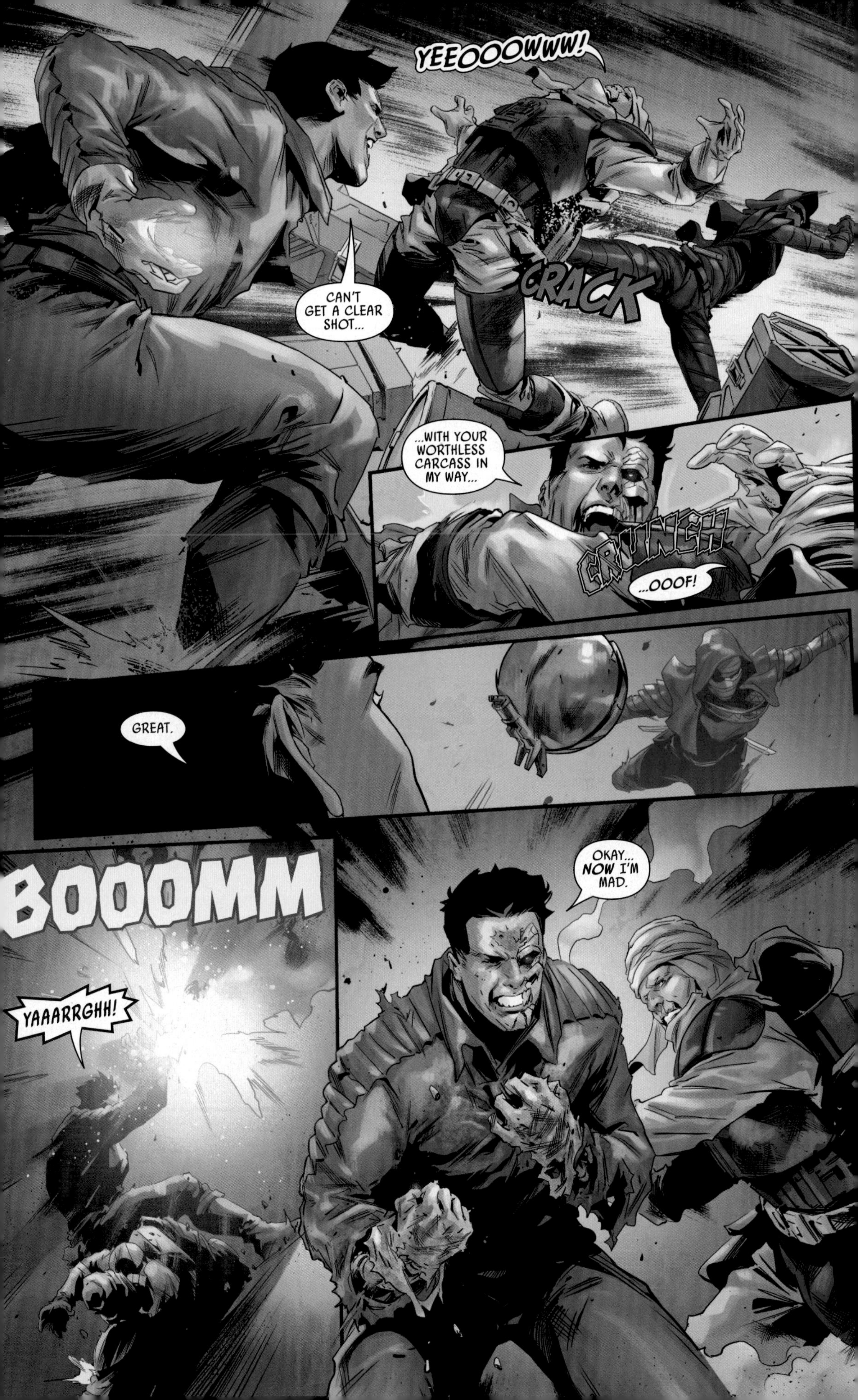

YEEOOOWWW!
CAN'T GET A CLEAR SHOT...
CRACK
...WITH YOUR WORTHLESS CARCASS IN MY WAY...
CRUNCH
...OOOF!
GREAT.
BOOOMM
YAAARRGHH!
OKAY... NOW I'M MAD.

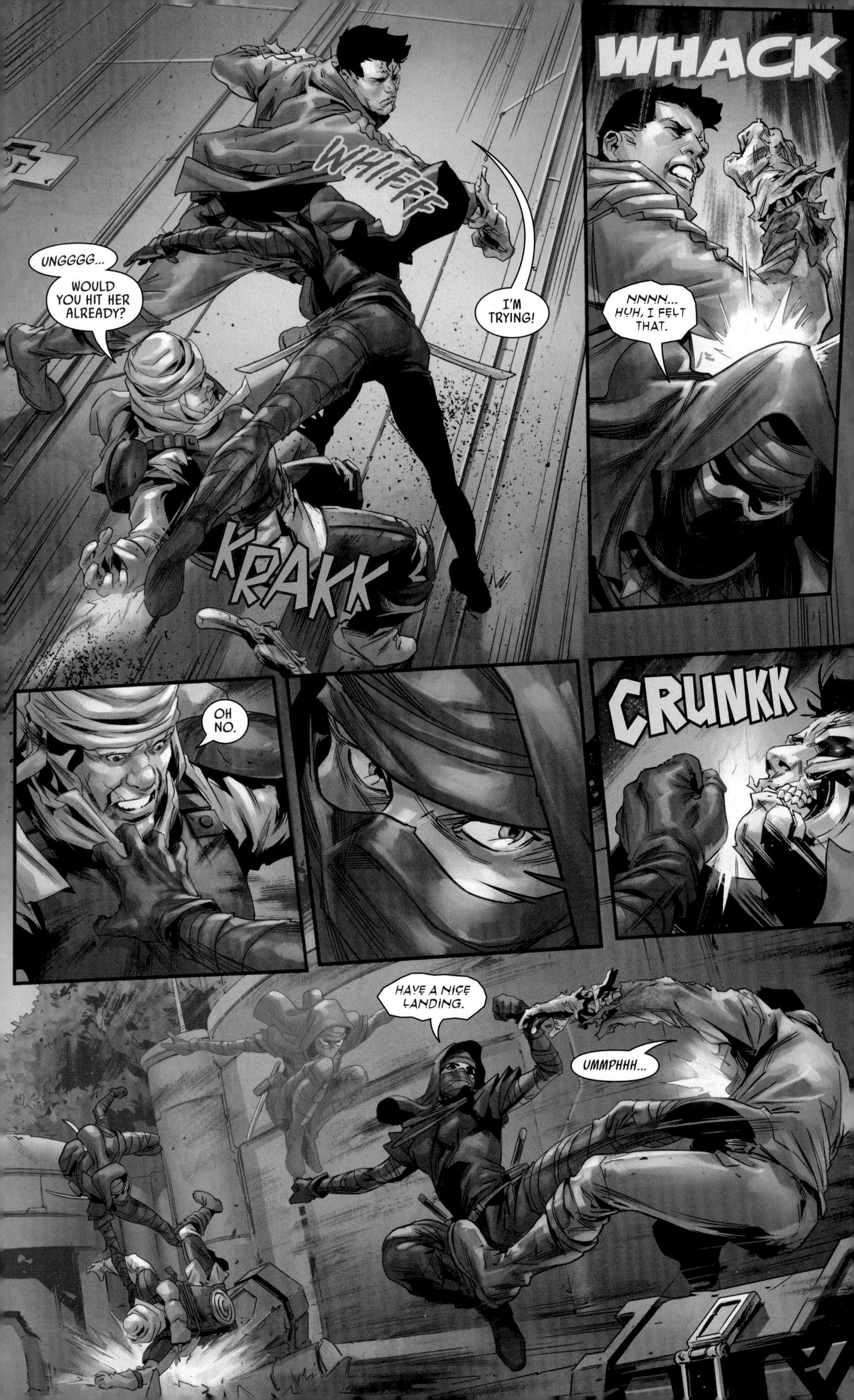
WHIFFF
UNGGGG... WOULD YOU HIT HER ALREADY?
I'M TRYING!
KRAKK
WHACK
NNNN... HUH, I FELT THAT.
OH NO.
CRUNKK
HAVE A NICE LANDING.
UMMPHHH...

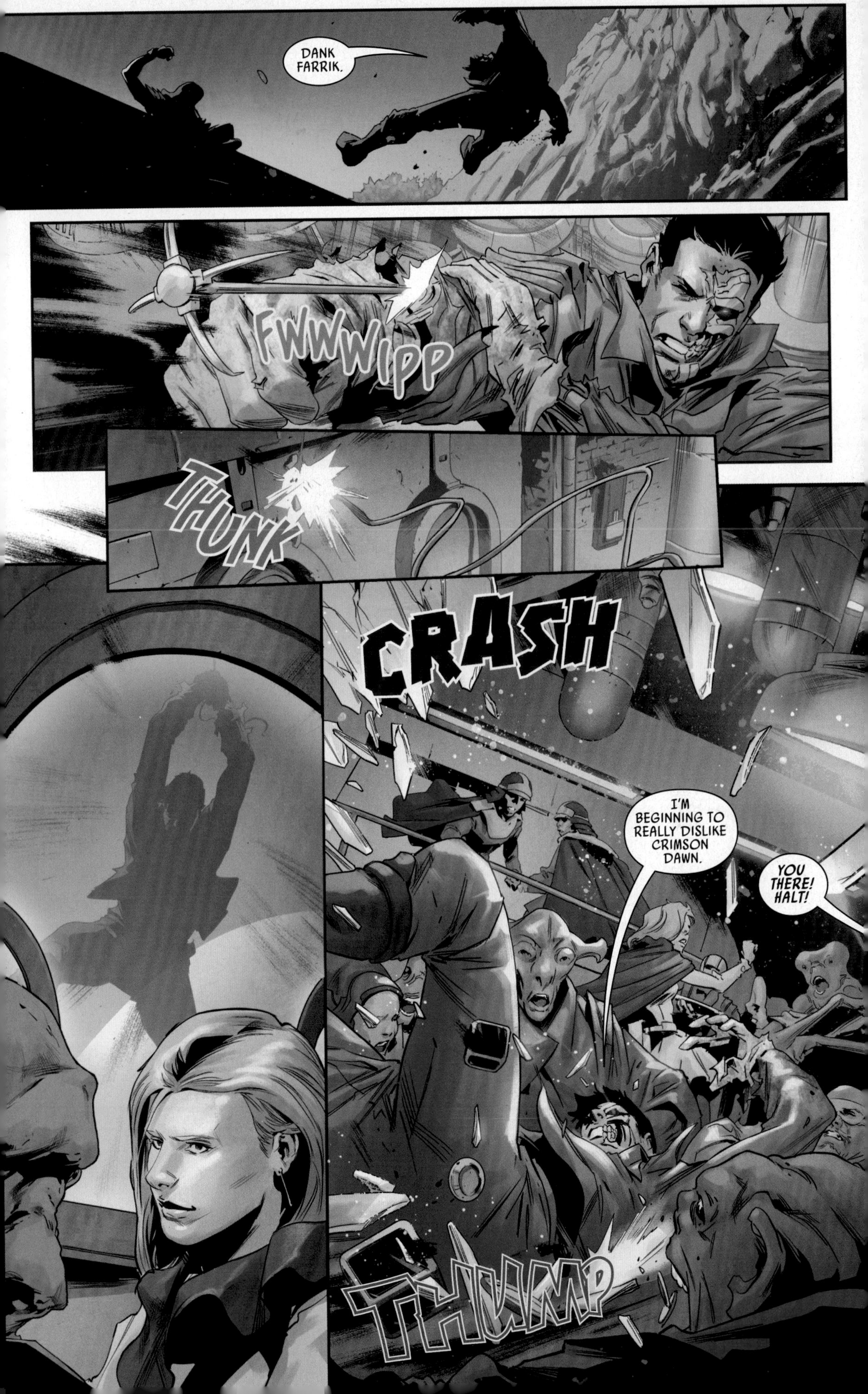
DANK FARRIK.
FWWWIPP
THUNK
CRASH
I'M BEGINNING TO REALLY DISLIKE CRIMSON DAWN.
YOU THERE! HALT!
THUMP

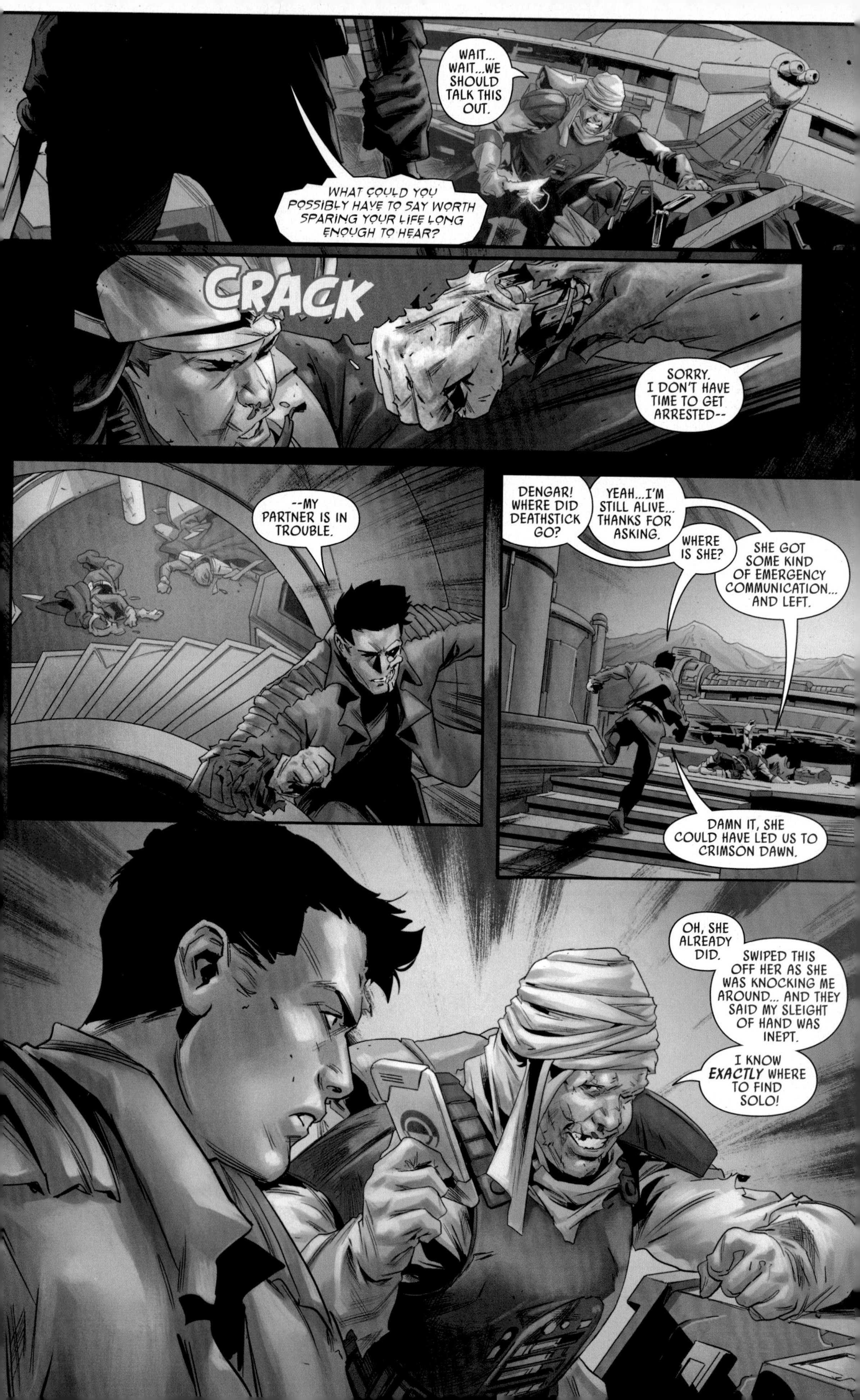
WAIT... WAIT...WE SHOULD TALK THIS OUT.
WHAT COULD YOU POSSIBLY HAVE TO SAY WORTH SPARING YOUR LIFE LONG ENOUGH TO HEAR?
CRACK
SORRY. I DON'T HAVE TIME TO GET ARRESTED--
--MY PARTNER IS IN TROUBLE.
DENGAR! WHERE DID DEATHSTICK GO?
YEAH...I'M STILL ALIVE... THANKS FOR ASKING.
WHERE IS SHE?
SHE GOT SOME KIND OF EMERGENCY COMMUNICATION... AND LEFT.
DAMN IT, SHE COULD HAVE LED US TO CRIMSON DAWN.
OH, SHE ALREADY DID.
SWIPED THIS OFF HER AS SHE WAS KNOCKING ME AROUND... AND THEY SAID MY SLEIGHT OF HAND WAS INEPT.
I KNOW *EXACTLY* WHERE TO FIND SOLO!

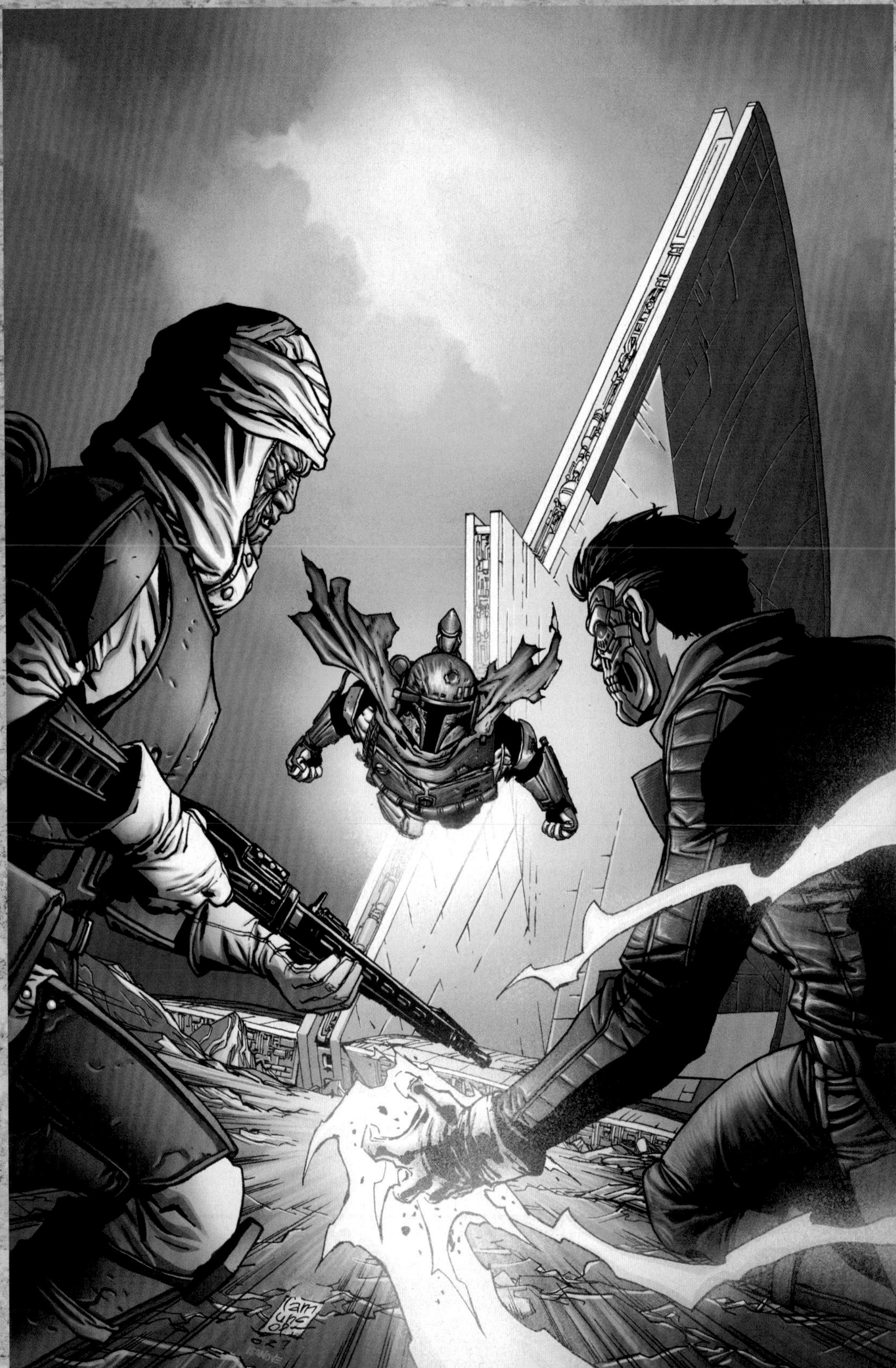

16 – SHADOW SOLDIERS

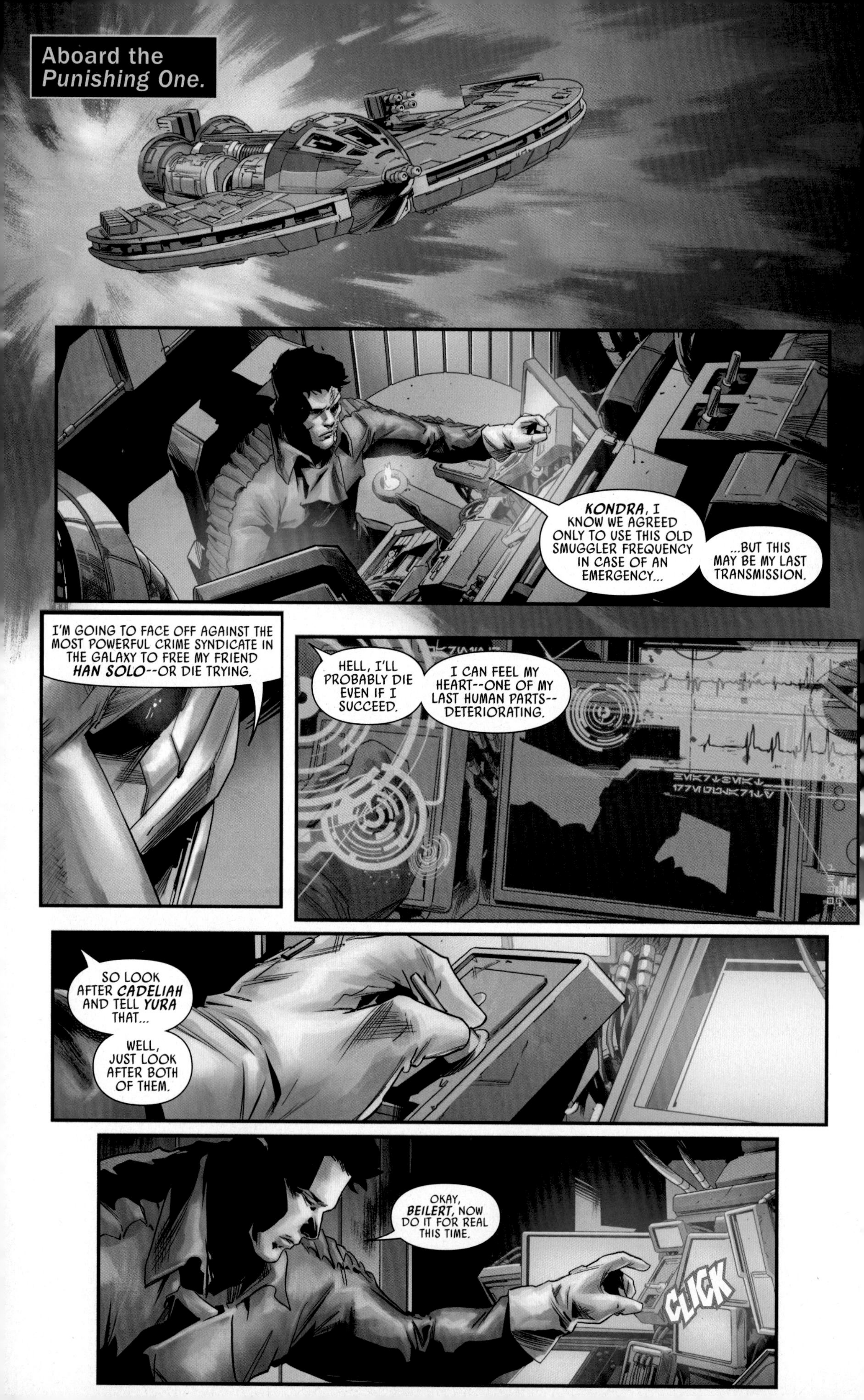
Aboard the *Punishing One.*
KONDRA, I KNOW WE AGREED ONLY TO USE THIS OLD SMUGGLER FREQUENCY IN CASE OF AN EMERGENCY...
...BUT THIS MAY BE MY LAST TRANSMISSION.
I'M GOING TO FACE OFF AGAINST THE MOST POWERFUL CRIME SYNDICATE IN THE GALAXY TO FREE MY FRIEND HAN SOLO--OR DIE TRYING.
HELL, I'LL PROBABLY DIE EVEN IF I SUCCEED.
I CAN FEEL MY HEART--ONE OF MY LAST HUMAN PARTS--DETERIORATING.
SO LOOK AFTER CADELIAH AND TELL YURA THAT...
WELL, JUST LOOK AFTER BOTH OF THEM.
OKAY, BEILERT, NOW DO IT FOR REAL THIS TIME.
CLICK

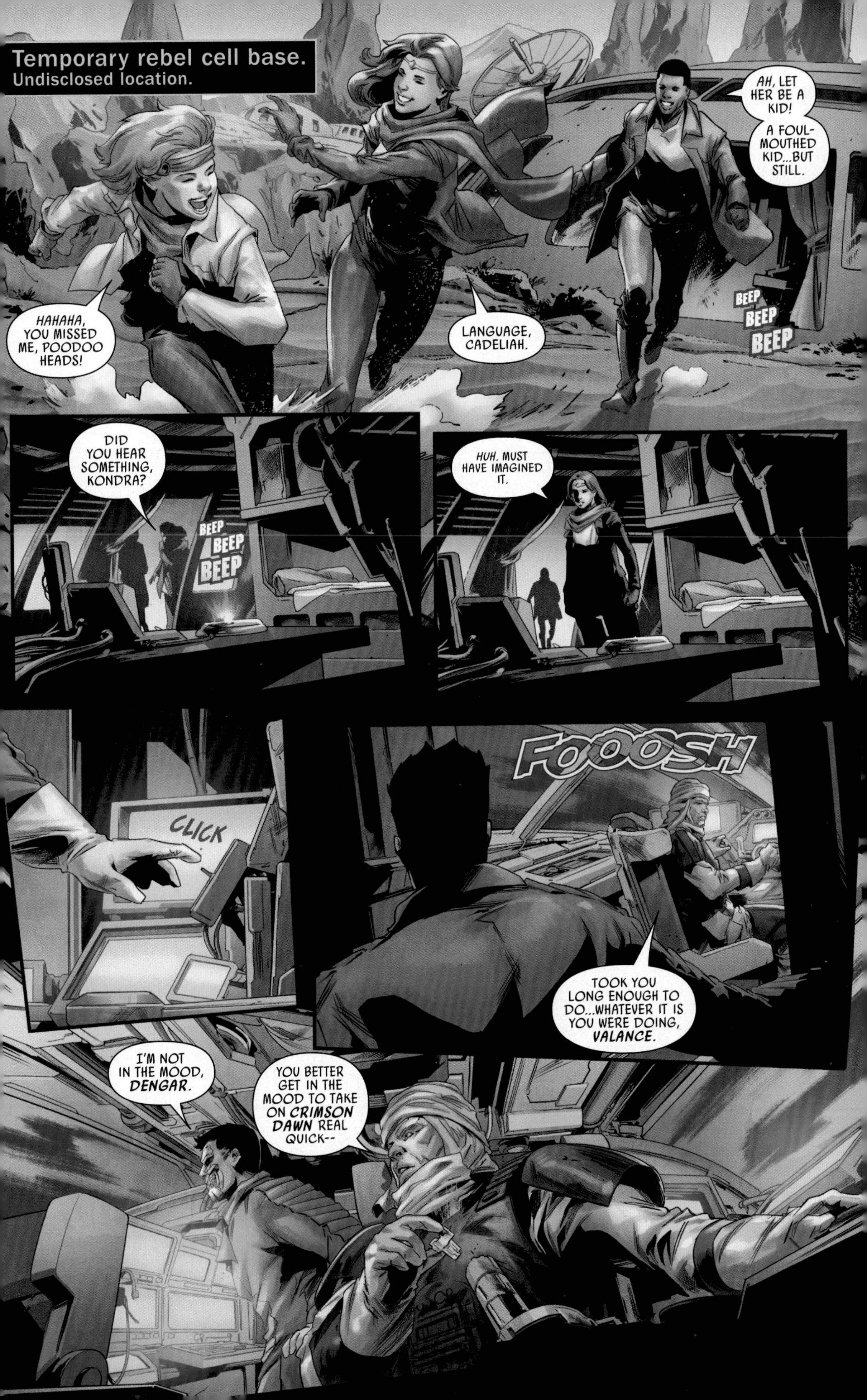
Temporary rebel cell base.
Undisclosed location.
HAHAHA, YOU MISSED ME, POODOO HEADS!
LANGUAGE, CADELIAH.
AH, LET HER BE A KID!
A FOUL-MOUTHED KID...BUT STILL.
BEEP BEEP BEEP
DID YOU HEAR SOMETHING, KONDRA?
BEEP BEEP BEEP
HUH. MUST HAVE IMAGINED IT.
CLICK
FOOOSH
TOOK YOU LONG ENOUGH TO DO...WHATEVER IT IS YOU WERE DOING, VALANCE.
I'M NOT IN THE MOOD, DENGAR.
YOU BETTER GET IN THE MOOD TO TAKE ON CRIMSON DAWN REAL QUICK--

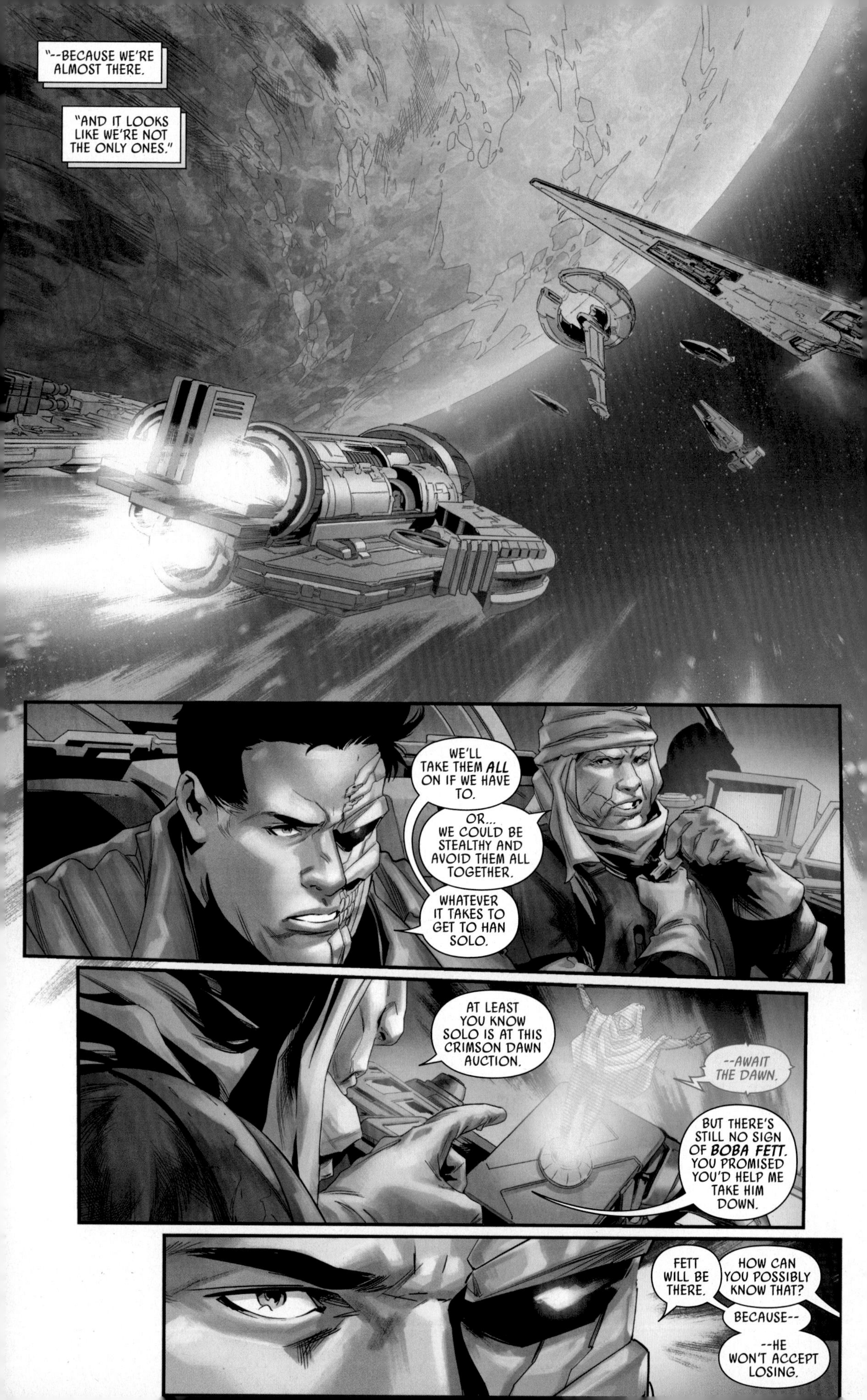
"--BECAUSE WE'RE ALMOST THERE.
"AND IT LOOKS LIKE WE'RE NOT THE ONLY ONES."
WE'LL TAKE THEM ALL ON IF WE HAVE TO.
OR... WE COULD BE STEALTHY AND AVOID THEM ALL TOGETHER.
WHATEVER IT TAKES TO GET TO HAN SOLO.
AT LEAST YOU KNOW SOLO IS AT THIS CRIMSON DAWN AUCTION.
--AWAIT THE DAWN.
BUT THERE'S STILL NO SIGN OF BOBA FETT. YOU PROMISED YOU'D HELP ME TAKE HIM DOWN.
FETT WILL BE THERE.
HOW CAN YOU POSSIBLY KNOW THAT?
BECAUSE--
--HE WON'T ACCEPT LOSING.

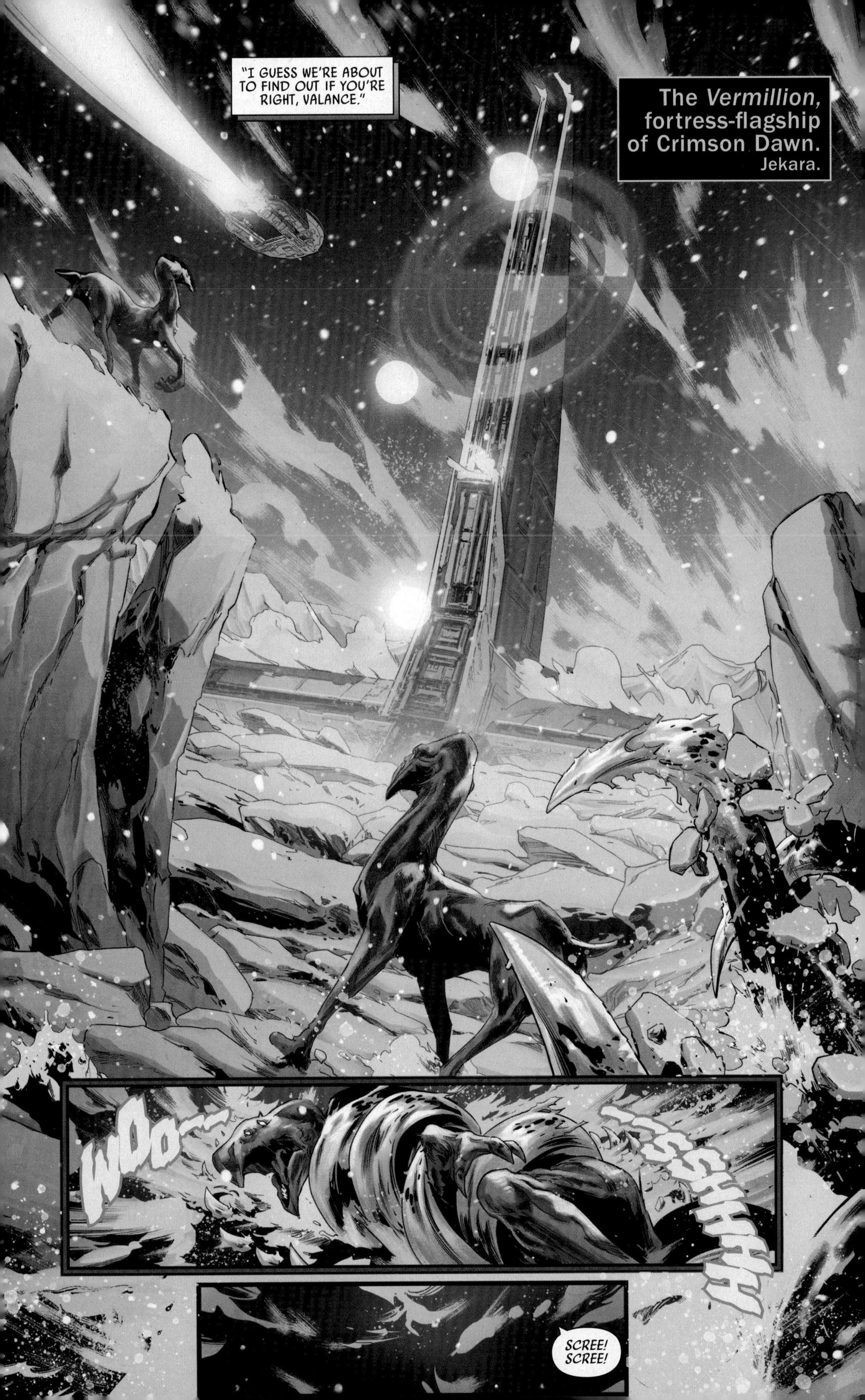
"I GUESS WE'RE ABOUT TO FIND OUT IF YOU'RE RIGHT, VALANCE."
The *Vermillion*, fortress-flagship of Crimson Dawn.
Jekara.
WOO—
SSSHHHHH
SCREE! SCREE!

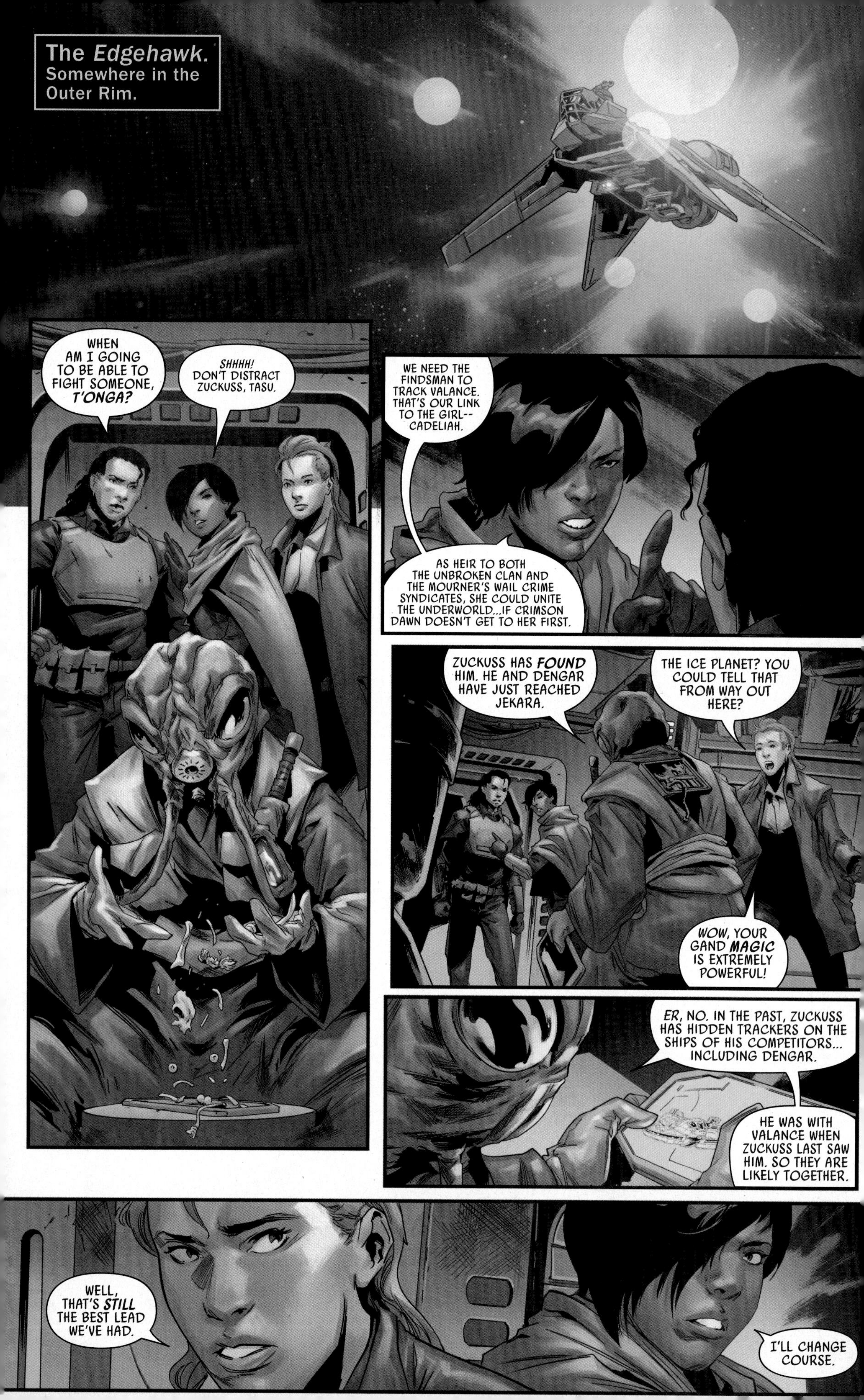
The *Edgehawk.*
Somewhere in the Outer Rim.
WHEN AM I GOING TO BE ABLE TO FIGHT SOMEONE, *T'ONGA?*
SHHHH! DON'T DISTRACT ZUCKUSS, TASU.
WE NEED THE FINDSMAN TO TRACK VALANCE. THAT'S OUR LINK TO THE GIRL--CADELIAH.
AS HEIR TO BOTH THE UNBROKEN CLAN AND THE MOURNER'S WAIL CRIME SYNDICATES, SHE COULD UNITE THE UNDERWORLD...IF CRIMSON DAWN DOESN'T GET TO HER FIRST.
ZUCKUSS HAS **FOUND** HIM. HE AND DENGAR HAVE JUST REACHED JEKARA.
THE ICE PLANET? YOU COULD TELL THAT FROM WAY OUT HERE?
WOW, YOUR GAND **MAGIC** IS EXTREMELY POWERFUL!
ER, NO. IN THE PAST, ZUCKUSS HAS HIDDEN TRACKERS ON THE SHIPS OF HIS COMPETITORS... INCLUDING DENGAR.
HE WAS WITH VALANCE WHEN ZUCKUSS LAST SAW HIM. SO THEY ARE LIKELY TOGETHER.
WELL, THAT'S ***STILL*** THE BEST LEAD WE'VE HAD.
I'LL CHANGE COURSE.

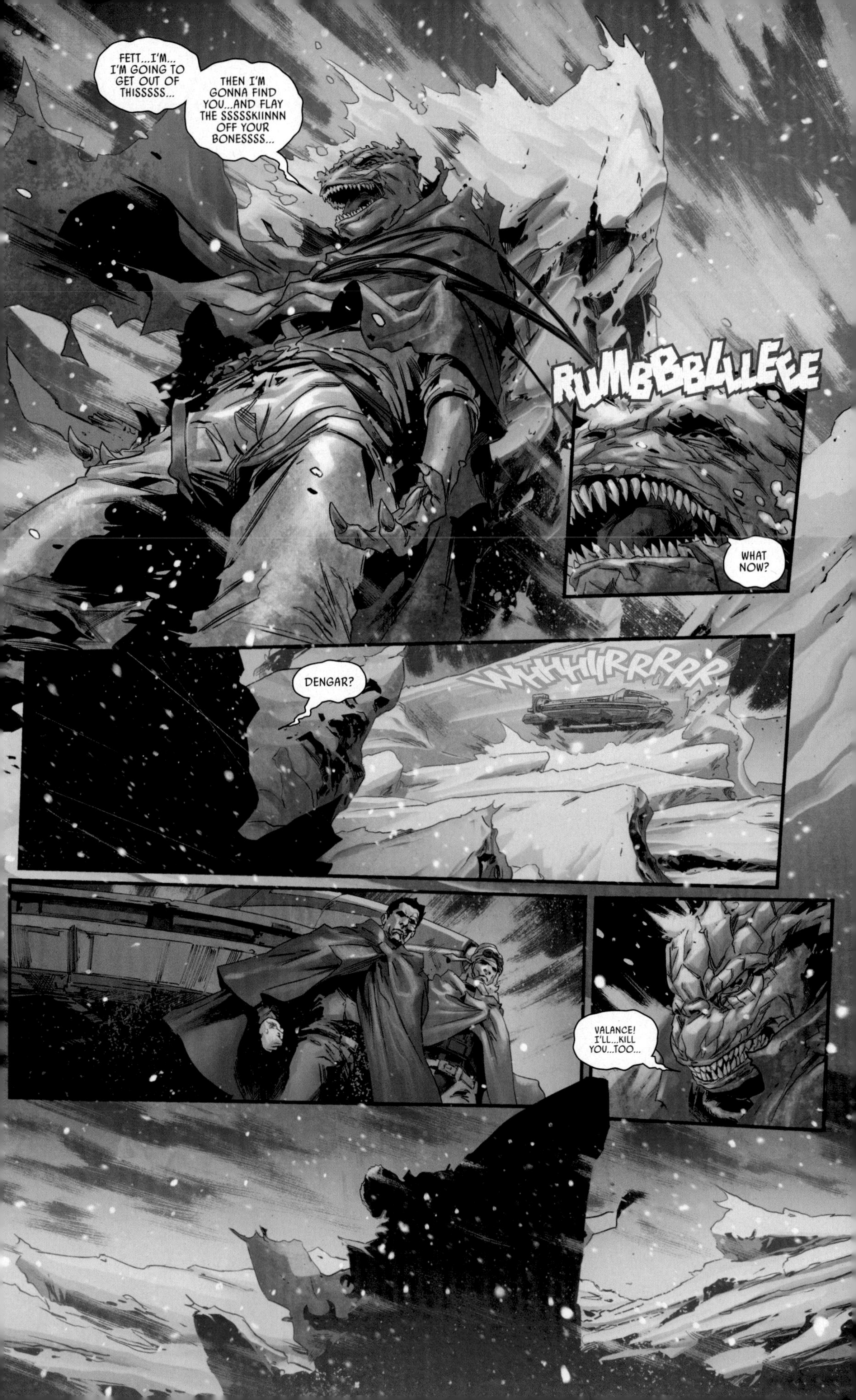
FETT...I'M... I'M GOING TO GET OUT OF THISSSSS...
THEN I'M GONNA FIND YOU...AND FLAY THE SSSSSKIINNN OFF YOUR BONESSSS...
RUMBBBLLEEE
WHAT NOW?
DENGAR?
WHHHIRRRRR
VALANCE! I'LL...KILL YOU...TOO...

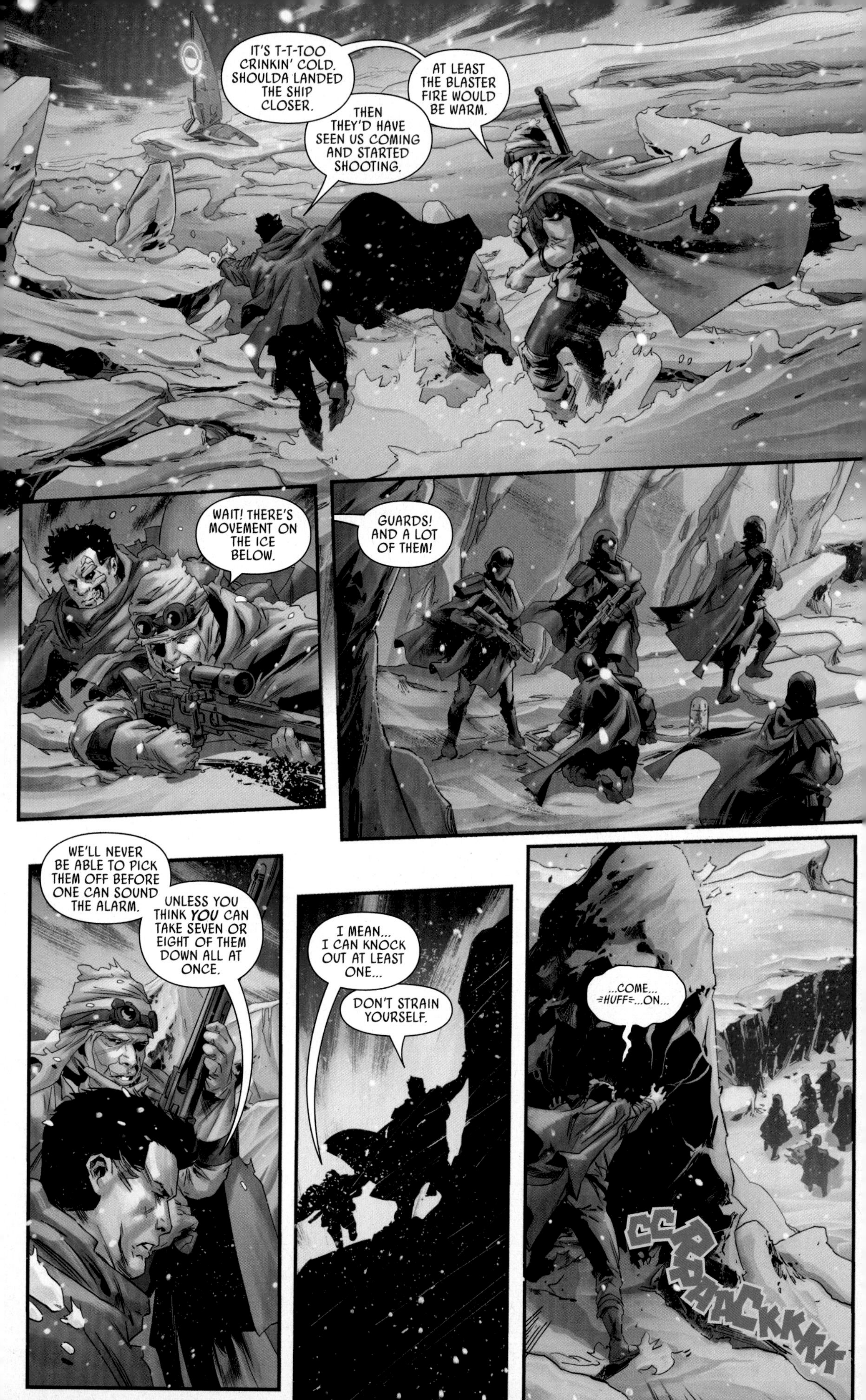
IT'S T-T-TOO CRINKIN' COLD. SHOULDA LANDED THE SHIP CLOSER.
AT LEAST THE BLASTER FIRE WOULD BE WARM.
THEN THEY'D HAVE SEEN US COMING AND STARTED SHOOTING.
WAIT! THERE'S MOVEMENT ON THE ICE BELOW.
GUARDS! AND A LOT OF THEM!
WE'LL NEVER BE ABLE TO PICK THEM OFF BEFORE ONE CAN SOUND THE ALARM.
UNLESS YOU THINK ***YOU*** CAN TAKE SEVEN OR EIGHT OF THEM DOWN ALL AT ONCE.
I MEAN... I CAN KNOCK OUT AT LEAST ONE...
DON'T STRAIN YOURSELF.
...COME... =HUFF=...ON...
CCRRAACKKKK

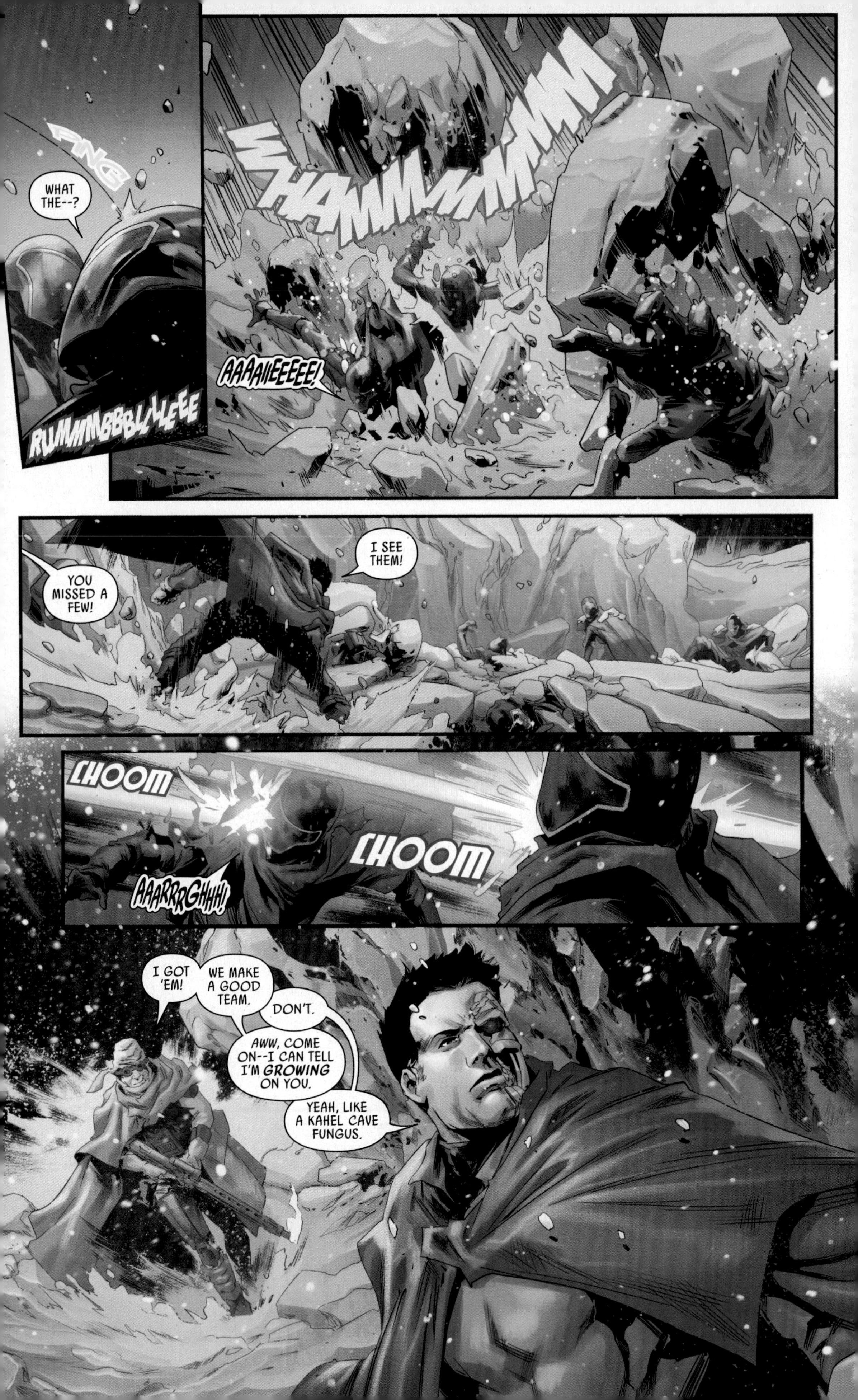
PING
WHAT THE--?
RUMMMBBBLLLLEEE
WHAMMMMMMM
AAAAIIEEEEE!
YOU MISSED A FEW!
I SEE THEM!
CHOOM
CHOOM
AAAARRRGHHH!
I GOT 'EM!
WE MAKE A GOOD TEAM.
DON'T.
AWW, COME ON--I CAN TELL I'M *GROWING* ON YOU.
YEAH, LIKE A KAHEL CAVE FUNGUS.

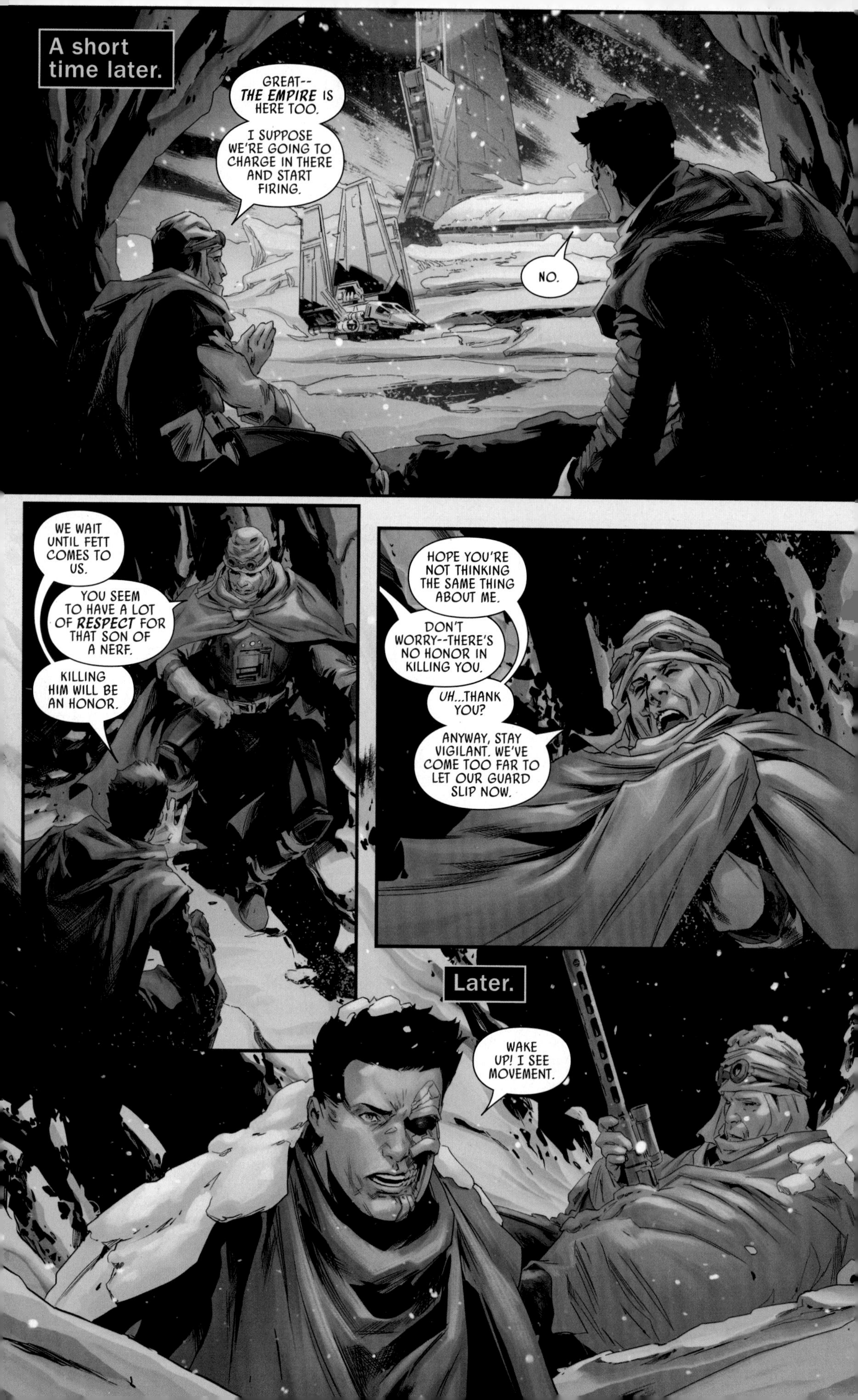
A short time later.
GREAT-- THE EMPIRE IS HERE TOO.
I SUPPOSE WE'RE GOING TO CHARGE IN THERE AND START FIRING.
NO.
WE WAIT UNTIL FETT COMES TO US.
YOU SEEM TO HAVE A LOT OF RESPECT FOR THAT SON OF A NERF.
KILLING HIM WILL BE AN HONOR.
HOPE YOU'RE NOT THINKING THE SAME THING ABOUT ME.
DON'T WORRY--THERE'S NO HONOR IN KILLING YOU.
UH...THANK YOU?
ANYWAY, STAY VIGILANT. WE'VE COME TOO FAR TO LET OUR GUARD SLIP NOW.
Later.
WAKE UP! I SEE MOVEMENT.

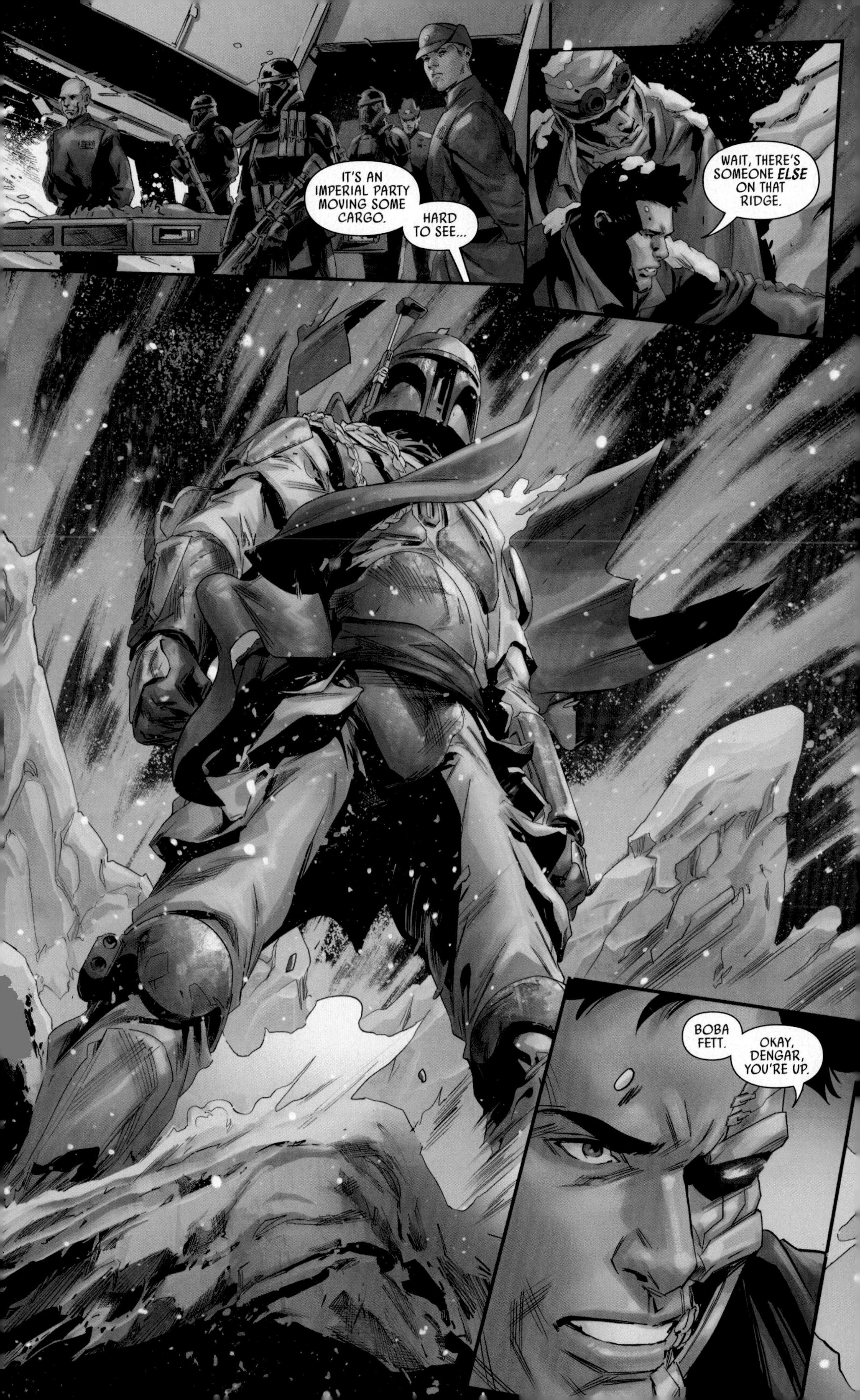
IT'S AN IMPERIAL PARTY MOVING SOME CARGO.
HARD TO SEE...
WAIT, THERE'S SOMEONE *ELSE* ON THAT RIDGE.
BOBA FETT.
OKAY, DENGAR, YOU'RE UP.

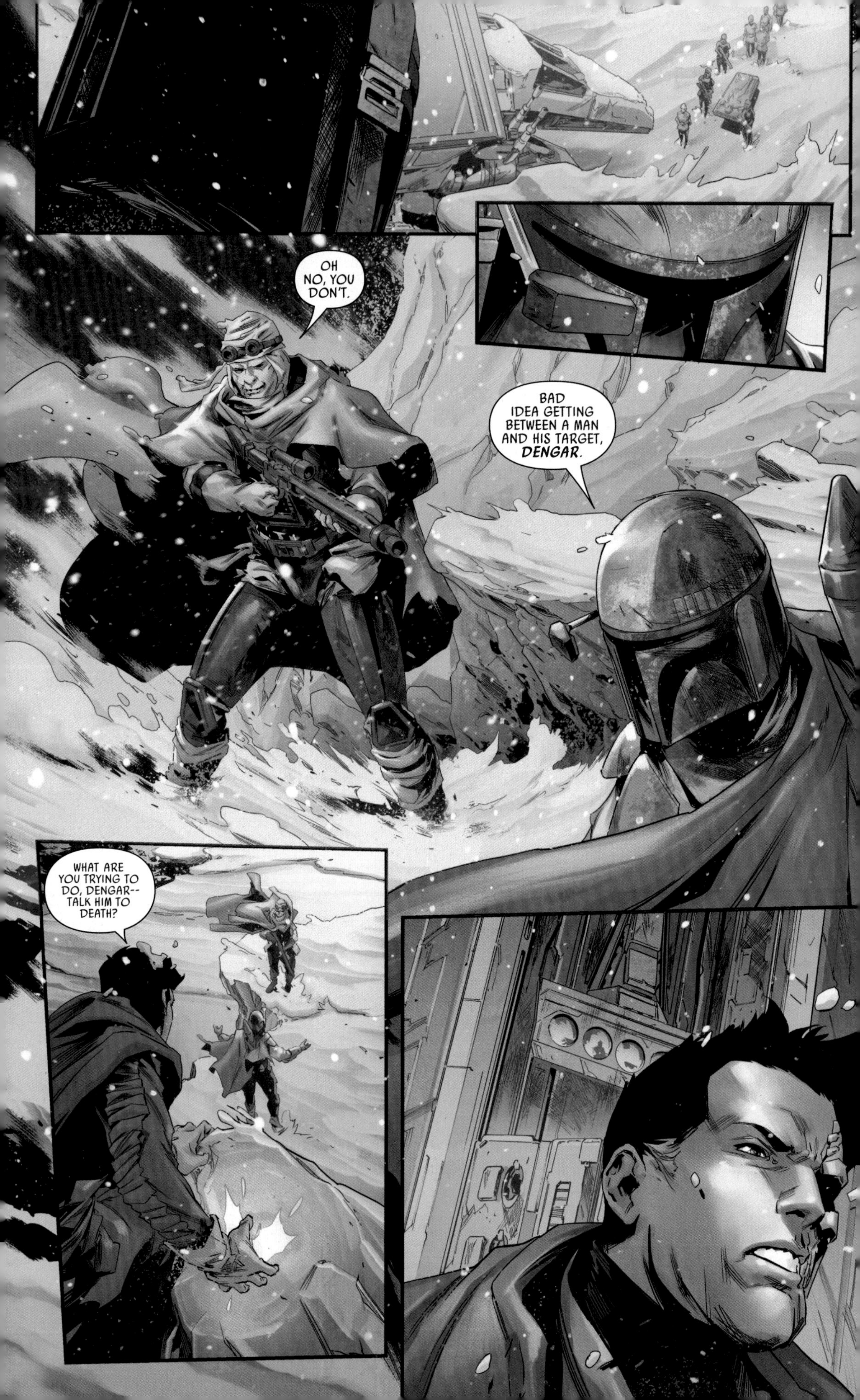
OH NO, YOU DON'T.
BAD IDEA GETTING BETWEEN A MAN AND HIS TARGET, DENGAR.
WHAT ARE YOU TRYING TO DO, DENGAR-- TALK HIM TO DEATH?

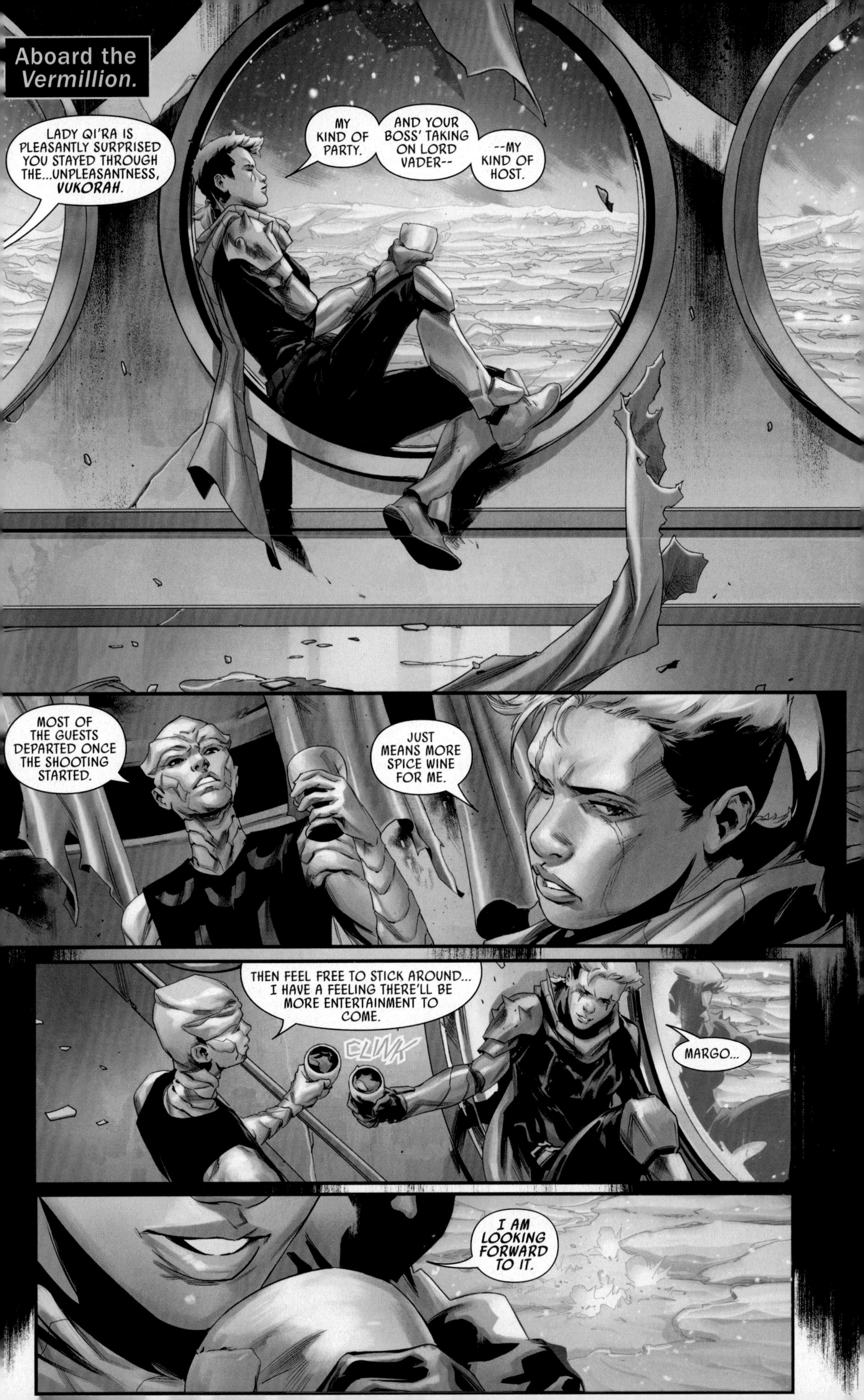
Aboard the *Vermillion.*
LADY QI'RA IS PLEASANTLY SURPRISED YOU STAYED THROUGH THE...UNPLEASANTNESS, VUKORAH.
MY KIND OF PARTY.
AND YOUR BOSS' TAKING ON LORD VADER--
--MY KIND OF HOST.
MOST OF THE GUESTS DEPARTED ONCE THE SHOOTING STARTED.
JUST MEANS MORE SPICE WINE FOR ME.
THEN FEEL FREE TO STICK AROUND... I HAVE A FEELING THERE'LL BE MORE ENTERTAINMENT TO COME.
CLINK
MARGO...
I AM LOOKING FORWARD TO IT.

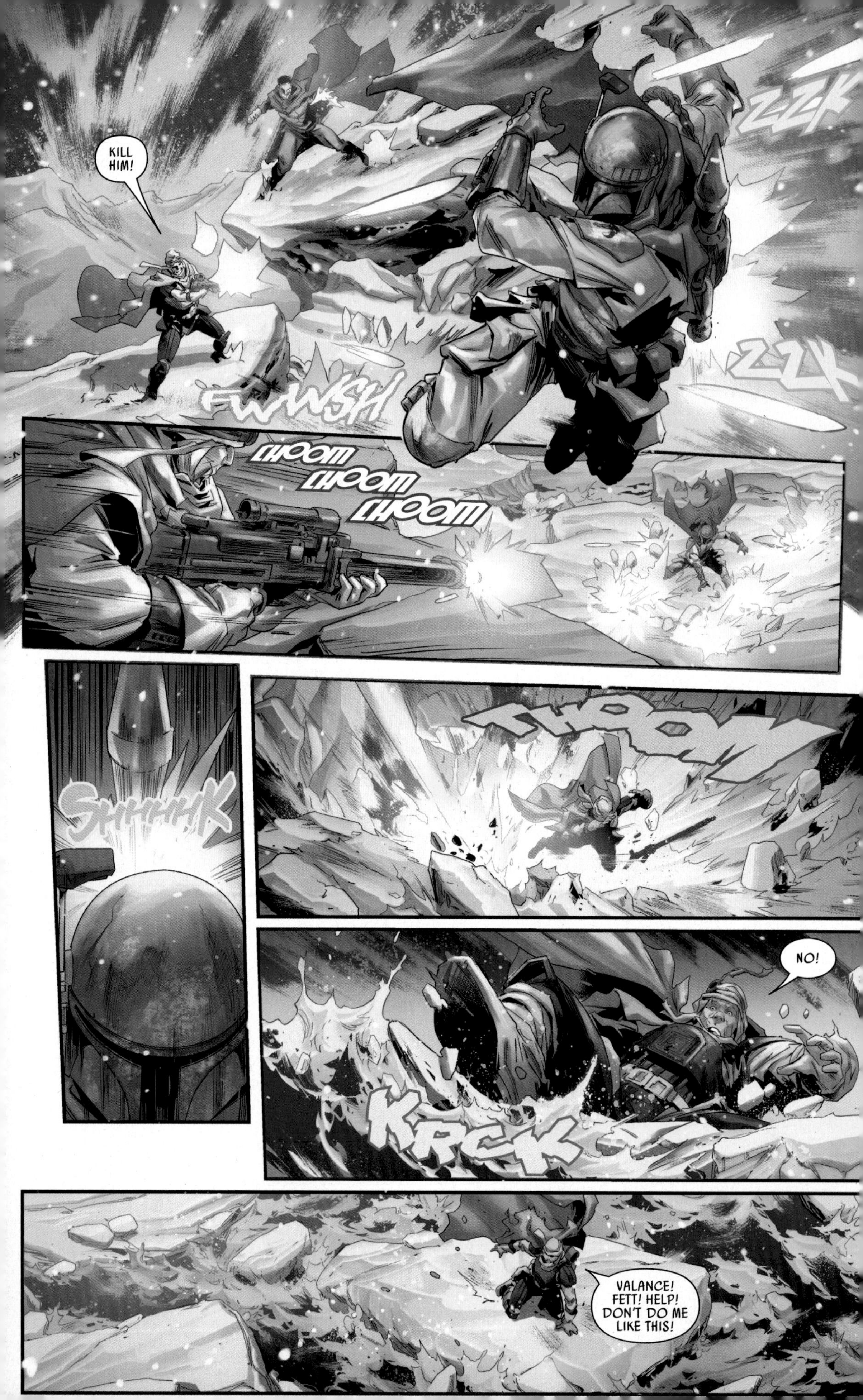
KILL HIM!
Z-ZK
FWWSH
ZZK
CHOOM
CHOOM
CHOOM
SHHHHK
NO!
KRCK
VALANCE! FETT! HELP! DON'T DO ME LIKE THIS!

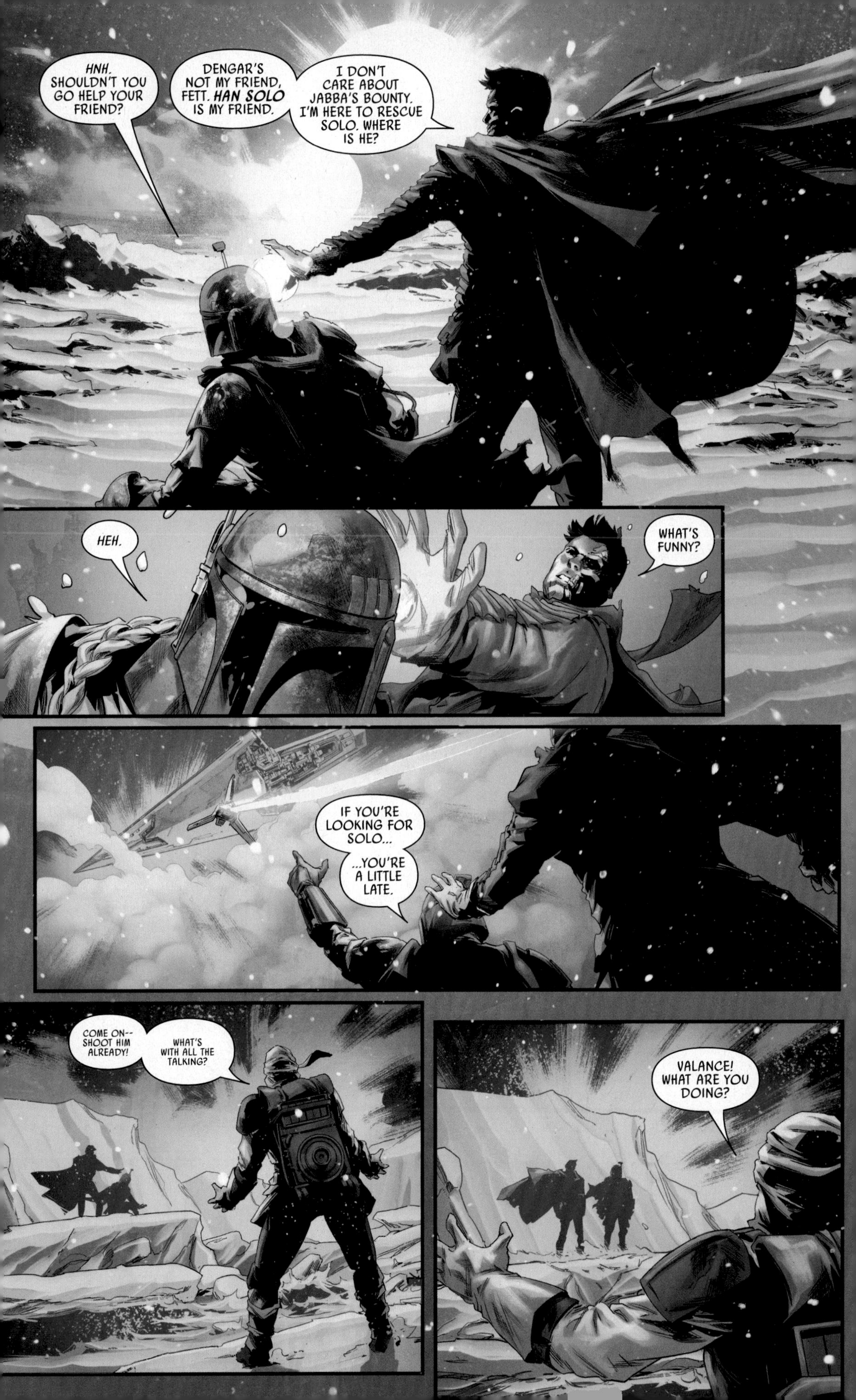
HNH. SHOULDN'T YOU GO HELP YOUR FRIEND?
DENGAR'S NOT MY FRIEND, FETT. HAN SOLO IS MY FRIEND.
I DON'T CARE ABOUT JABBA'S BOUNTY. I'M HERE TO RESCUE SOLO. WHERE IS HE?
HEH.
WHAT'S FUNNY?
IF YOU'RE LOOKING FOR SOLO...
...YOU'RE A LITTLE LATE.
COME ON-- SHOOT HIM ALREADY!
WHAT'S WITH ALL THE TALKING?
VALANCE! WHAT ARE YOU DOING?

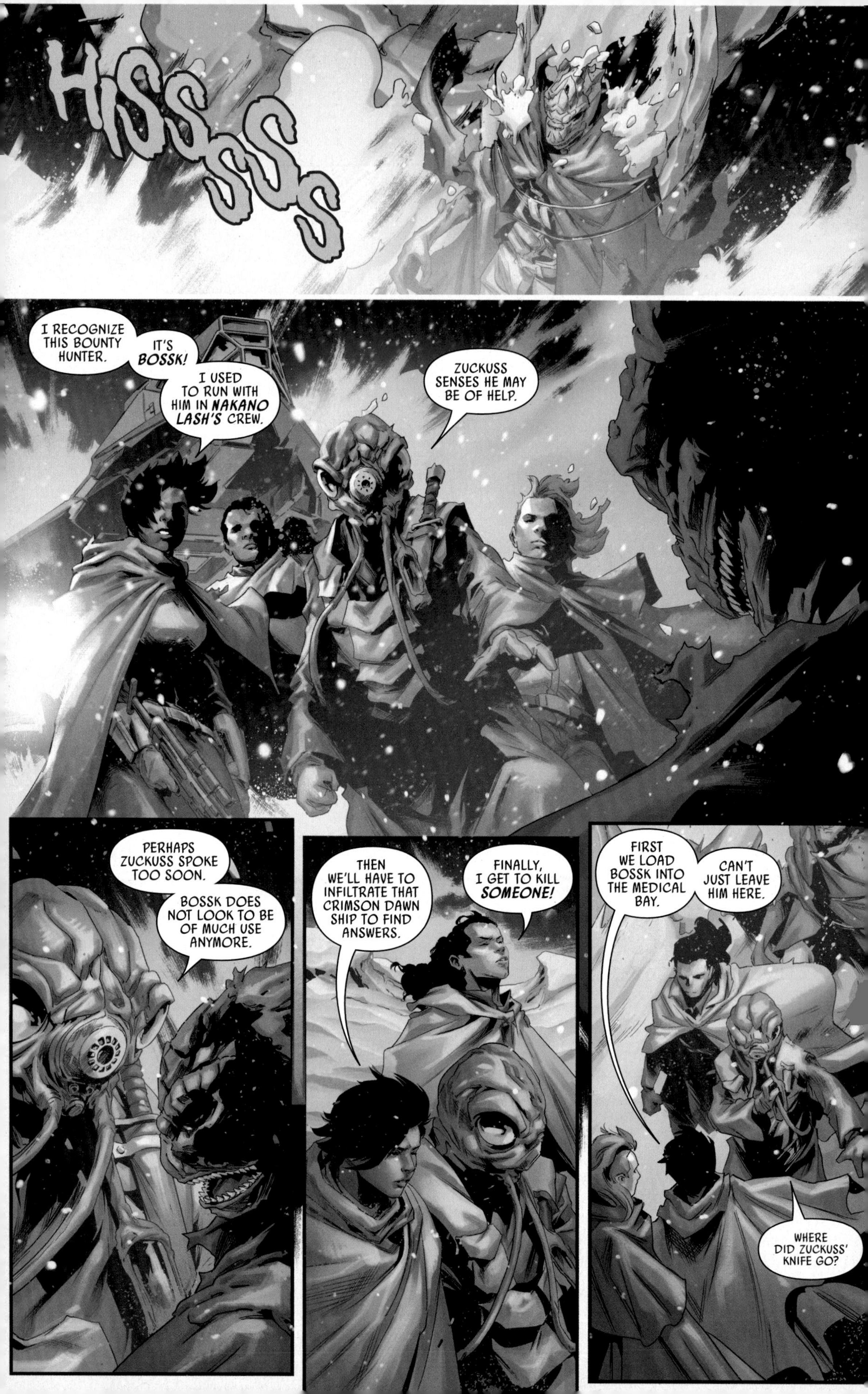
HISSSSS
I RECOGNIZE THIS BOUNTY HUNTER.
IT'S BOSSK!
I USED TO RUN WITH HIM IN NAKANO LASH'S CREW.
ZUCKUSS SENSES HE MAY BE OF HELP.
PERHAPS ZUCKUSS SPOKE TOO SOON.
BOSSK DOES NOT LOOK TO BE OF MUCH USE ANYMORE.
THEN WE'LL HAVE TO INFILTRATE THAT CRIMSON DAWN SHIP TO FIND ANSWERS.
FINALLY, I GET TO KILL SOMEONE!
FIRST WE LOAD BOSSK INTO THE MEDICAL BAY.
CAN'T JUST LEAVE HIM HERE.
WHERE DID ZUCKUSS' KNIFE GO?

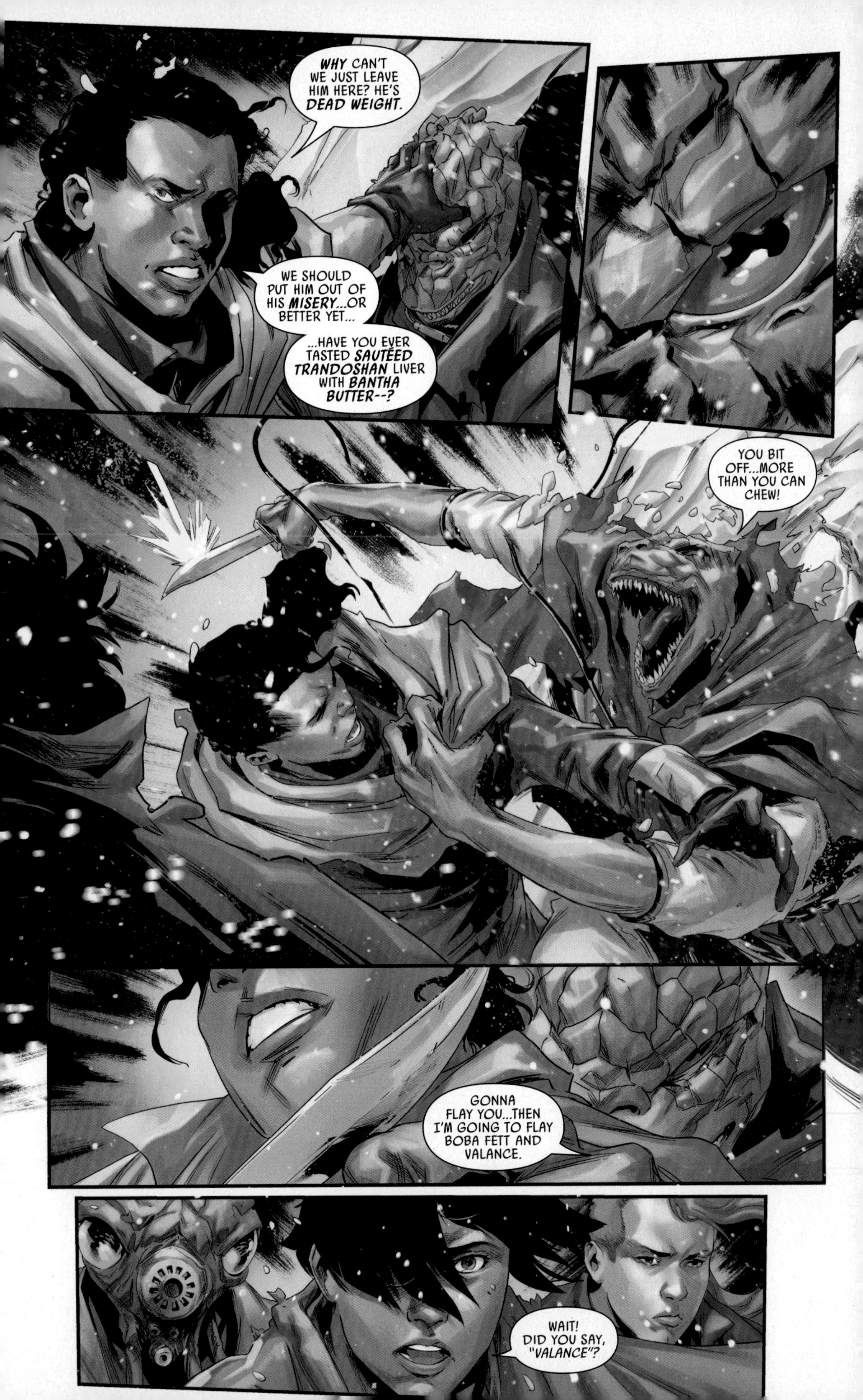
WHY CAN'T WE JUST LEAVE HIM HERE? HE'S DEAD WEIGHT.
WE SHOULD PUT HIM OUT OF HIS MISERY...OR BETTER YET...
...HAVE YOU EVER TASTED SAUTÉED TRANDOSHAN LIVER WITH BANTHA BUTTER--?
YOU BIT OFF...MORE THAN YOU CAN CHEW!
GONNA FLAY YOU...THEN I'M GOING TO FLAY BOBA FETT AND VALANCE.
WAIT! DID YOU SAY, "VALANCE"?

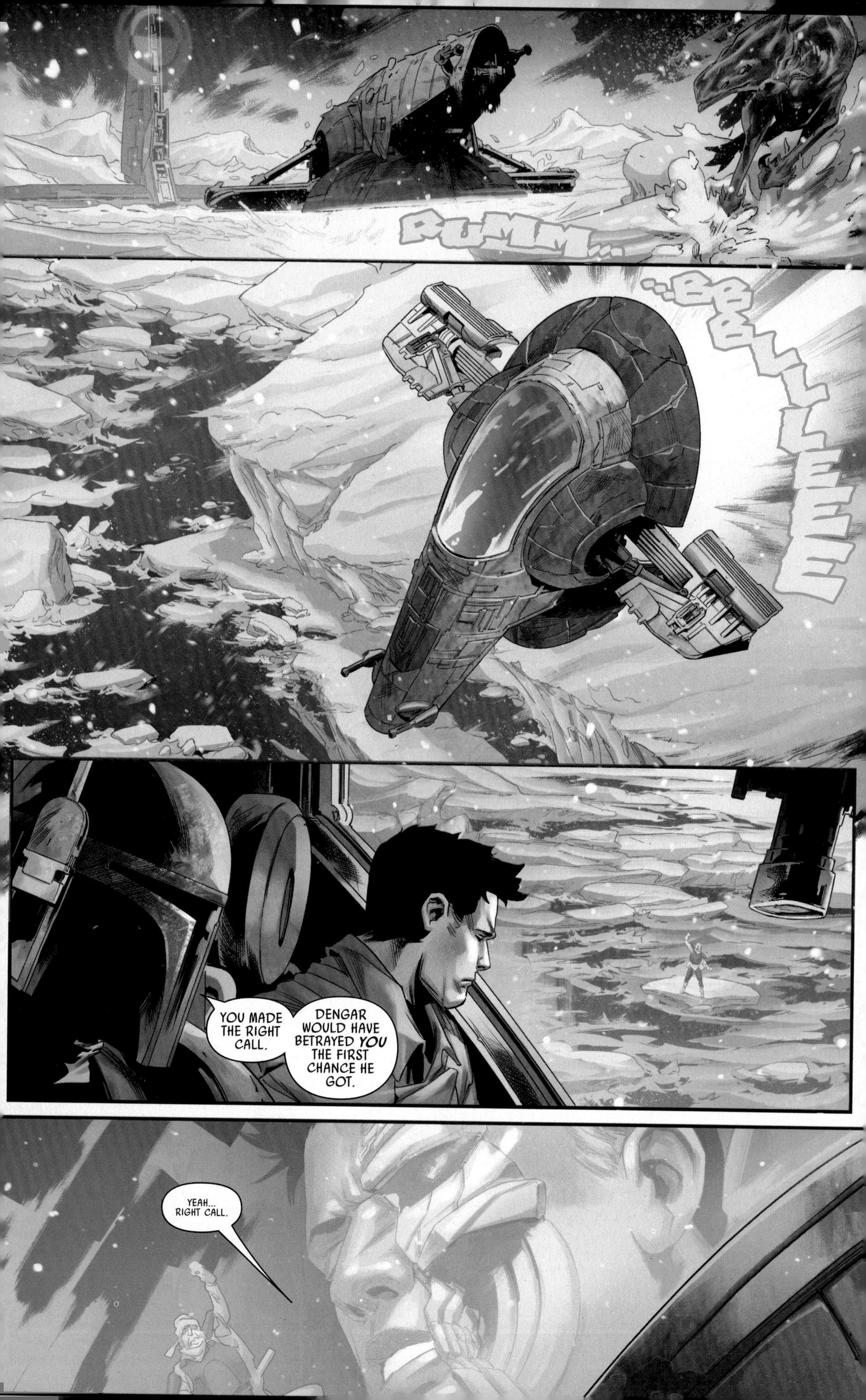
BUMM...
...BBBLLLEEEEE
YOU MADE THE RIGHT CALL.
DENGAR WOULD HAVE BETRAYED YOU THE FIRST CHANCE HE GOT.
YEAH... RIGHT CALL.

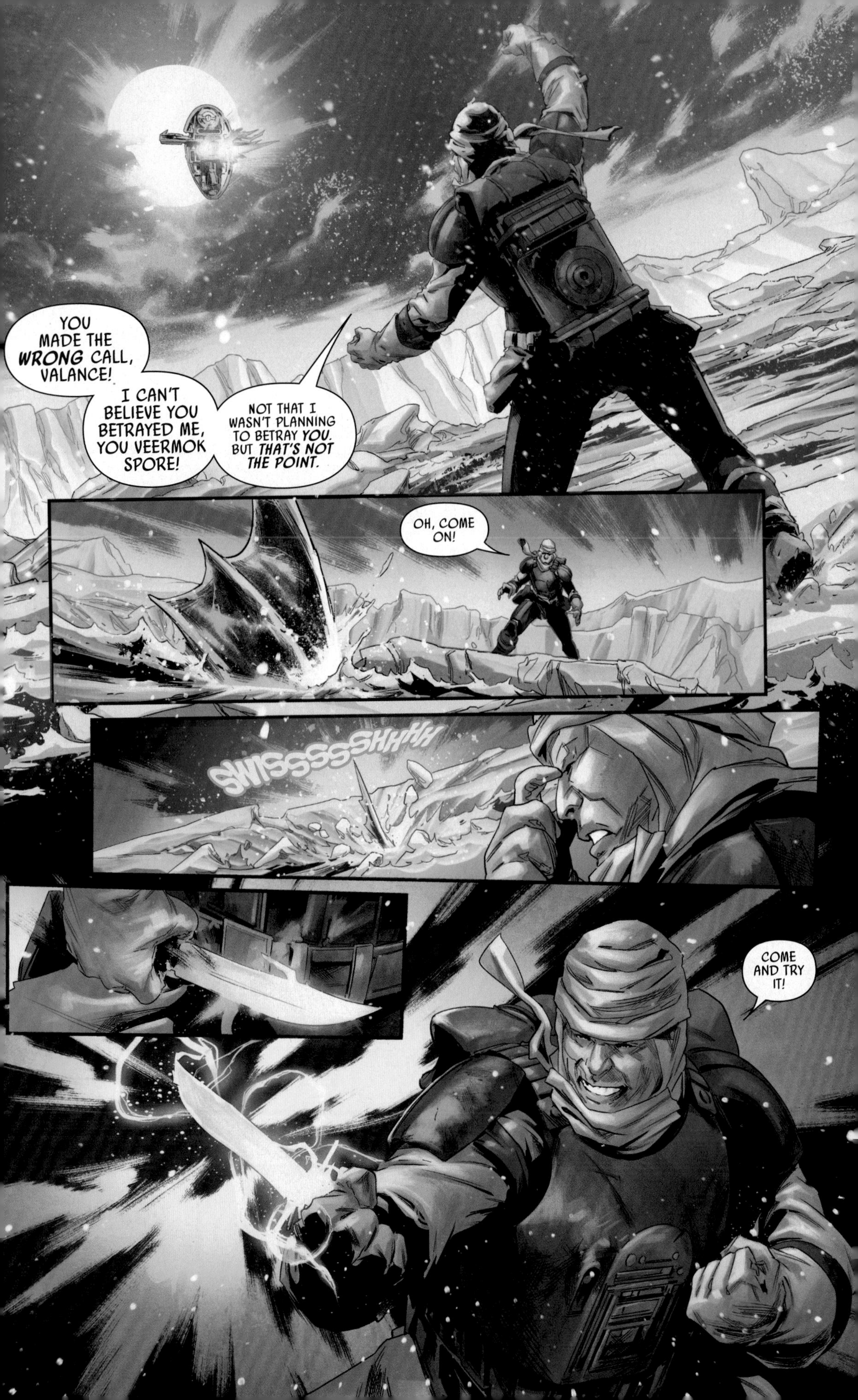

YOU MADE THE WRONG CALL, VALANCE!
I CAN'T BELIEVE YOU BETRAYED ME, YOU VEERMOK SPORE!
NOT THAT I WASN'T PLANNING TO BETRAY YOU. BUT THAT'S NOT THE POINT.
OH, COME ON!
SWISSSSSSHHHH
COME AND TRY IT!

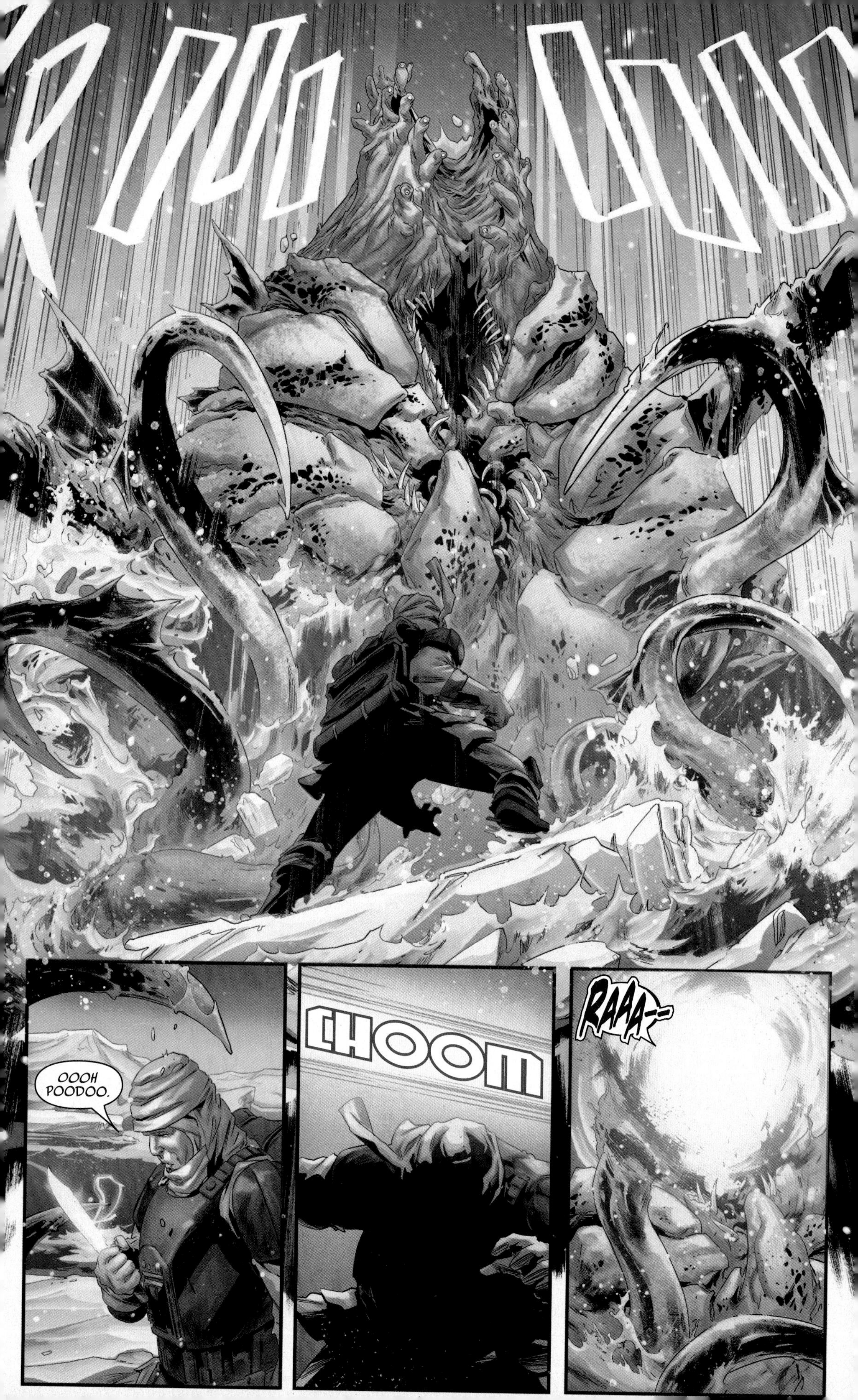
OOOH
POODOO.
CHOOM
RAAA--

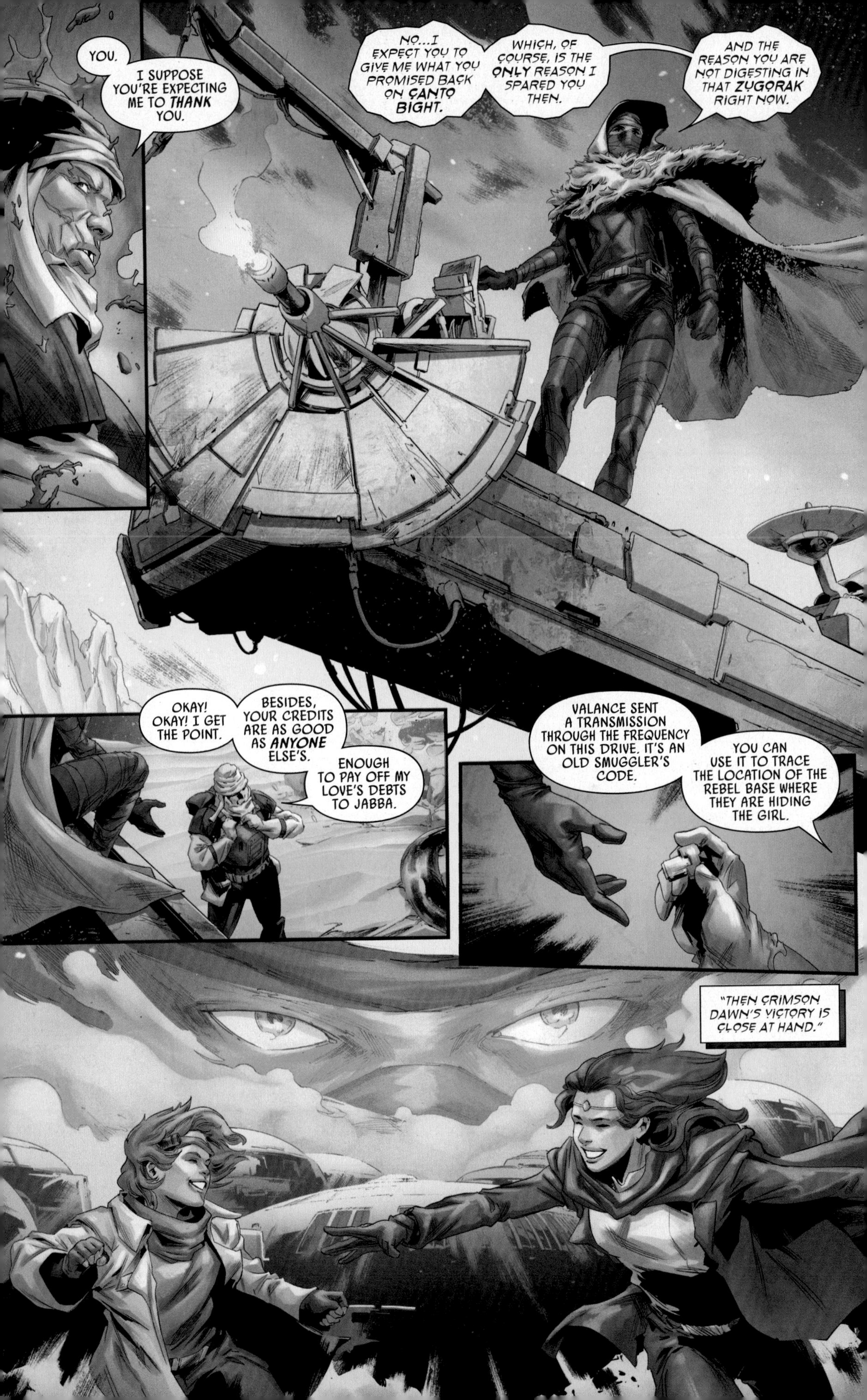
YOU.
I SUPPOSE YOU'RE EXPECTING ME TO *THANK* YOU.
NO...I EXPECT YOU TO GIVE ME WHAT YOU PROMISED BACK ON *CANTO BIGHT.*
WHICH, OF COURSE, IS THE *ONLY* REASON I SPARED YOU THEN.
AND THE REASON YOU ARE NOT DIGESTING IN THAT *ZUGORAK* RIGHT NOW.
OKAY! OKAY! I GET THE POINT.
BESIDES, YOUR CREDITS ARE AS GOOD AS *ANYONE* ELSE'S.
ENOUGH TO PAY OFF MY LOVE'S DEBTS TO JABBA.
VALANCE SENT A TRANSMISSION THROUGH THE FREQUENCY ON THIS DRIVE. IT'S AN OLD SMUGGLER'S CODE.
YOU CAN USE IT TO TRACE THE LOCATION OF THE REBEL BASE WHERE THEY ARE HIDING THE GIRL.
"THEN CRIMSON DAWN'S VICTORY IS CLOSE AT HAND."

17 — LAST STAND

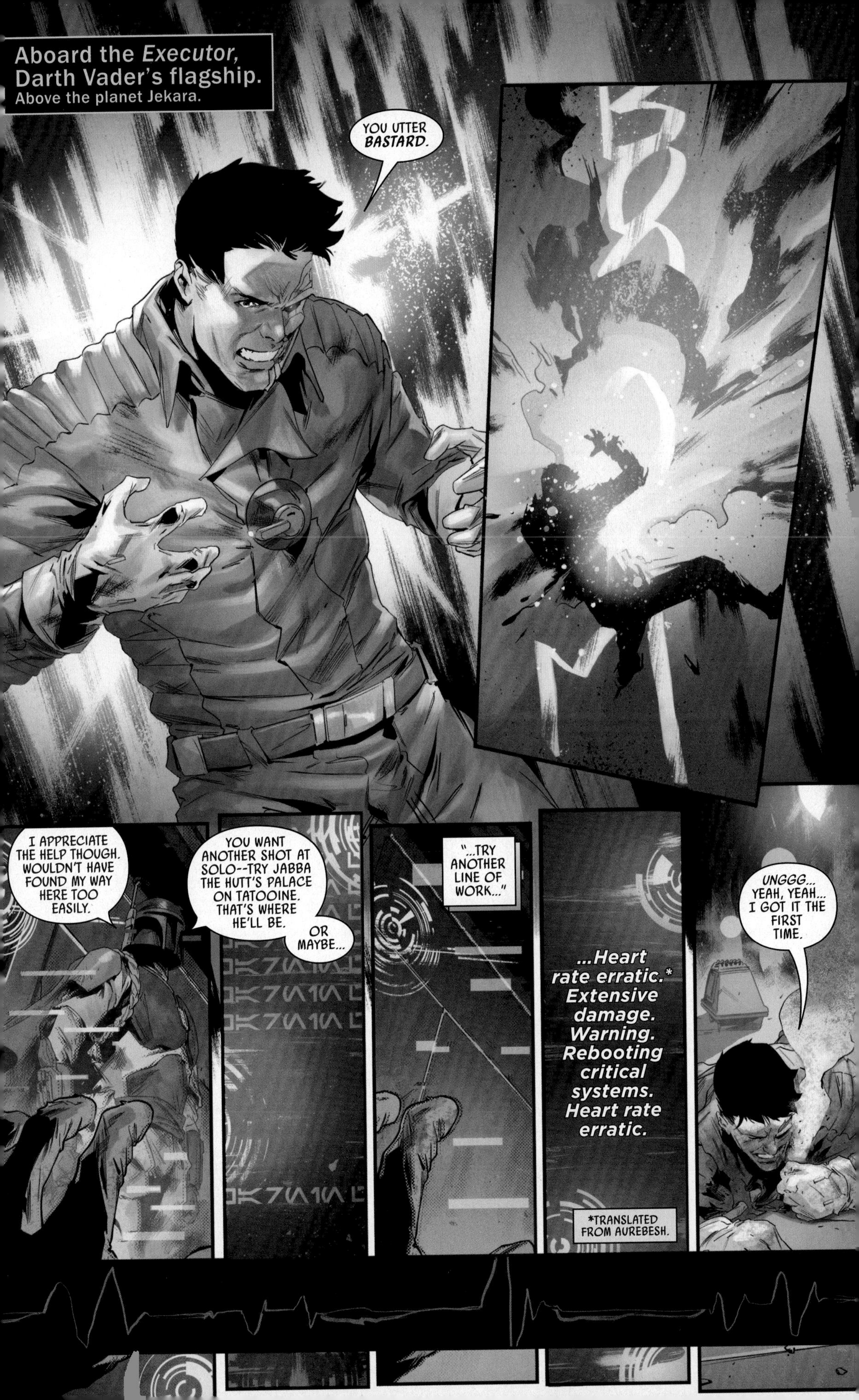

Aboard the *Executor*, Darth Vader's flagship.
Above the planet Jekara.
YOU UTTER BASTARD.
I APPRECIATE THE HELP THOUGH. WOULDN'T HAVE FOUND MY WAY HERE TOO EASILY.
YOU WANT ANOTHER SHOT AT SOLO--TRY JABBA THE HUTT'S PALACE ON TATOOINE. THAT'S WHERE HE'LL BE.
OR MAYBE...
"...TRY ANOTHER LINE OF WORK..."
...Heart rate erratic.* Extensive damage. Warning. Rebooting critical systems. Heart rate erratic.
*TRANSLATED FROM AUREBESH.
UNGGG... YEAH, YEAH... I GOT IT THE FIRST TIME.

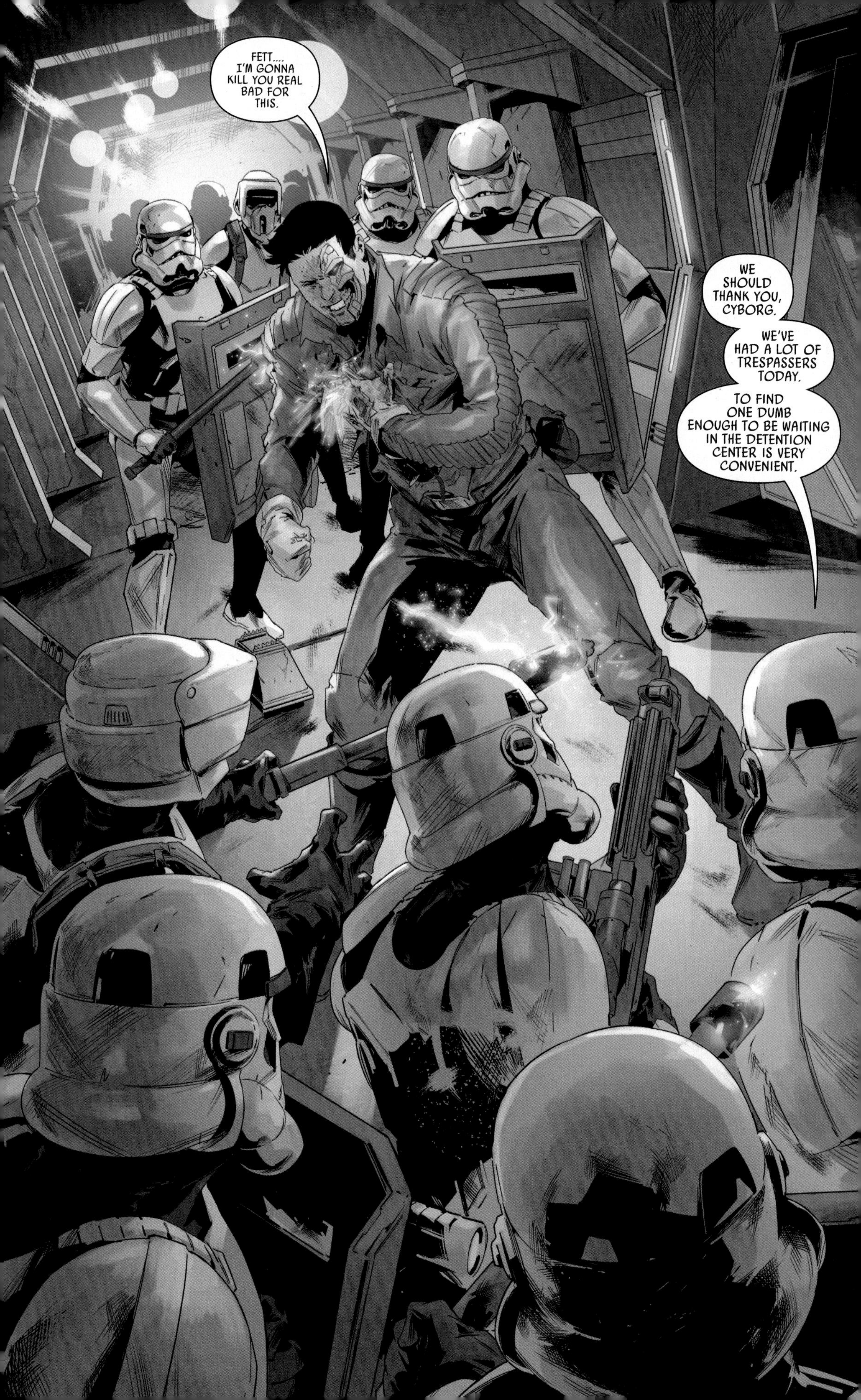
FETT.... I'M GONNA KILL YOU REAL BAD FOR THIS.
WE SHOULD THANK YOU, CYBORG.
WE'VE HAD A LOT OF TRESPASSERS TODAY.
TO FIND ONE DUMB ENOUGH TO BE WAITING IN THE DETENTION CENTER IS VERY CONVENIENT.

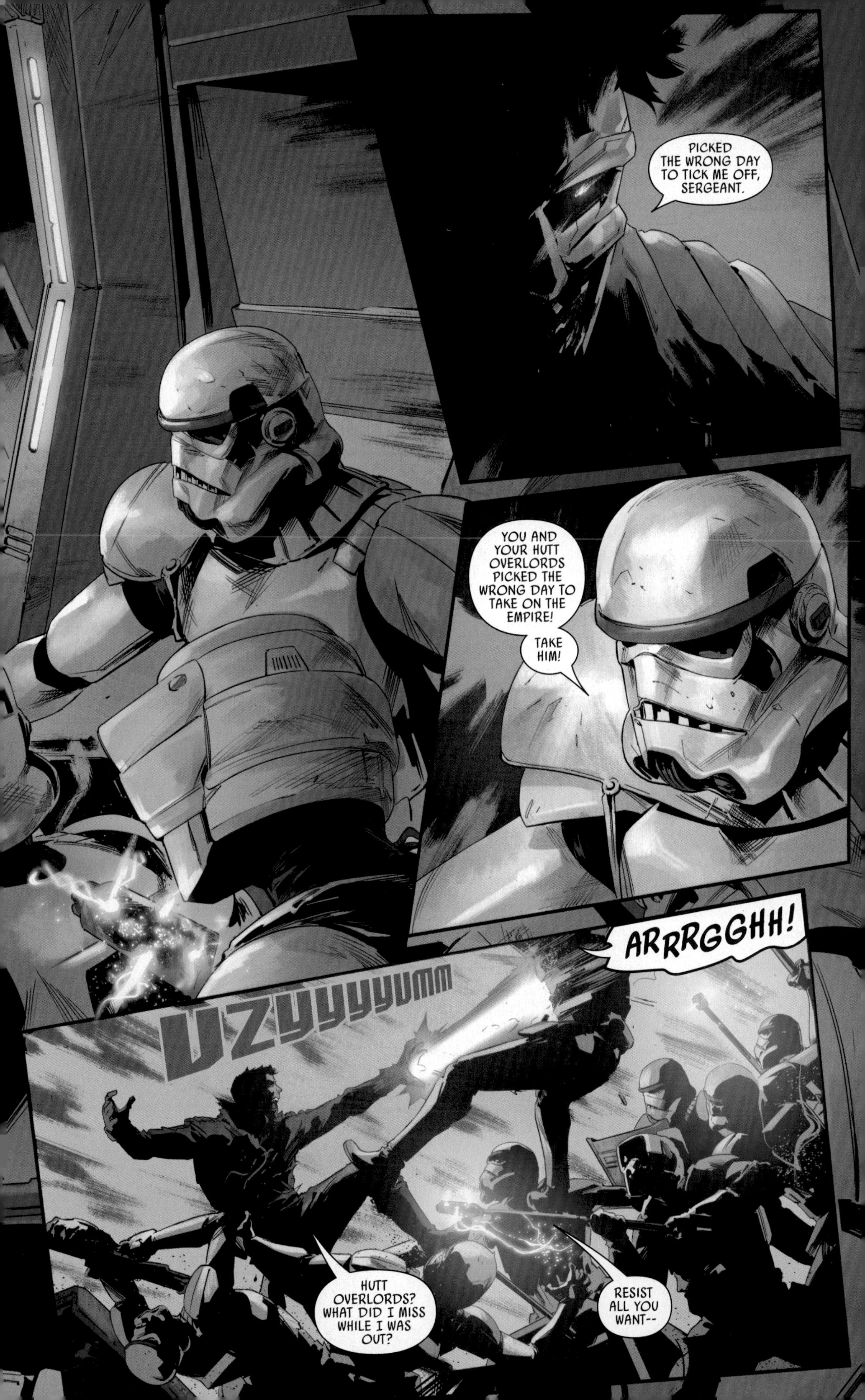
PICKED THE WRONG DAY TO TICK ME OFF, SERGEANT.
YOU AND YOUR HUTT OVERLORDS PICKED THE WRONG DAY TO TAKE ON THE EMPIRE!
TAKE HIM!
ARRRGGHH!
UZYYYYYUMM
HUTT OVERLORDS? WHAT DID I MISS WHILE I WAS OUT?
RESIST ALL YOU WANT--

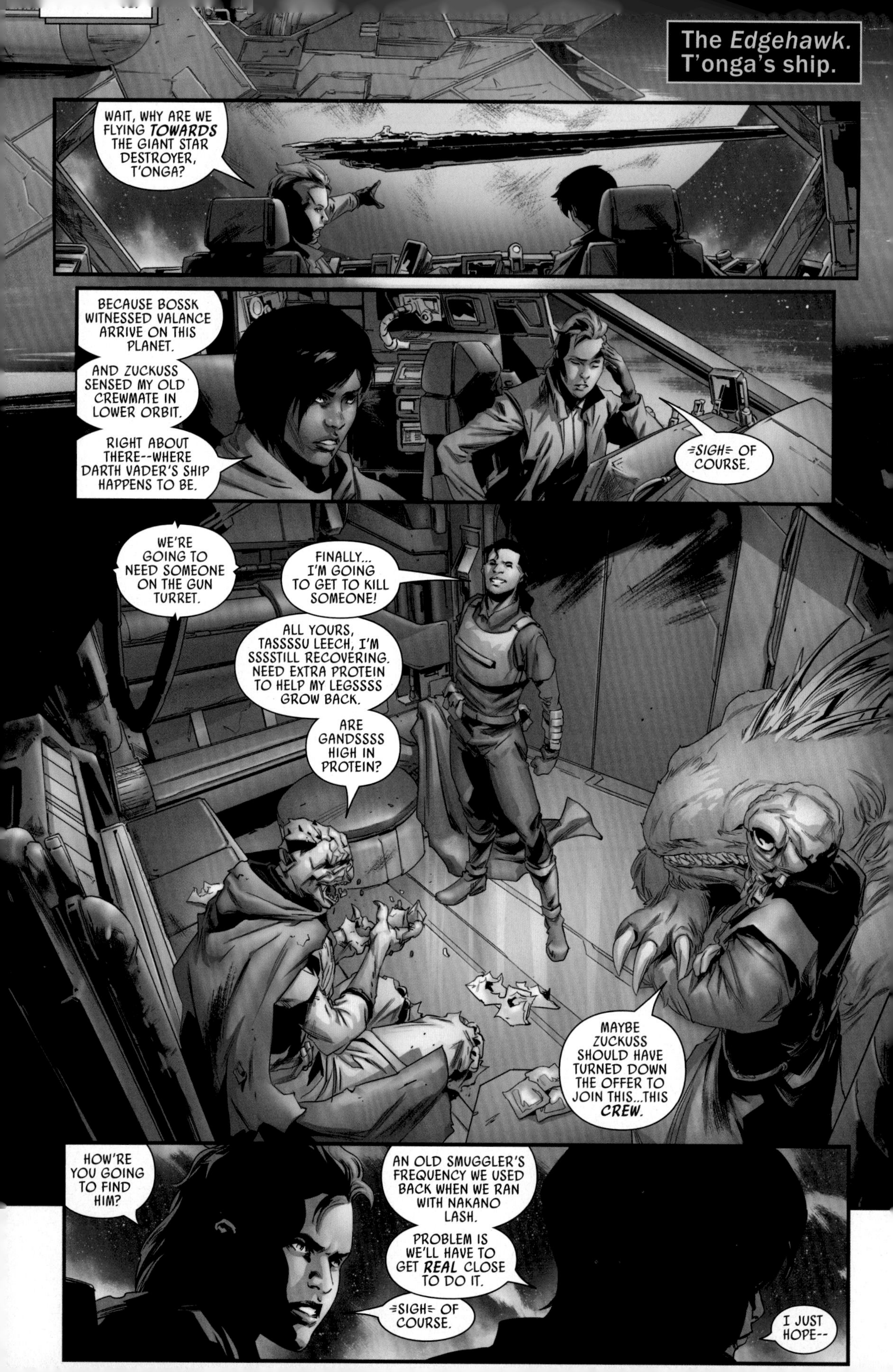
The *Edgehawk.* T'onga's ship.
WAIT, WHY ARE WE FLYING **TOWARDS** THE GIANT STAR DESTROYER, T'ONGA?
BECAUSE BOSSK WITNESSED VALANCE ARRIVE ON THIS PLANET.
AND ZUCKUSS SENSED MY OLD CREWMATE IN LOWER ORBIT.
RIGHT ABOUT THERE--WHERE DARTH VADER'S SHIP HAPPENS TO BE.
=SIGH= OF COURSE.
WE'RE GOING TO NEED SOMEONE ON THE GUN TURRET.
FINALLY... I'M GOING TO GET TO KILL SOMEONE!
ALL YOURS, TASSSSU LEECH, I'M SSSSTILL RECOVERING. NEED EXTRA PROTEIN TO HELP MY LEGSSSS GROW BACK.
ARE GANDSSSS HIGH IN PROTEIN?
MAYBE ZUCKUSS SHOULD HAVE TURNED DOWN THE OFFER TO JOIN THIS...THIS **CREW.**
HOW'RE YOU GOING TO FIND HIM?
AN OLD SMUGGLER'S FREQUENCY WE USED BACK WHEN WE RAN WITH NAKANO LASH.
PROBLEM IS WE'LL HAVE TO GET **REAL** CLOSE TO DO IT.
=SIGH= OF COURSE.
I JUST HOPE--

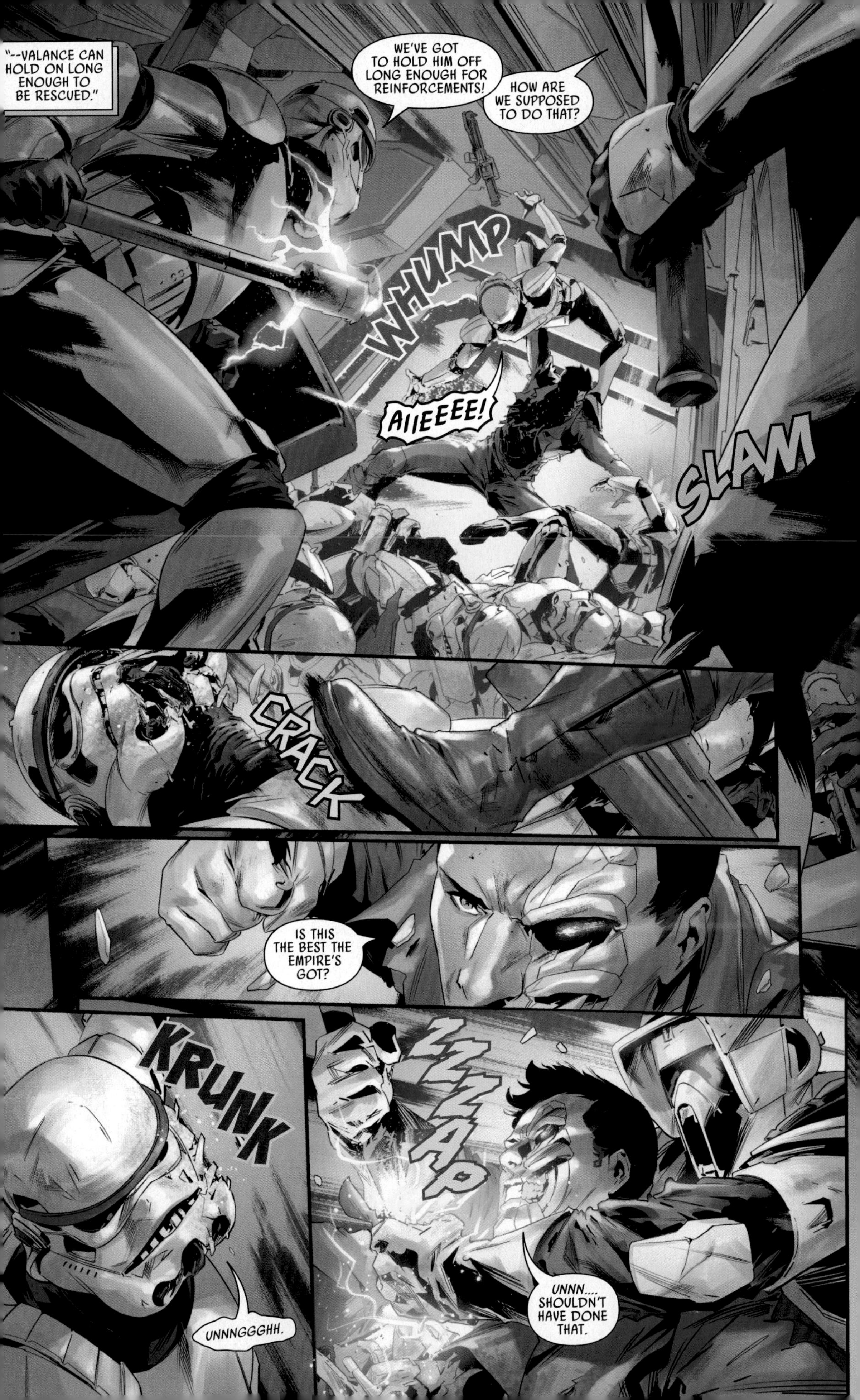
"--VALANCE CAN HOLD ON LONG ENOUGH TO BE RESCUED."
WE'VE GOT TO HOLD HIM OFF LONG ENOUGH FOR REINFORCEMENTS!
HOW ARE WE SUPPOSED TO DO THAT?
WHUMP
AIIEEEE!
SLAM
CRACK
IS THIS THE BEST THE EMPIRE'S GOT?
KRUNK
ZZZZAP
UNNNGGGHH.
UNNN.... SHOULDN'T HAVE DONE THAT.

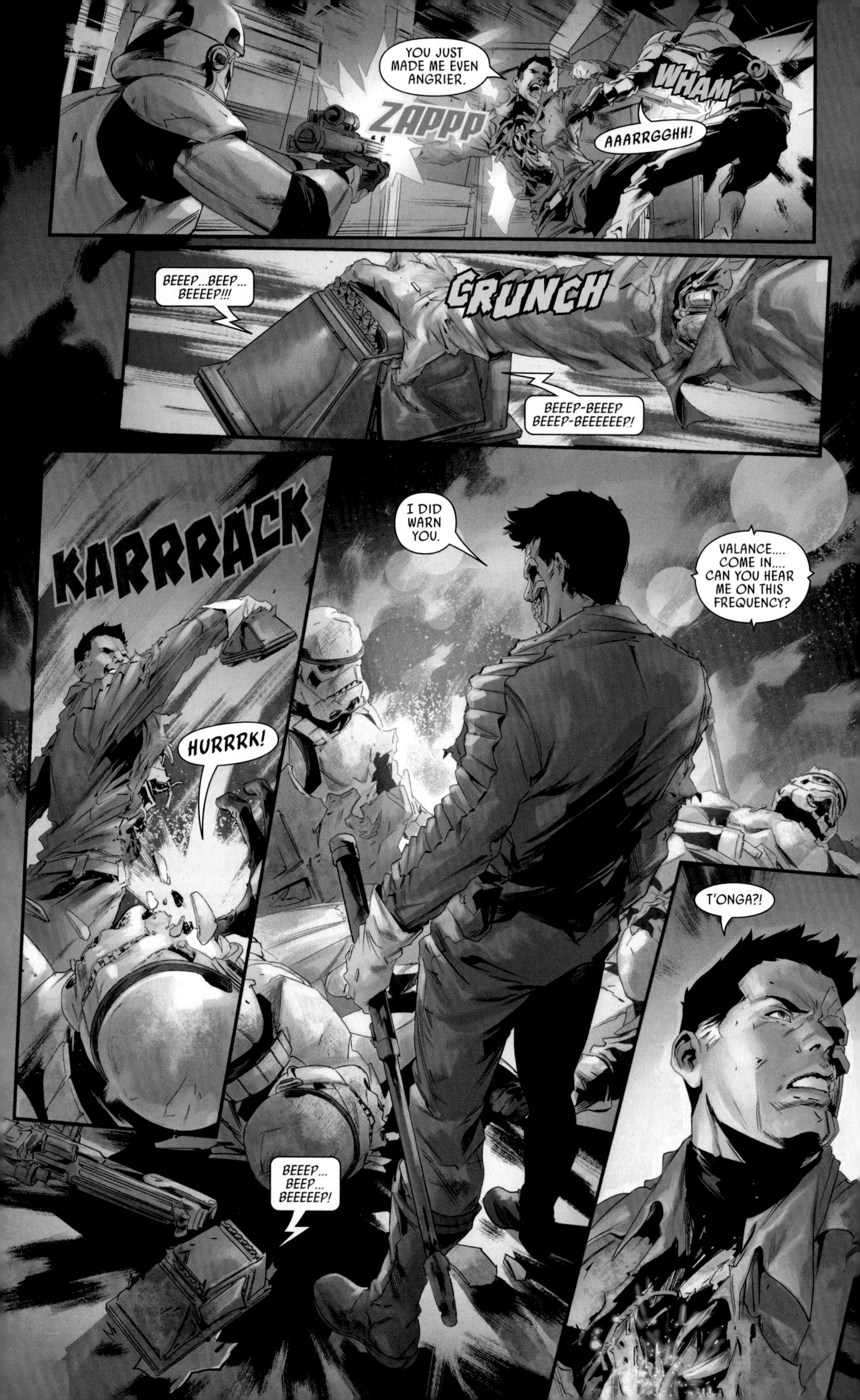
YOU JUST MADE ME EVEN ANGRIER.
ZAPPP
WHAM
AAARRGGHH!
BEEEP...BEEP... BEEEEP!!!
CRUNCH
BEEEP-BEEEP BEEEP-BEEEEEEP!
KARRRACK
HURRRK!
BEEEP... BEEP... BEEEEEP!
I DID WARN YOU.
VALANCE.... COME IN.... CAN YOU HEAR ME ON THIS FREQUENCY?
T'ONGA?!

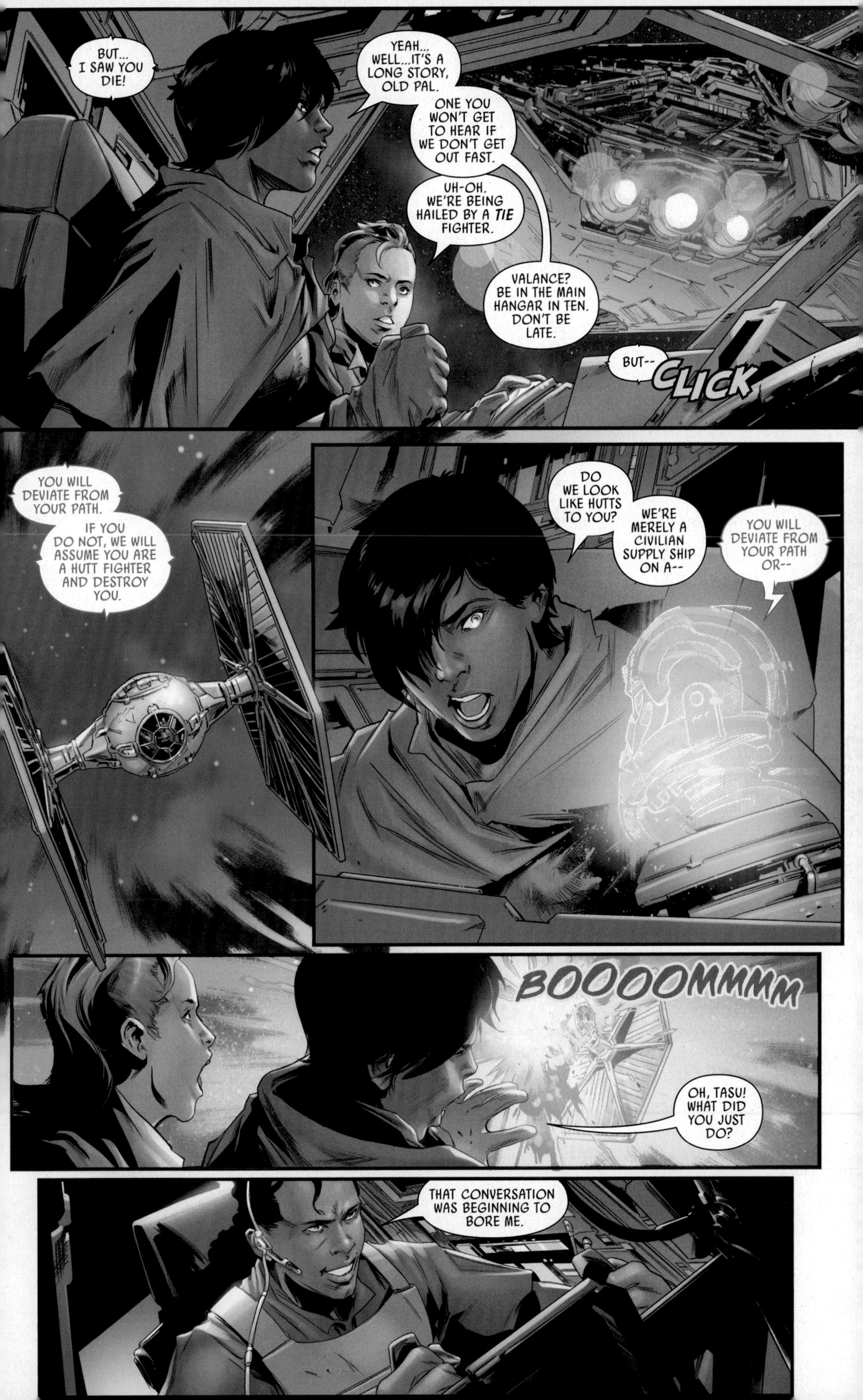

BUT... I SAW YOU DIE!
YEAH... WELL...IT'S A LONG STORY, OLD PAL.
ONE YOU WON'T GET TO HEAR IF WE DON'T GET OUT FAST.
UH-OH. WE'RE BEING HAILED BY A TIE FIGHTER.
VALANCE? BE IN THE MAIN HANGAR IN TEN. DON'T BE LATE.
BUT--
CLICK
YOU WILL DEVIATE FROM YOUR PATH.
IF YOU DO NOT, WE WILL ASSUME YOU ARE A HUTT FIGHTER AND DESTROY YOU.
DO WE LOOK LIKE HUTTS TO YOU?
WE'RE MERELY A CIVILIAN SUPPLY SHIP ON A--
YOU WILL DEVIATE FROM YOUR PATH OR--
BOOOOMMMM
OH, TASU! WHAT DID YOU JUST DO?
THAT CONVERSATION WAS BEGINNING TO BORE ME.

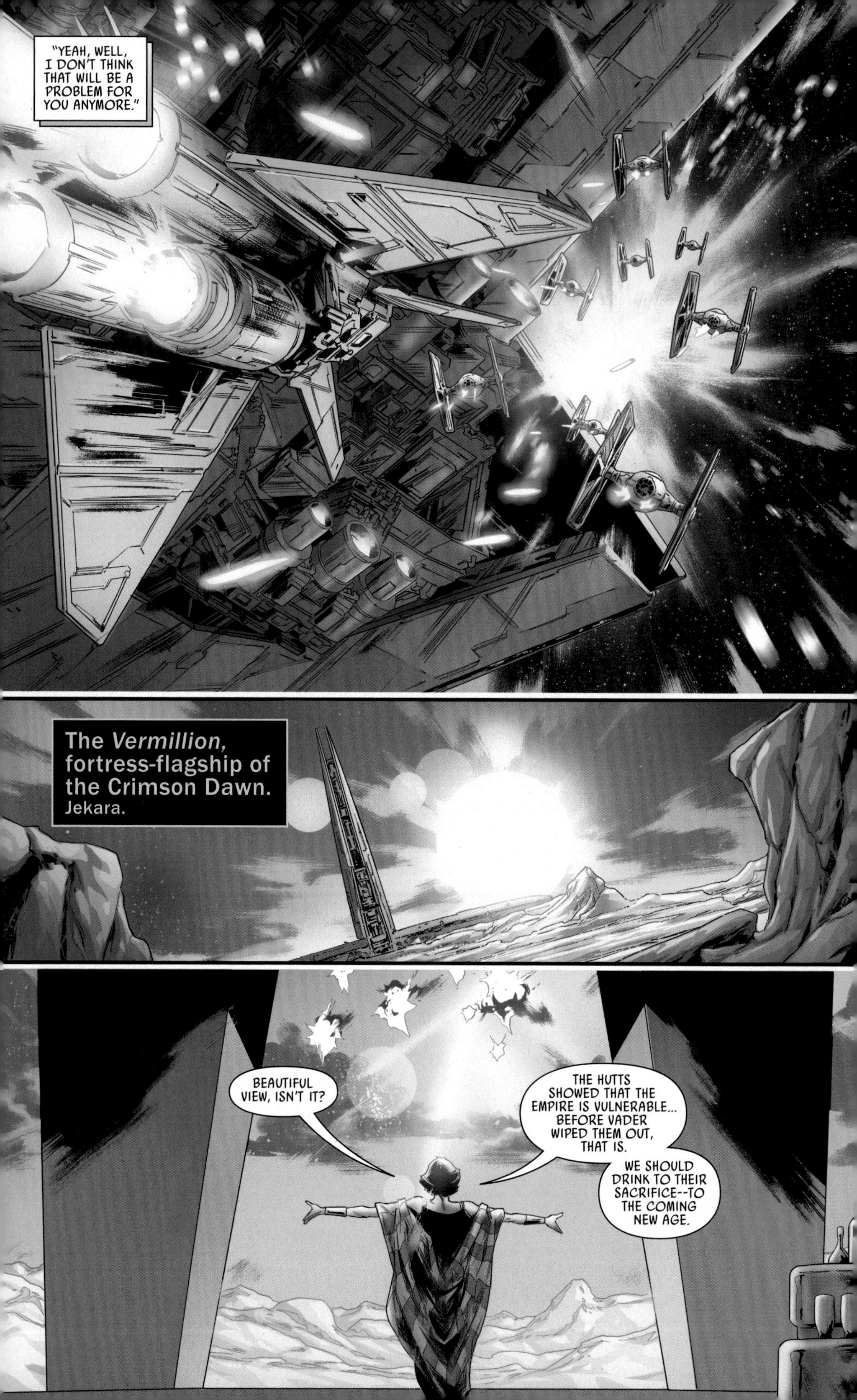
"YEAH, WELL, I DON'T THINK THAT WILL BE A PROBLEM FOR YOU ANYMORE."
The *Vermillion*, fortress-flagship of the Crimson Dawn. Jekara.
BEAUTIFUL VIEW, ISN'T IT?
THE HUTTS SHOWED THAT THE EMPIRE IS VULNERABLE... BEFORE VADER WIPED THEM OUT, THAT IS.
WE SHOULD DRINK TO THEIR SACRIFICE--TO THE COMING NEW AGE.

IT'S NOT WHAT I WANT *FROM* YOU. IT'S WHAT I WANT *FOR* YOU.

CRIMSON DAWN IS GOING TO UNITE THE UNDERWORLD.

BUT TO BRING A NEW ORDER...WE WILL HAVE TO CRUSH THOSE SYNDICATES THAT STAND IN OUR WAY.

I AM HONORED THAT YOU WANTED AN AUDIENCE WITH ME, LADY QI'RA.

IF I WERE A PARANOID PERSON, I WOULD THINK YOU WANTED SOMETHING FROM ME.

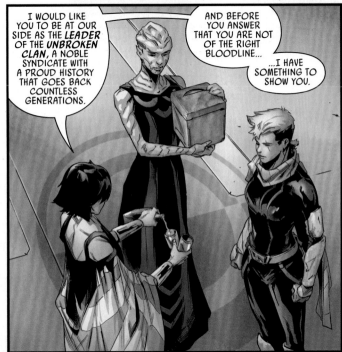

I WOULD LIKE YOU TO BE AT OUR SIDE AS THE *LEADER* OF THE *UNBROKEN CLAN*, A NOBLE SYNDICATE WITH A PROUD HISTORY THAT GOES BACK COUNTLESS GENERATIONS.

AND BEFORE YOU ANSWER THAT YOU ARE NOT OF THE RIGHT BLOODLINE...

...I HAVE SOMETHING TO SHOW YOU.

IS THAT WHAT I THINK IT IS?

YOUR CLAN HAS A STORIED PAST...BUT CRIMSON DAWN IS ABOUT THE FUTURE.

SO, WHAT IS YOUR ANSWER?

I...

...AWAIT THE DAWN.

CLINK

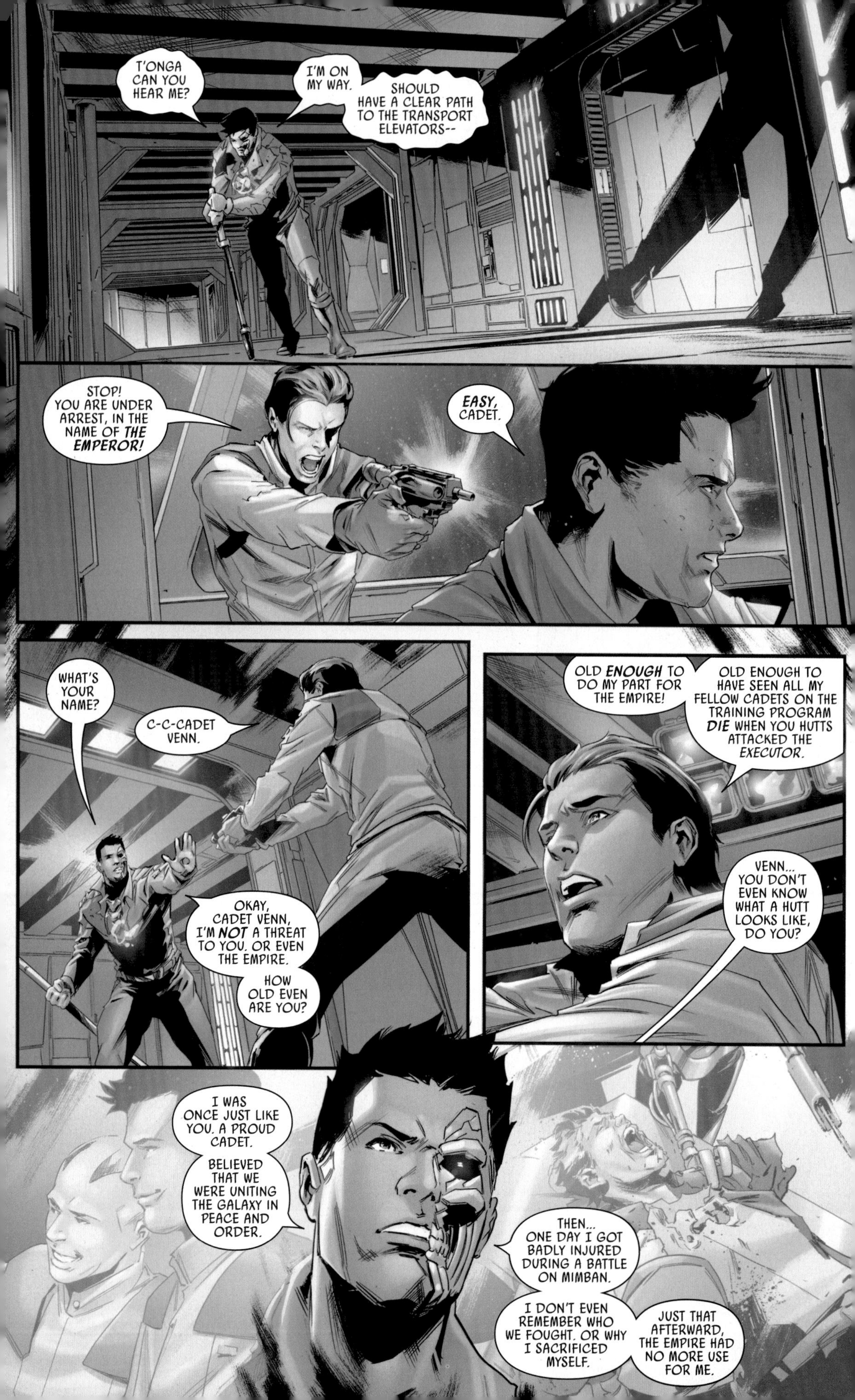
T'ONGA CAN YOU HEAR ME?
I'M ON MY WAY.
SHOULD HAVE A CLEAR PATH TO THE TRANSPORT ELEVATORS--
STOP! YOU ARE UNDER ARREST, IN THE NAME OF *THE EMPEROR!*
EASY, CADET.
WHAT'S YOUR NAME?
C-C-CADET VENN.
OKAY, CADET VENN, I'M *NOT* A THREAT TO YOU. OR EVEN THE EMPIRE.
HOW OLD EVEN ARE YOU?
OLD *ENOUGH* TO DO MY PART FOR THE EMPIRE!
OLD ENOUGH TO HAVE SEEN ALL MY FELLOW CADETS ON THE TRAINING PROGRAM *DIE* WHEN YOU HUTTS ATTACKED THE *EXECUTOR.*
VENN... YOU DON'T EVEN KNOW WHAT A HUTT LOOKS LIKE, DO YOU?
I WAS ONCE JUST LIKE YOU. A PROUD CADET.
BELIEVED THAT WE WERE UNITING THE GALAXY IN PEACE AND ORDER.
THEN... ONE DAY I GOT BADLY INJURED DURING A BATTLE ON MIMBAN.
I DON'T EVEN REMEMBER WHO WE FOUGHT. OR WHY I SACRIFICED MYSELF.
JUST THAT AFTERWARD, THE EMPIRE HAD NO MORE USE FOR ME.

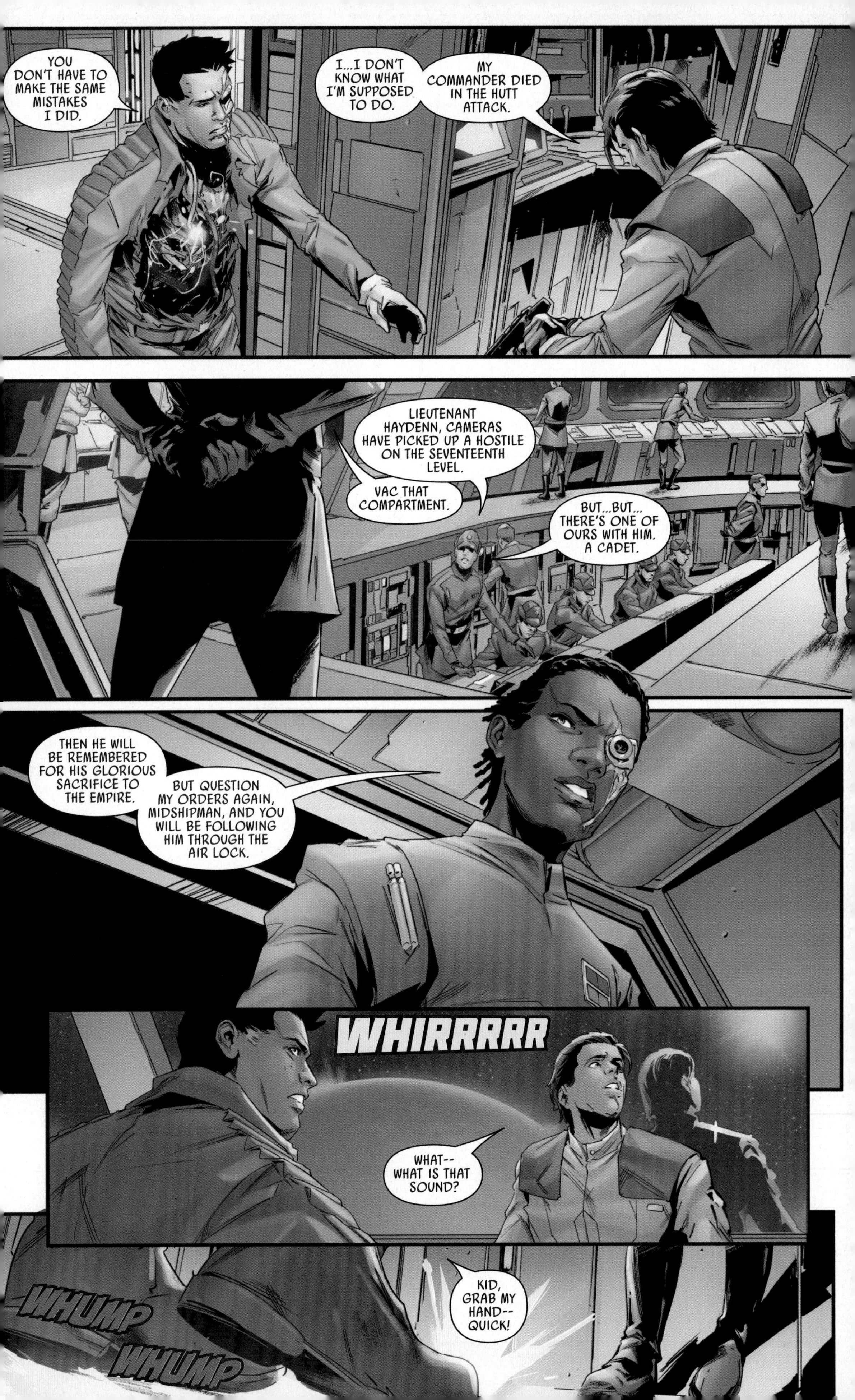
YOU DON'T HAVE TO MAKE THE SAME MISTAKES I DID.
I...I DON'T KNOW WHAT I'M SUPPOSED TO DO.
MY COMMANDER DIED IN THE HUTT ATTACK.
LIEUTENANT HAYDENN, CAMERAS HAVE PICKED UP A HOSTILE ON THE SEVENTEENTH LEVEL.
VAC THAT COMPARTMENT.
BUT...BUT... THERE'S ONE OF OURS WITH HIM. A CADET.
THEN HE WILL BE REMEMBERED FOR HIS GLORIOUS SACRIFICE TO THE EMPIRE.
BUT QUESTION MY ORDERS AGAIN, MIDSHIPMAN, AND YOU WILL BE FOLLOWING HIM THROUGH THE AIR LOCK.
WHIRRRRR
WHAT-- WHAT IS THAT SOUND?
WHUMP
WHUMP
KID, GRAB MY HAND-- QUICK!

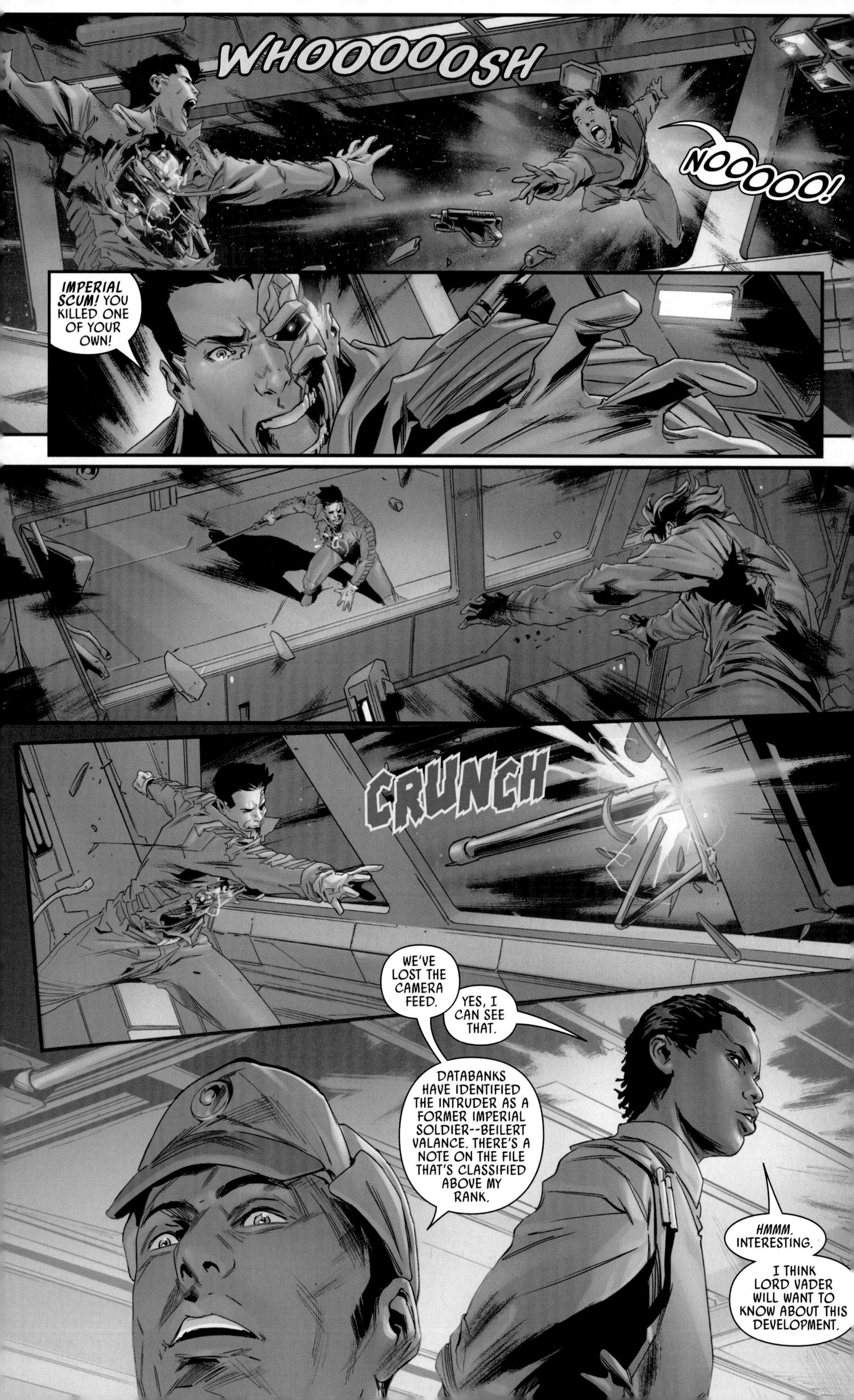
WHOOOOOOSH
NOOOOO!
IMPERIAL SCUM! YOU KILLED ONE OF YOUR OWN!
CRUNCH
WE'VE LOST THE CAMERA FEED.
YES, I CAN SEE THAT.
DATABANKS HAVE IDENTIFIED THE INTRUDER AS A FORMER IMPERIAL SOLDIER--BEILERT VALANCE. THERE'S A NOTE ON THE FILE THAT'S CLASSIFIED ABOVE MY RANK.
HMMM. INTERESTING.
I THINK LORD VADER WILL WANT TO KNOW ABOUT THIS DEVELOPMENT.

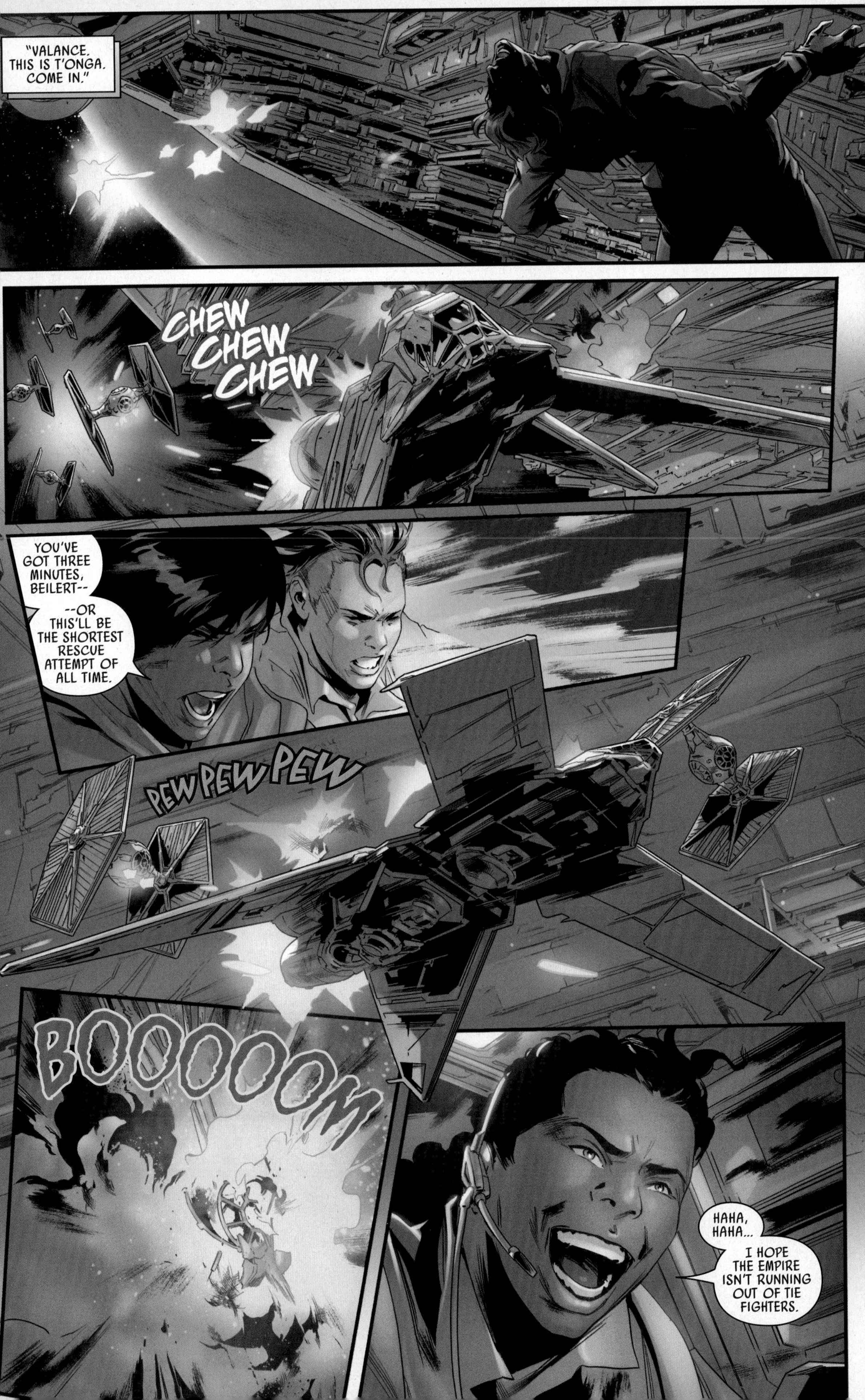
"VALANCE. THIS IS T'ONGA. COME IN."
CHEW CHEW CHEW
YOU'VE GOT THREE MINUTES, BEILERT--
--OR THIS'LL BE THE SHORTEST RESCUE ATTEMPT OF ALL TIME.
PEW PEW PEW
BOOOOOM
HAHA, HAHA...
I HOPE THE EMPIRE ISN'T RUNNING OUT OF TIE FIGHTERS.

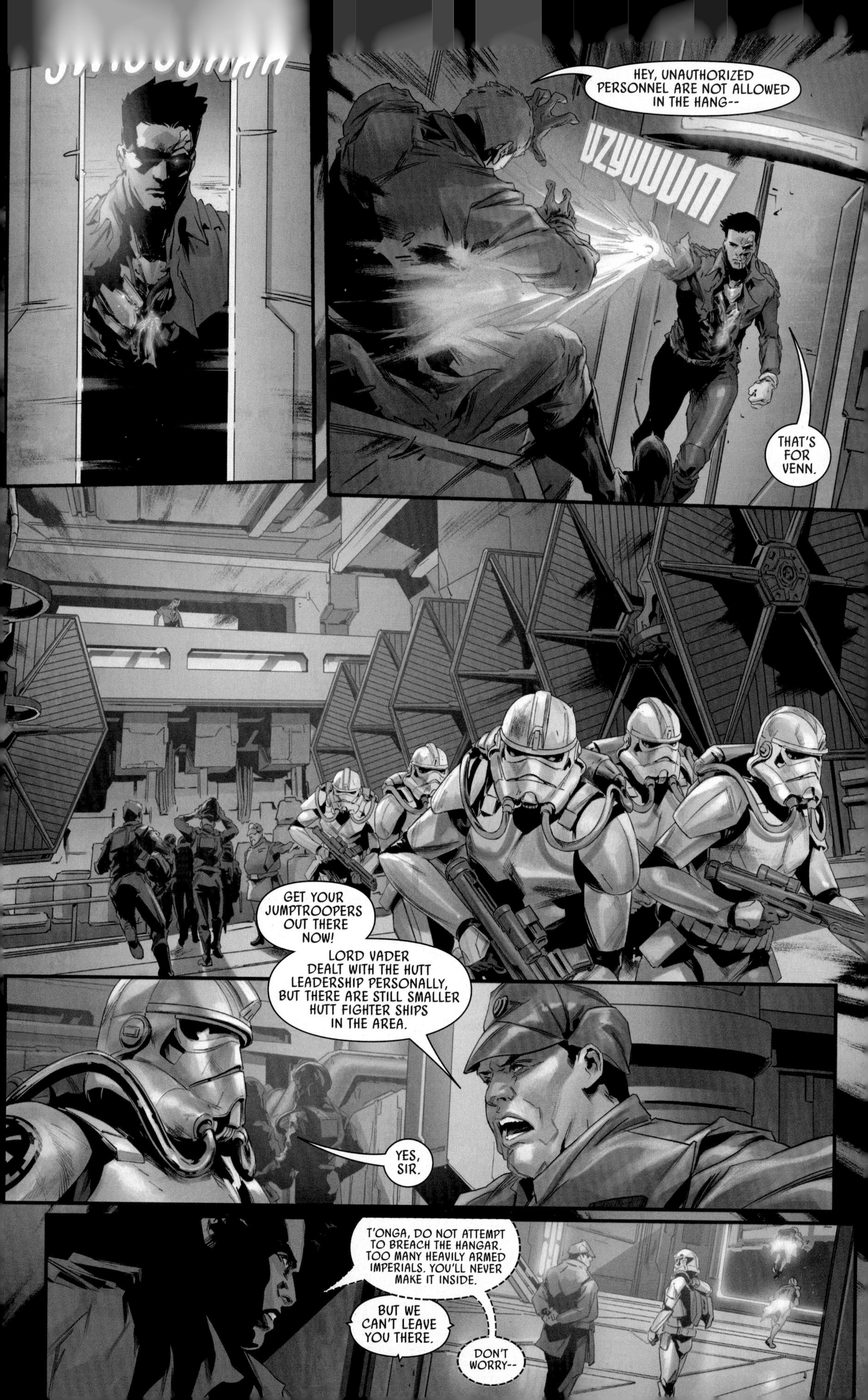
HEY, UNAUTHORIZED PERSONNEL ARE NOT ALLOWED IN THE HANG--
THAT'S FOR VENN.
GET YOUR JUMPTROOPERS OUT THERE NOW!
LORD VADER DEALT WITH THE HUTT LEADERSHIP PERSONALLY, BUT THERE ARE STILL SMALLER HUTT FIGHTER SHIPS IN THE AREA.
YES, SIR.
T'ONGA, DO NOT ATTEMPT TO BREACH THE HANGAR. TOO MANY HEAVILY ARMED IMPERIALS. YOU'LL NEVER MAKE IT INSIDE.
BUT WE CAN'T LEAVE YOU THERE.
DON'T WORRY--

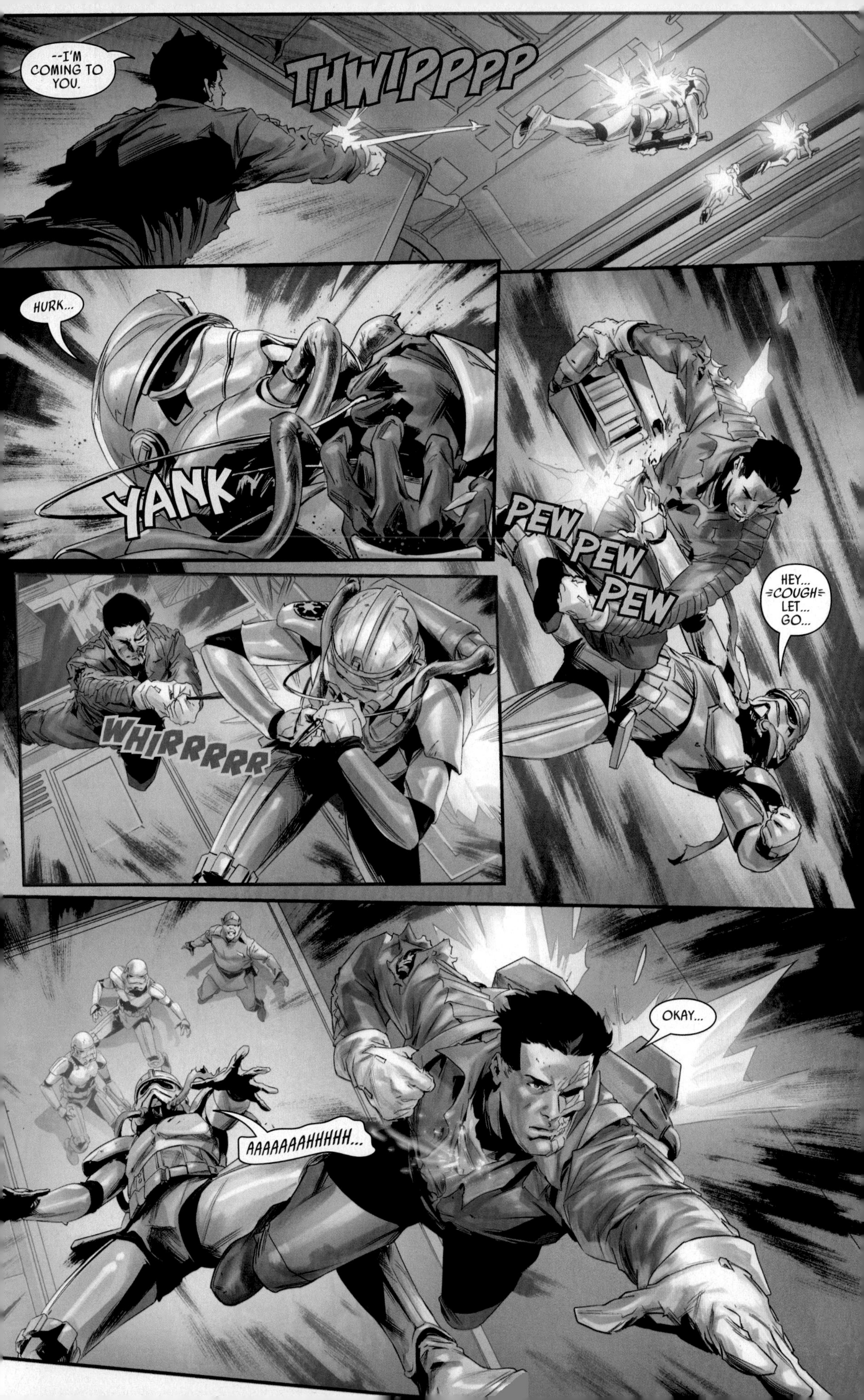
--I'M COMING TO YOU.
THWIPPPP
HURK...
YANK
PEW PEW PEW
HEY... COUGH LET... GO...
WHIRRRRR
OKAY...
AAAAAAAHHHHH...

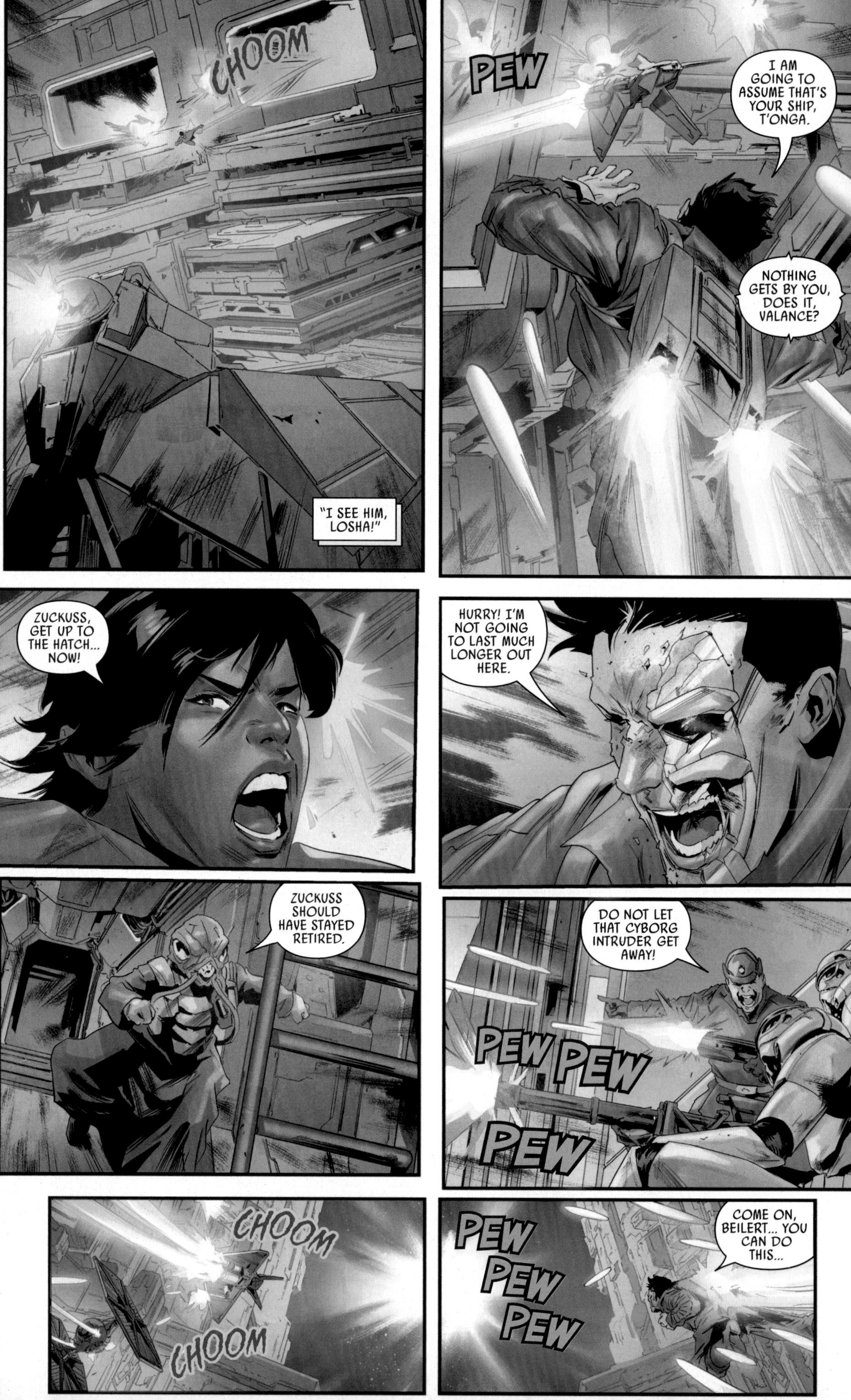
CHOOM
"I SEE HIM, LOSHA!"
PEW
I AM GOING TO ASSUME THAT'S YOUR SHIP, T'ONGA.
NOTHING GETS BY YOU, DOES IT, VALANCE?
ZUCKUSS, GET UP TO THE HATCH... NOW!
HURRY! I'M NOT GOING TO LAST MUCH LONGER OUT HERE.
ZUCKUSS SHOULD HAVE STAYED RETIRED.
DO NOT LET THAT CYBORG INTRUDER GET AWAY!
PEW PEW
PEW
CHOOM
CHOOM
PEW
PEW
PEW
COME ON, BEILERT... YOU CAN DO THIS...

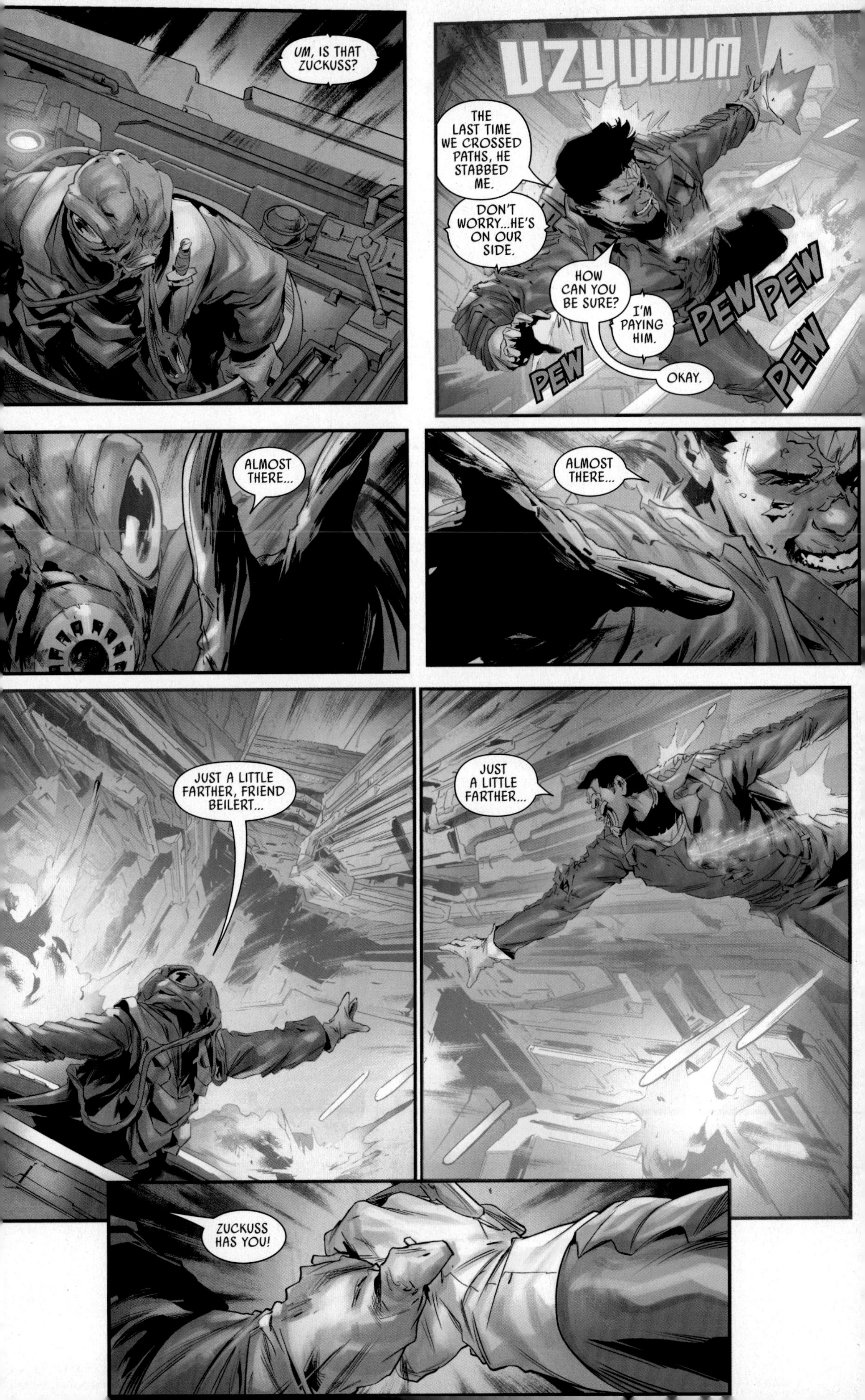
UM, IS THAT ZUCKUSS?
VZYVVVVM
THE LAST TIME WE CROSSED PATHS, HE STABBED ME.
DON'T WORRY...HE'S ON OUR SIDE.
HOW CAN YOU BE SURE?
I'M PAYING HIM.
OKAY.
PEW
PEW PEW
PEW
ALMOST THERE...
ALMOST THERE...
JUST A LITTLE FARTHER, FRIEND BEILERT...
JUST A LITTLE FARTHER...
ZUCKUSS HAS YOU!

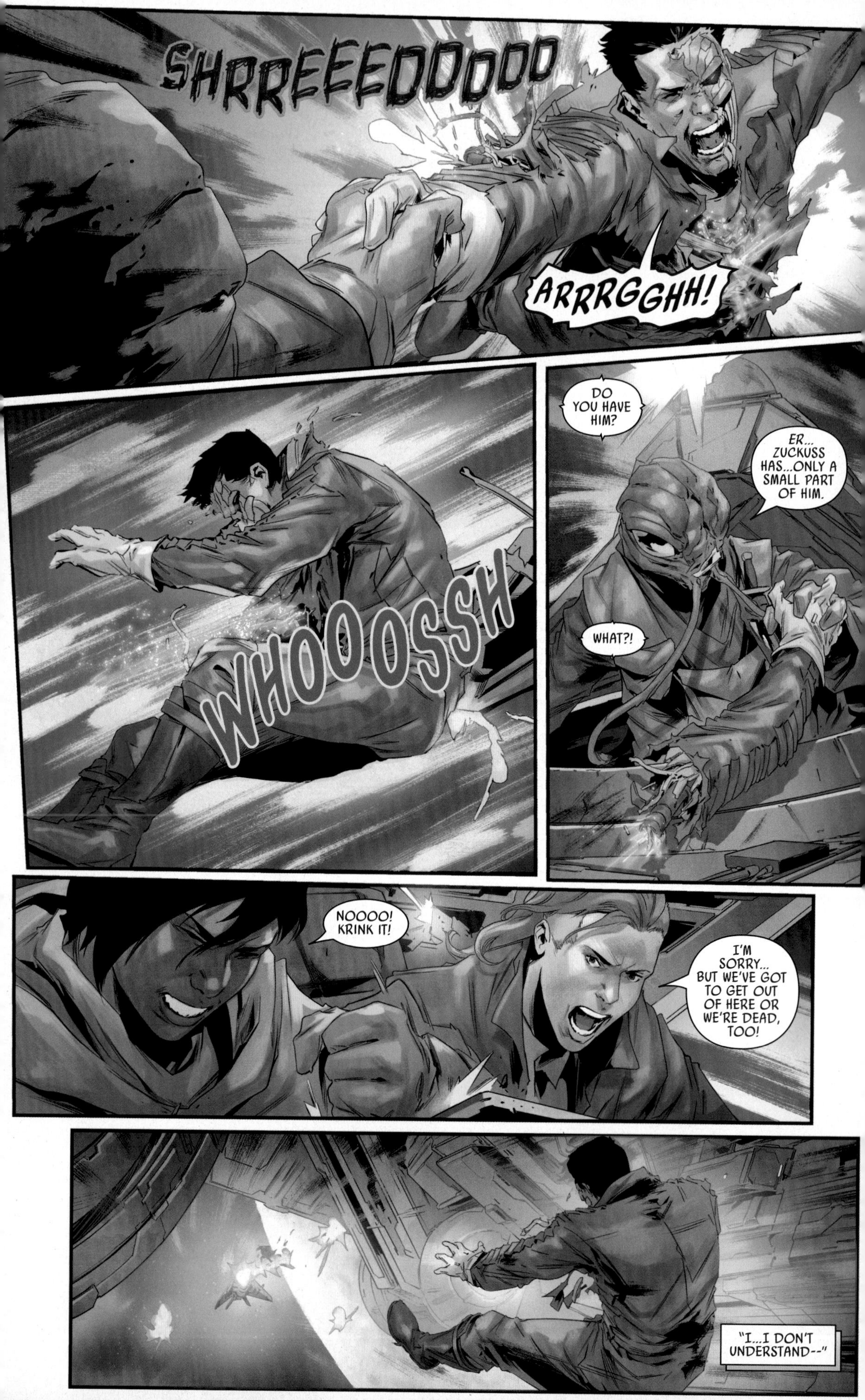
SHRREEEDDDDDD
ARRRGGHH!
WHOOOSSH
DO YOU HAVE HIM?
ER... ZUCKUSS HAS...ONLY A SMALL PART OF HIM.
WHAT?!
NOOOO! KRINK IT!
I'M SORRY... BUT WE'VE GOT TO GET OUT OF HERE OR WE'RE DEAD, TOO!
"I...I DON'T UNDERSTAND--"

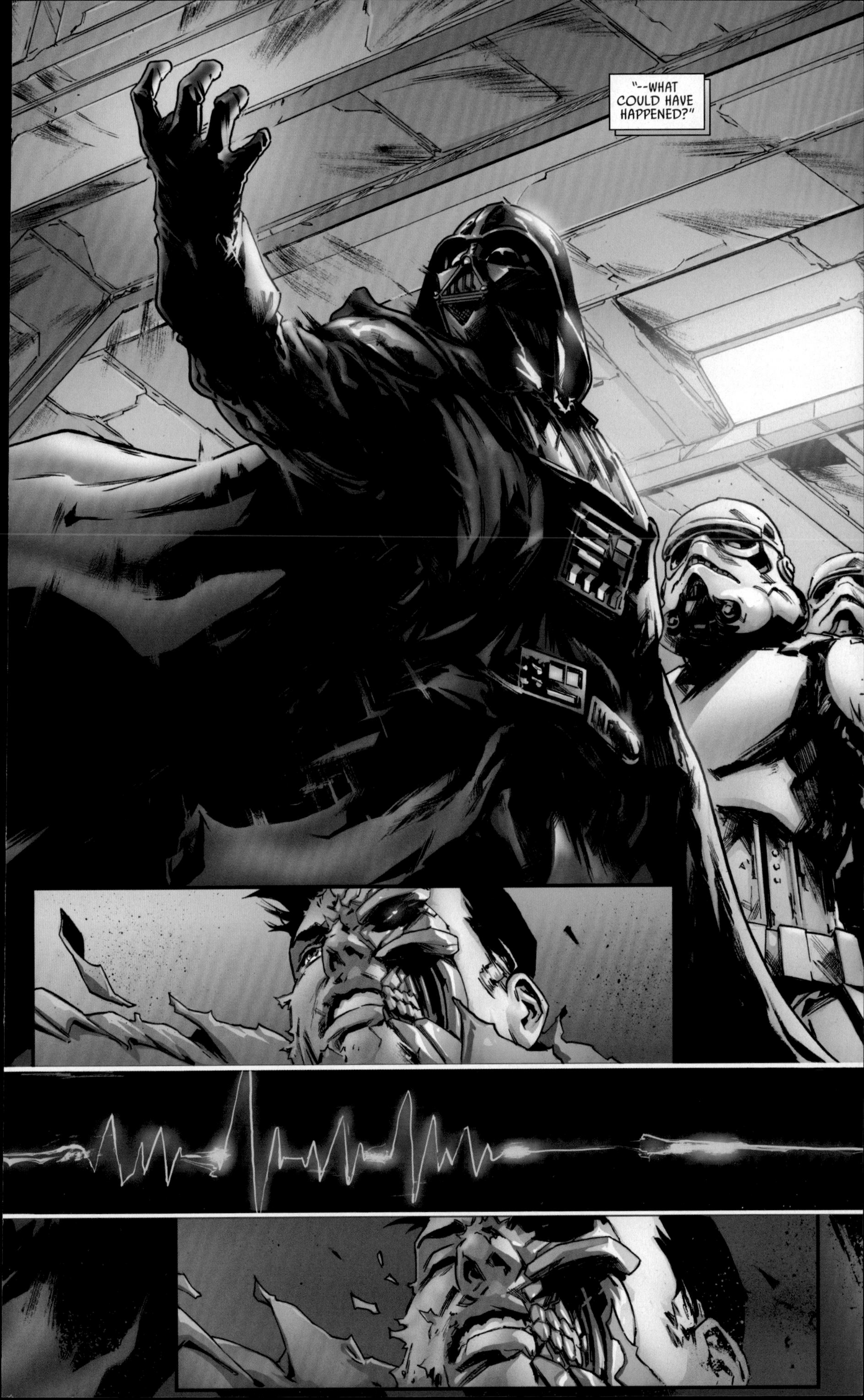
"--WHAT COULD HAVE HAPPENED?"

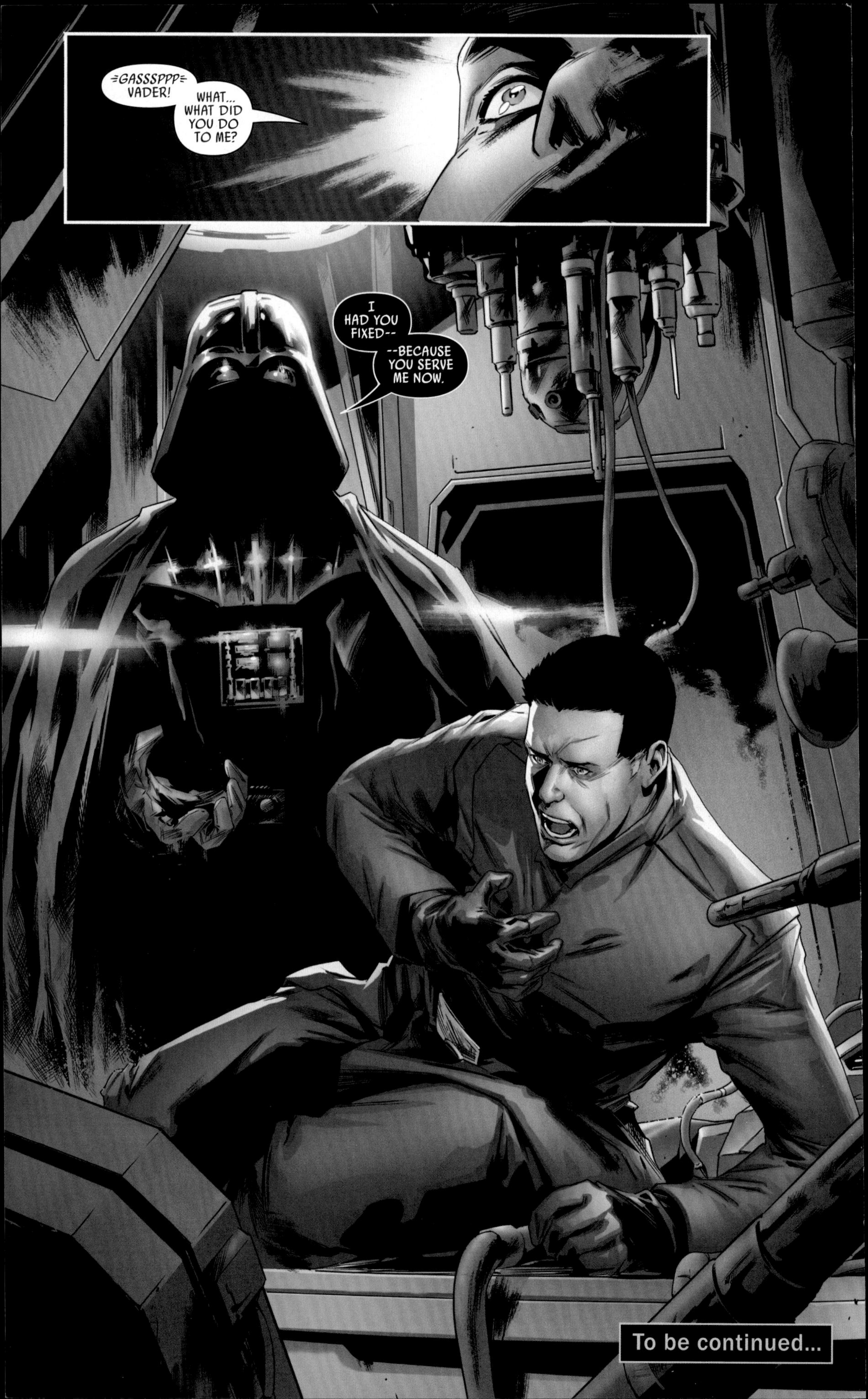
=GASSSPPP=
VADER!
WHAT...
WHAT DID
YOU DO
TO ME?
I
HAD YOU
FIXED--
--BECAUSE
YOU SERVE
ME NOW.
To be continued...

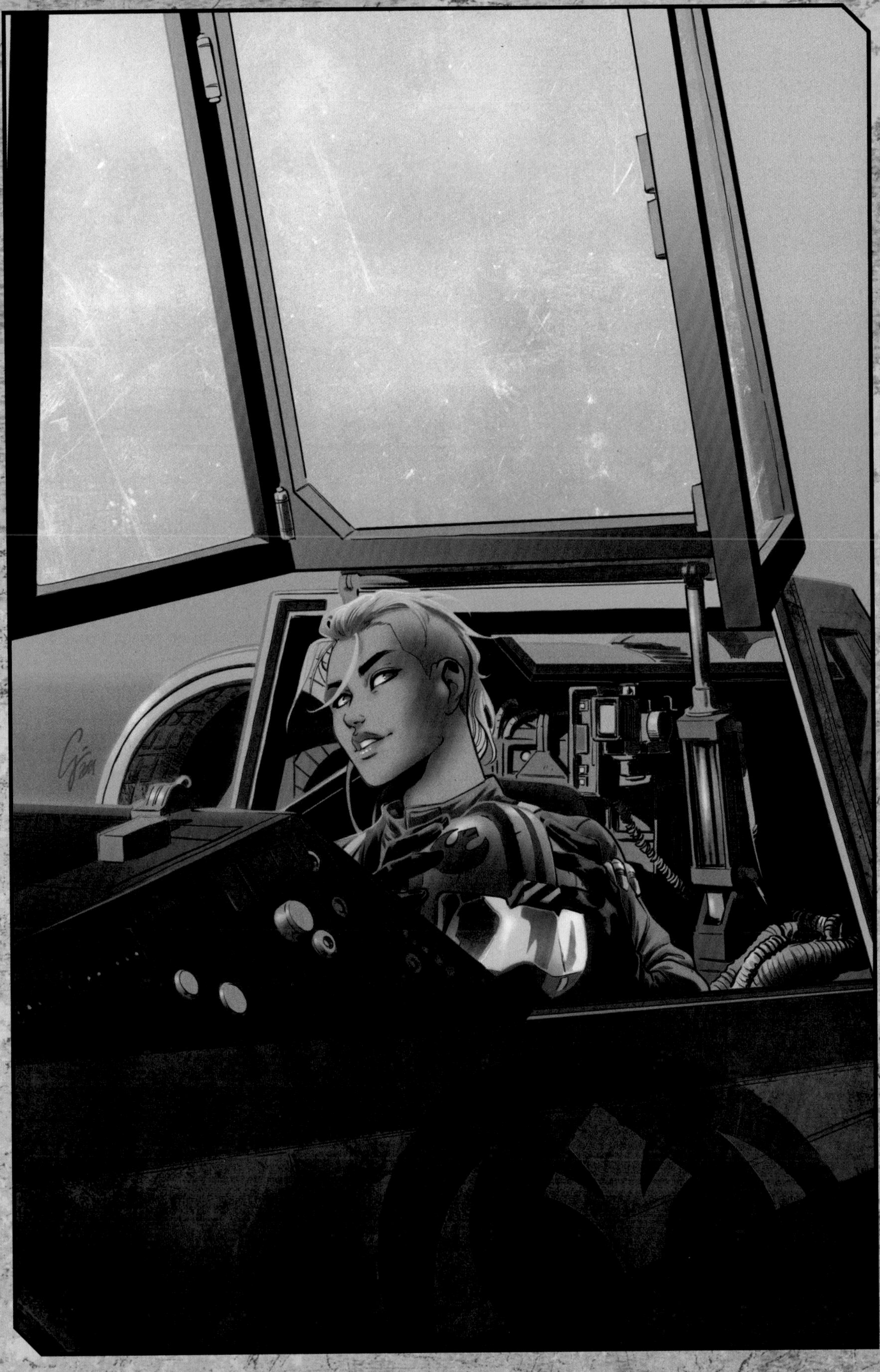

#13 Pride Variant by
JACOPO CAMAGNI

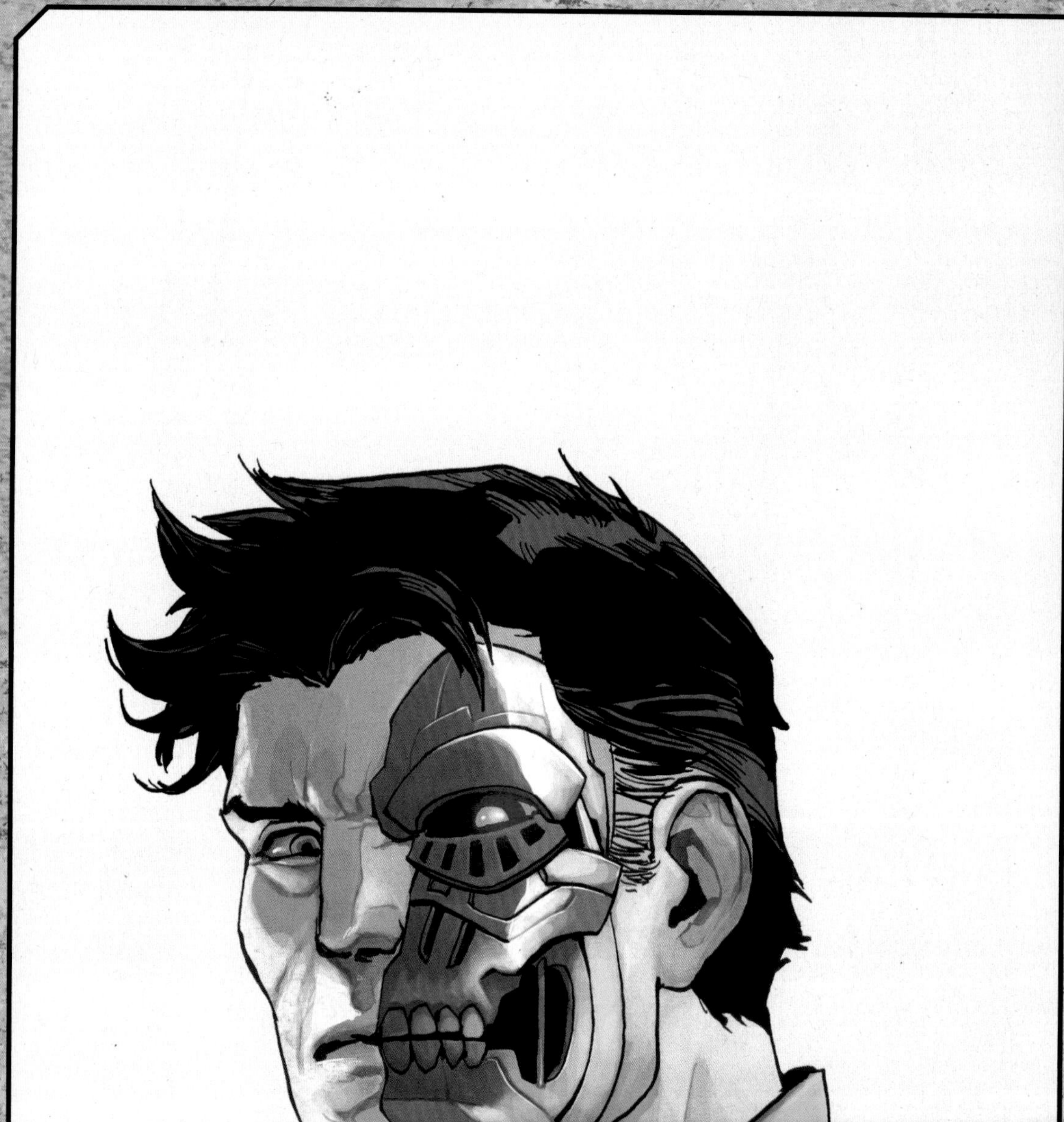

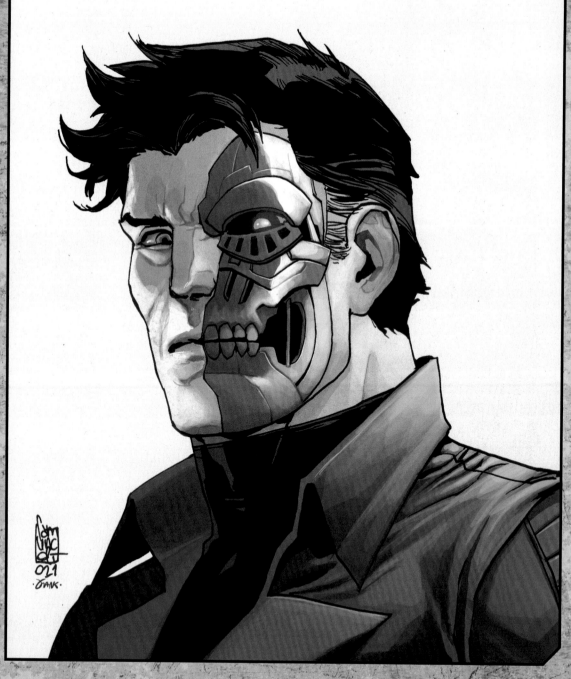

#14 Headshot Variant by
GIUSEPPE CAMUNCOLI & FRANK MARTIN

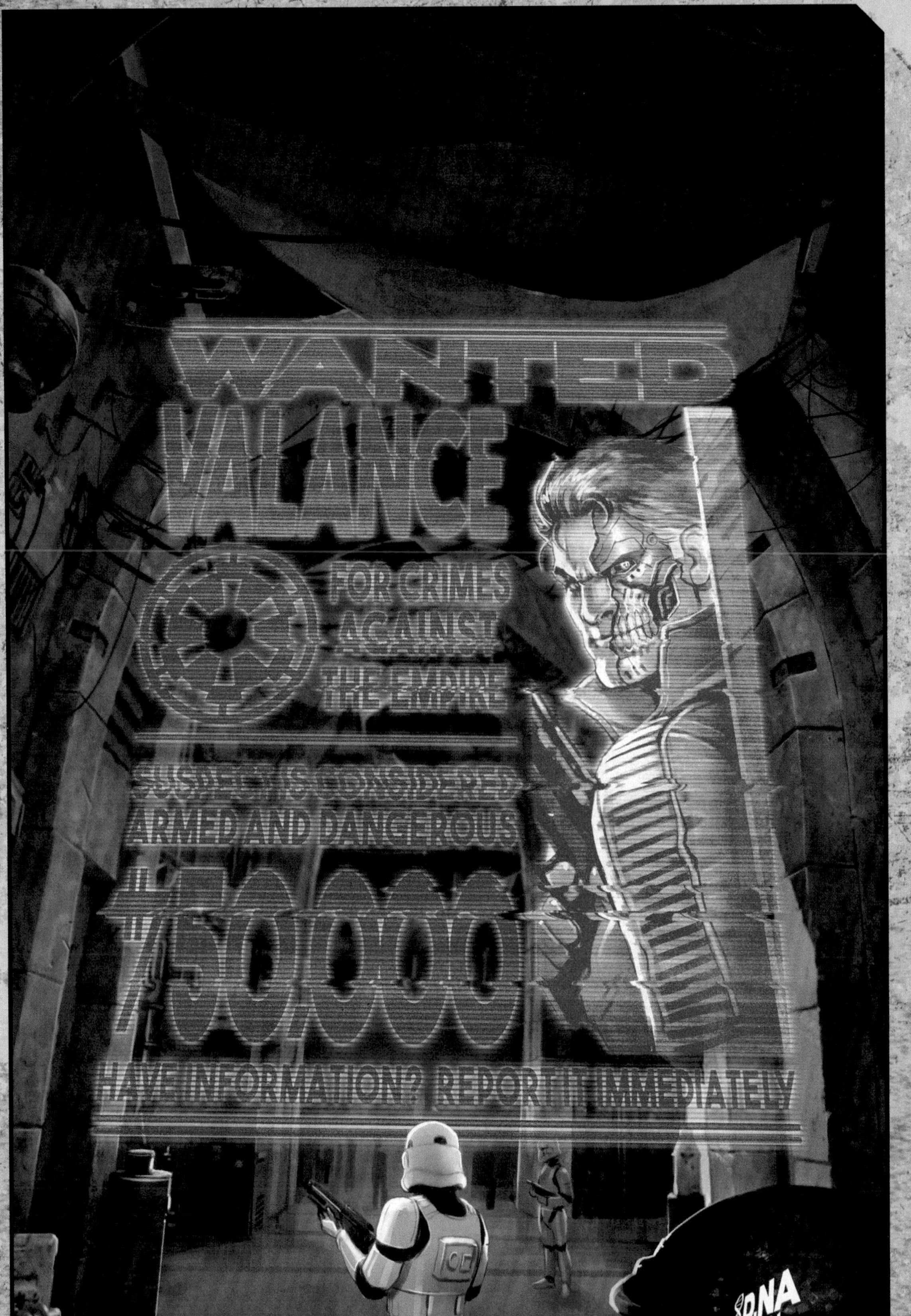
WANTED
VALANCE
FOR CRIMES AGAINST THE EMPIRE
SUSPECT IS CONSIDERED ARMED AND DANGEROUS
HAVE INFORMATION? REPORT IT IMMEDIATELY
D.NA 6.21

#15 Variant by
DAVID NAKAYAMA

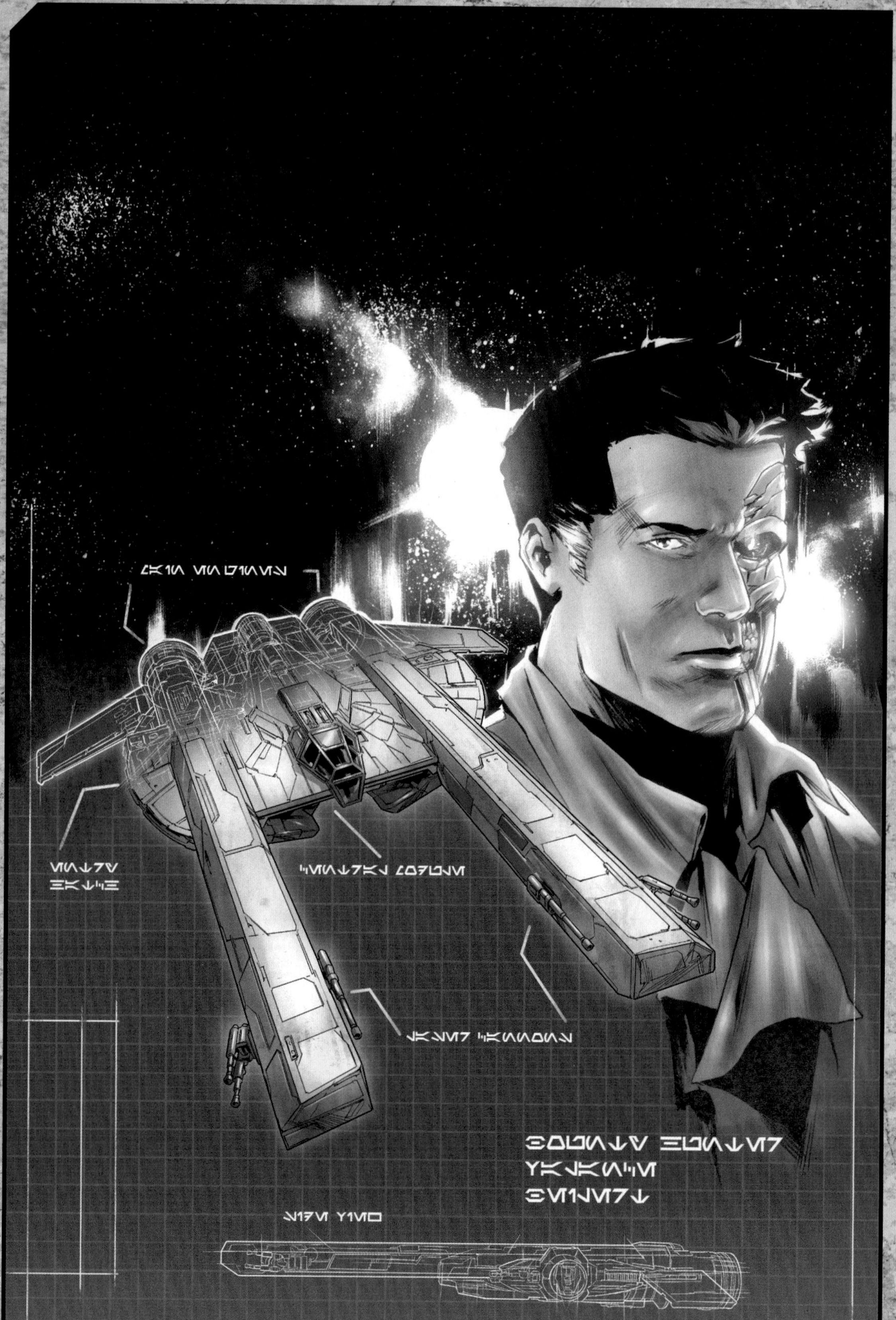

#16 Blueprint Variant by
PAOLO VILLANELLI & MATTIA IACONO

STAR WARS

WAR OF THE BOUNTY HUNTERS

BOUNTY HUNTERS

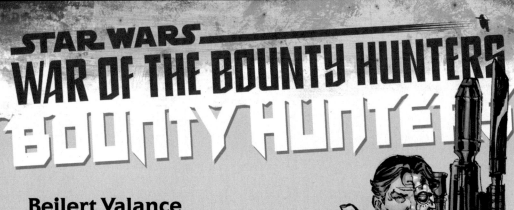

Beilert Valance

Homeworld: **Chorin**
Species: **Human (cyborg)**
First Appearance: ***Star Wars #16***
(Marvel Comics 1978)

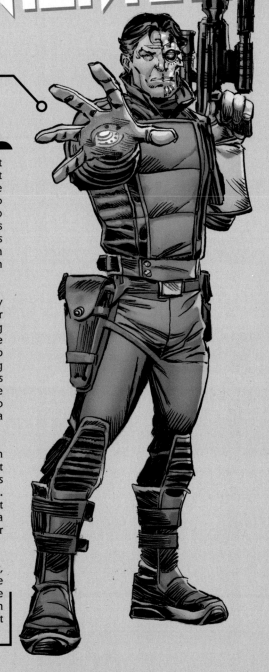

Believing in the cause of the Empire, Beilert Valance left his homeworld, the mining planet of Chorin, to enlist in the Imperial Navy. There he met a fellow cadet named Han Solo who did not share his enthusiasm. Han ended up saving Valance's life after his TIE fighter was shot down during an early mission. Valance's ideals were eventually crushed along with his body in an explosion during an incursion on Mimban.

Cast out of the Imperial service after they deemed it not worth the cost to fully repair him, Valance was left a broken man, struggling to find his place in the galaxy. After a chance encounter with famed mercenary Nakano Lash and her crew, Valance found a new calling as a bounty hunter. With improved cybernetics and his experience in combat, he became known in the galaxy's underworld as a force to be reckoned with...and avoided if you had a price on your head.

Valance's ship is the *Broken Wing*. He often uses former mentor Lash's custom bayonet blaster rifle in battle but has many weapons built into his cybernetic body at his disposal. Most infamous are his palm blasters, but his arsenal also includes concussion discs, a vibroblade, grappling hooks and a beskar knife hidden in his artificial shinbone.

During the *War of the Bounty Hunters*, Valance saw an opportunity to return the favor and tried to save Han Solo from the hands of Crimson Dawn. He joined forces with adversaries Dengar and Boba Fett. The attempt would change the course of his destiny.

#17 Handbook Variant by
RON FRENZ, TOM PALMER & NOLAN WOODARD WITH CARLOS LAO

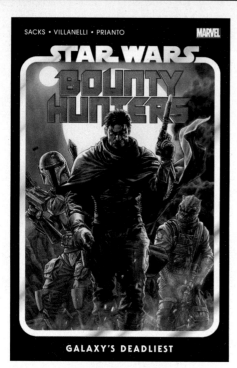

**Star Wars: Bounty Hunters
Vol. 1 — Galaxy's Deadliest**
ISBN 978-1-302-92083-8

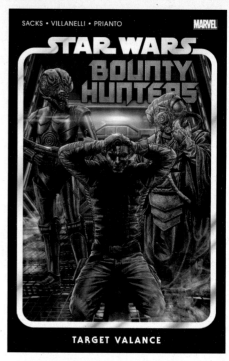

**Star Wars: Bounty Hunters
Vol. 2 — Target Valance**
ISBN 978-1-302-92084-5

**Star Wars Vol. 1:
The Destiny Path**
ISBN 978-1-302-92078-4

**Star Wars: Darth Vader by Greg Pak
Vol. 1 — Dark Heart of the Sith**
ISBN 978-1-302-92081-4

© & TM 2020 Lucasfilm Ltd.   © 2020 MARVEL

ROGUE ARCHAEOLOGIST DOCTOR APHRA THIEVES HER WAY ACROSS THE GALAXY!

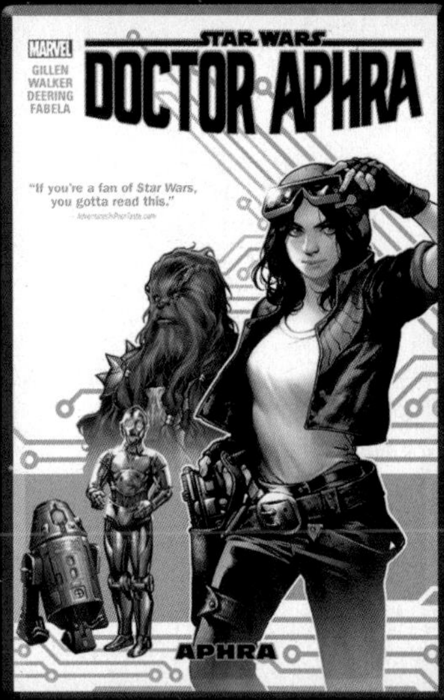
MARVEL
STAR WARS
DOCTOR APHRA
GILLEN
WALKER
DEERING
FABELA
"If you're a fan of Star Wars, you gotta read this."
APHRA

STAR WARS: DOCTOR APHRA VOL. 1 – APHRA TPB
ISBN: 978-1302913212

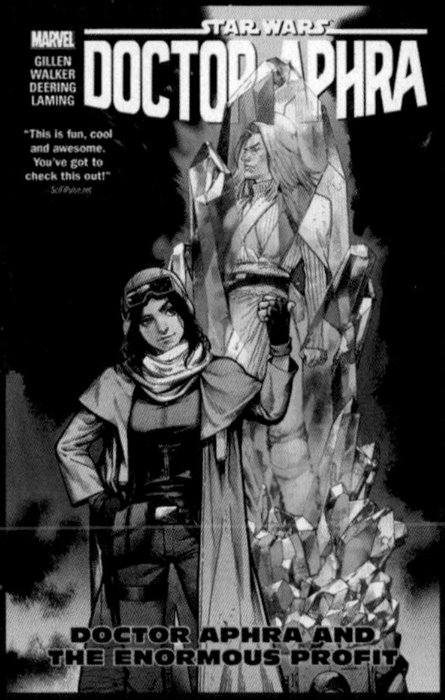
MARVEL
STAR WARS
DOCTOR APHRA
GILLEN
WALKER
DEERING
LAMING
"This is fun, cool and awesome. You've got to check this out!"
DOCTOR APHRA AND THE ENORMOUS PROFIT

STAR WARS: DOCTOR APHRA VOL. 2 – DOCTOR APHRA AND THE ENORMOUS PROFIT TPB
ISBN: 978-1302907631

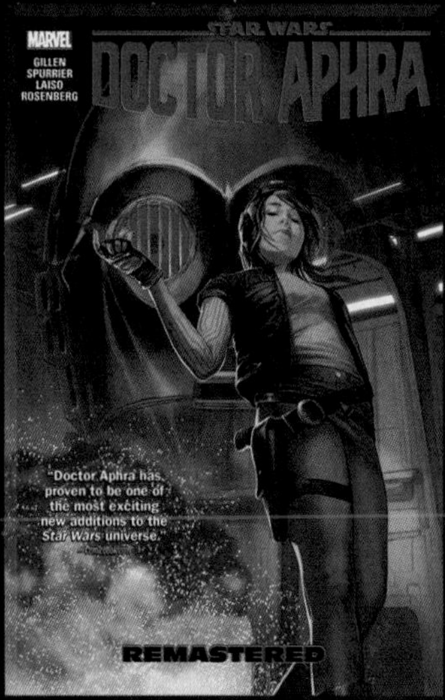
MARVEL
STAR WARS
DOCTOR APHRA
GILLEN
SPURRIER
LAISO
ROSENBERG
"Doctor Aphra has proven to be one of the most exciting new additions to the Star Wars universe."
REMASTERED

STAR WARS: DOCTOR APHRA VOL. 3 – REMASTERED TPB
ISBN: 978-1302911522

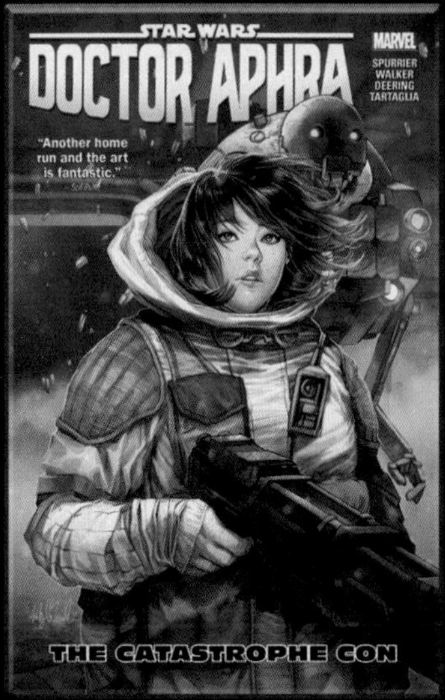
STAR WARS
DOCTOR APHRA
MARVEL
SPURRIER
WALKER
DEERING
TARTAGLIA
"Another home run and the art is fantastic."
THE CATASTROPHE CON

STAR WARS: DOCTOR APHRA VOL. 4 – THE CATASTROPHE CON TPB
ISBN: 978-1302911539

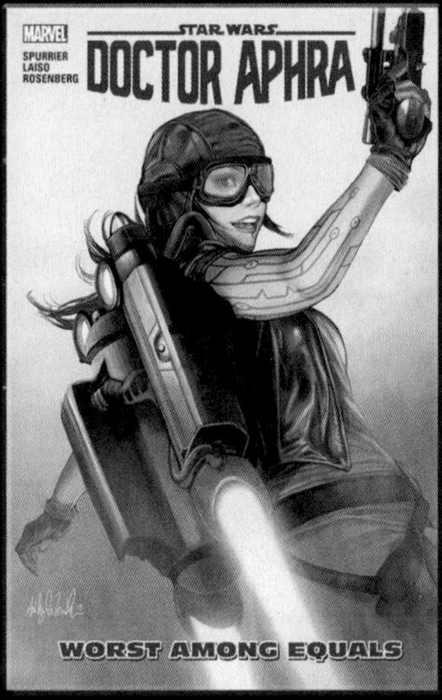
MARVEL
STAR WARS
DOCTOR APHRA
SPURRIER
LAISO
ROSENBERG
WORST AMONG EQUALS

STAR WARS: DOCTOR APHRA VOL. 5 – WORST AMONG EQUALS TPB
ISBN: 978-1302914875

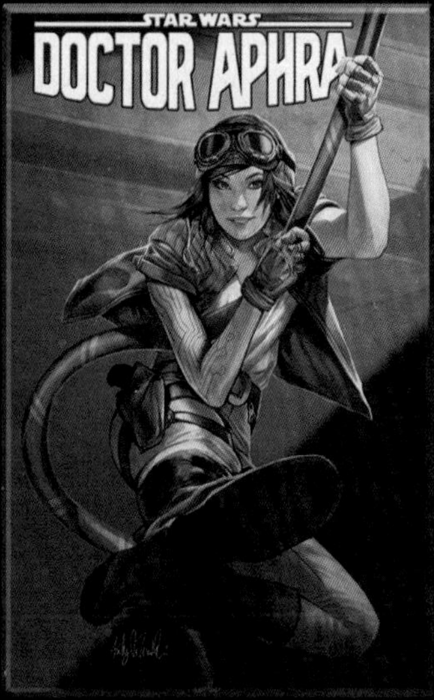
STAR WARS
DOCTOR APHRA

STAR WARS: DOCTOR APHRA VOL. 6 – UNSPEAKABLE REBEL SUPERWEAPON TPB
ISBN: 978-1302914882

ON SALE NOW
AVAILABLE IN PRINT AND DIGITAL WHEREVER BOOKS ARE SOLD

Disney · LUCASFILM · MARVEL

TO FIND A COMIC SHOP NEAR YOU, VISIT COMICSHOPLOCATOR.COM

WANT TO KNOW THE BEST WAY TO EXPLORE THE MARVEL *STAR WARS* UNIVERSE?
THIS GUIDE WILL SHOW YOU WHERE TO BEGIN!

FOLLOW THE ADVENTURES OF LUKE, HAN AND LEIA IN THESE

STAR WARS™

COLLECTED EDITIONS!

START HERE

**Star Wars Vol. 1:
Skywalker Strikes**
ISBN 978-0-7851-9213-8

**Star Wars Vol. 2:
Showdown on the Smuggler's Moon**
ISBN 978-0-7851-9214-5

**Star Wars:
Vader Down**
ISBN 978-0-7851-9789-8

**Star Wars Vol. 3:
Rebel Jail**
ISBN 978-0-7851-9983-0

**Star Wars Vol. 4:
Last Flight of the Harbinger**
ISBN 978-0-7851-9984-7

**Star Wars Vol. 5:
Yoda's Secret War**
ISBN 978-1-302-90265-0

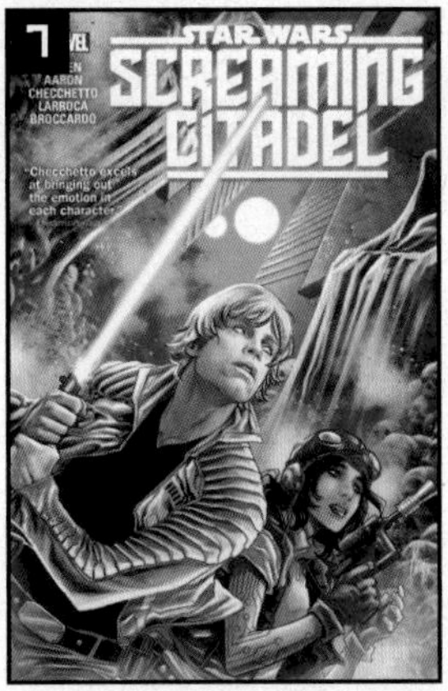
7
STAR WARS
SCREAMING CITADEL
AARON
CHECCHETTO
LARROCA
BROCCARDO

Star Wars:
The Screaming Citadel
ISBN 978-1-302-90678-8

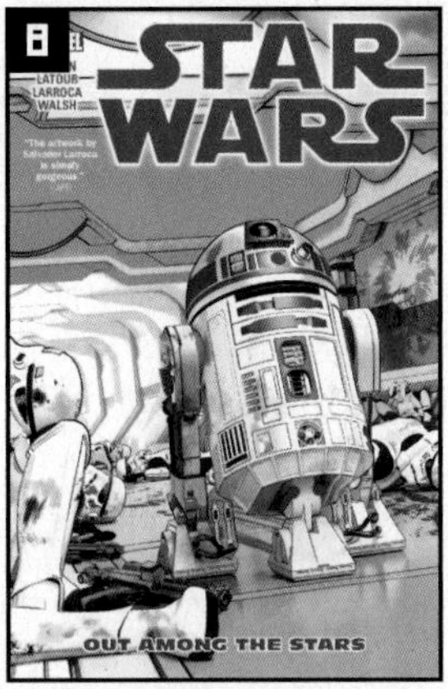
8
LATOUR
LARROCA
WALSH
STAR WARS
OUT AMONG THE STARS

Star Wars Vol. 6:
Out Among the Stars
ISBN 978-1-302-90553-8

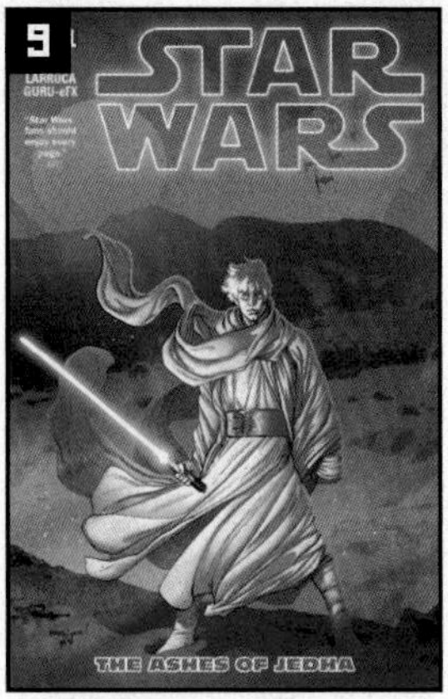
9
LARROCA
GURU-eFX
STAR WARS
THE ASHES OF JEDHA

Star Wars Vol. 7:
The Ashes of Jedha
ISBN 978-1-302-91052-5

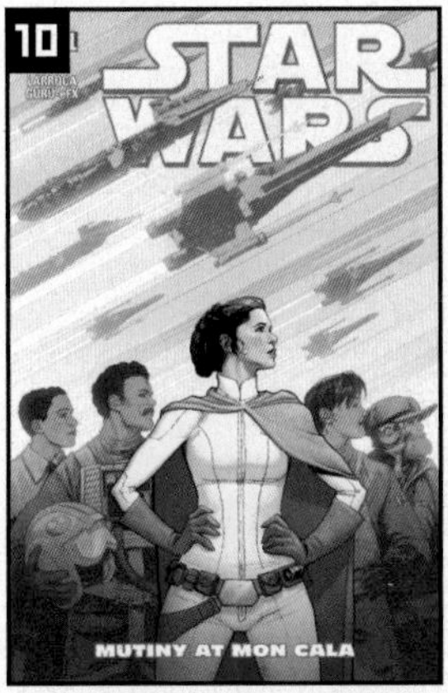
10
LARROCA
GURU-eFX
STAR WARS
MUTINY AT MON CALA

Star Wars Vol. 8:
Mutiny at Mon Cala
ISBN 978-1-302-91053-2

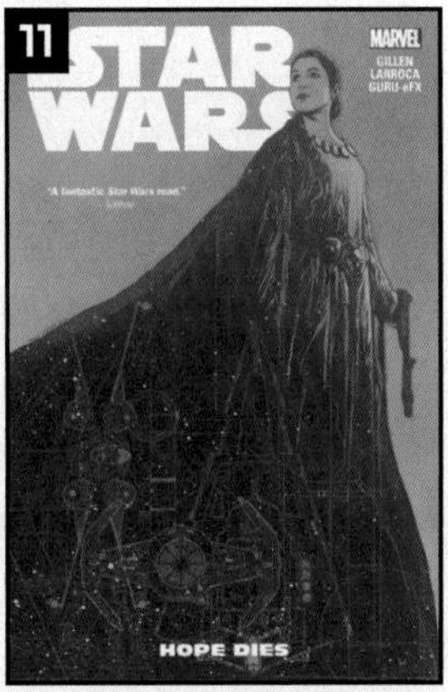
11
STAR WARS
MARVEL
GILLEN
LARROCA
GURU-eFX
HOPE DIES

Star Wars Vol. 9:
Hope Dies
ISBN 978-1-302-91054-9

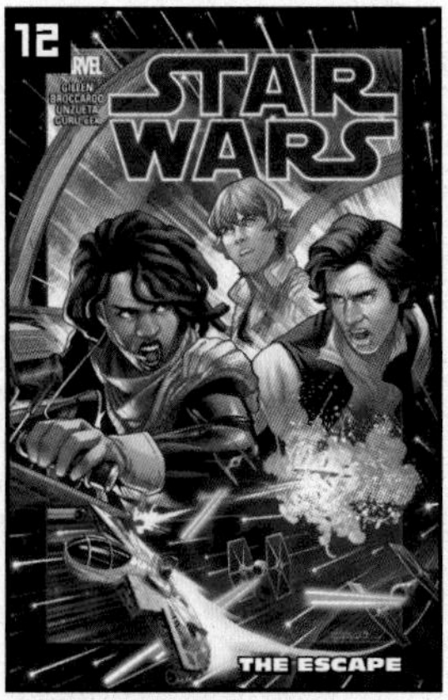
12
STAR WARS
THE ESCAPE

Star Wars Vol. 10:
The Escape
ISBN 978-1-302-91449-3

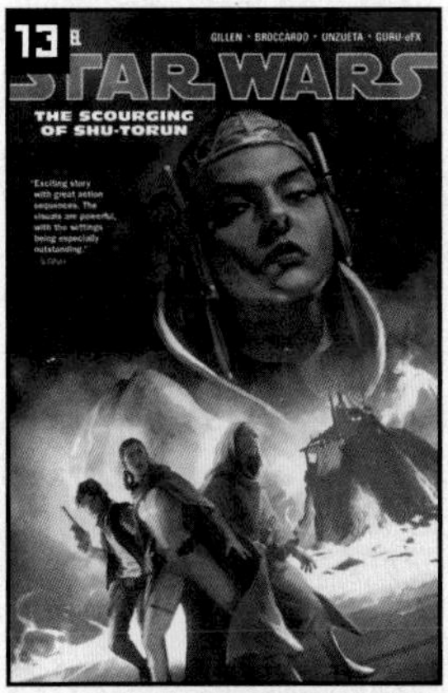
13
GILLEN · BROCCARDO · UNZUETA · GURU-eFX
STAR WARS
THE SCOURGING OF SHU-TORUN

Star Wars Vol. 11:
The Scourging of Shu-Torun
ISBN 978-1-302-91450-9

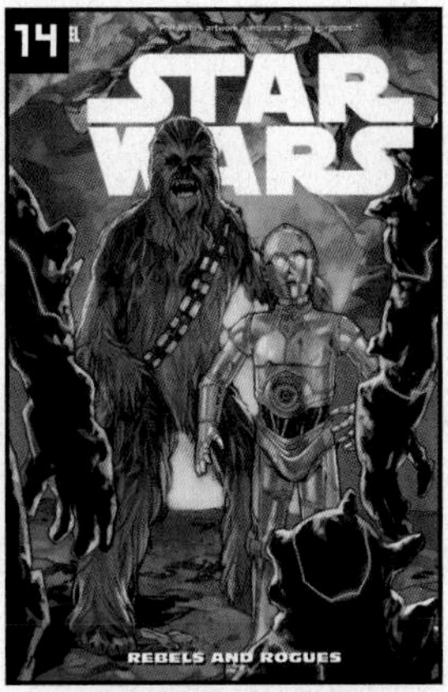
14
STAR WARS
REBELS AND ROGUES

Star Wars Vol. 12:
Rebels and Rogues
ISBN 978-1-302-91451-6

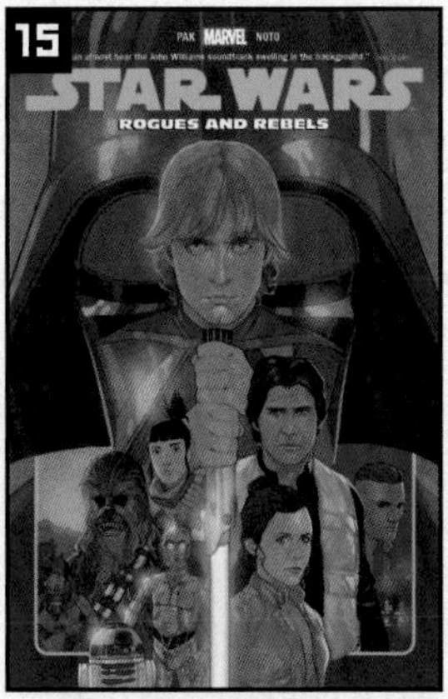
15
PAK
MARVEL
NOTO
STAR WARS
ROGUES AND REBELS

Star Wars Vol. 13:
Rogues and Rebels
ISBN 978-1-302-91450-9

DARTH VADER: DARK LORD OR SHINING KNIGHT?

STAR WARS: VADER - DARK VISIONS TPB
ISBN: 978-1302919009

ON SALE NOW
AVAILABLE IN PRINT AND DIGITAL
WHEREVER BOOKS ARE SOLD

TO FIND A COMIC SHOP NEAR YOU
VISIT COMICSHOPLOCATOR.COM

THE SECRET HISTORY OF GRAND ADMIRAL THRAWN IS REVEALED!

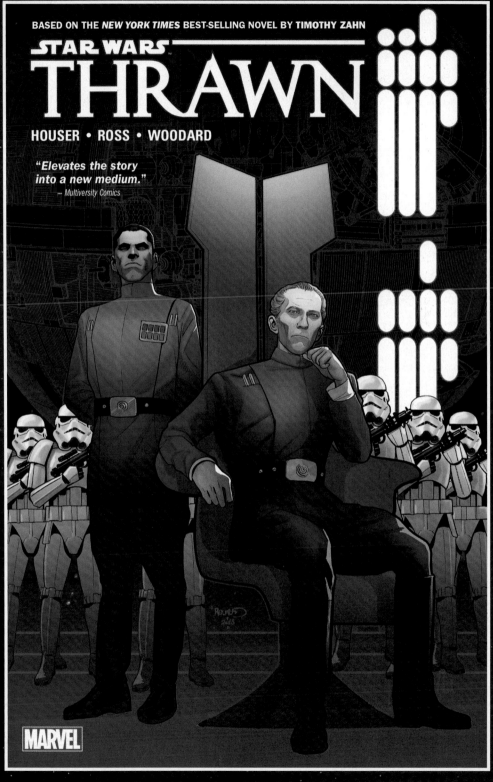

BASED ON THE *NEW YORK TIMES* BEST-SELLING NOVEL BY TIMOTHY ZAHN

STAR WARS THRAWN

HOUSER • ROSS • WOODARD

"Elevates the story into a new medium."
— Multiversity Comics

STAR WARS: THRAWN TPB

ISBN: 978-1302911560

ON SALE NOW

AVAILABLE IN PRINT AND DIGITAL WHEREVER BOOKS ARE SOLD

TO FIND A COMIC SHOP NEAR YOU VISIT COMICSHOPLOCATOR.COM

STAR WARS
THE HIGH REPUBLIC

Centuries before the Skywalker saga, a new adventure begins....

Books, Comics, ebooks, and Audiobooks Available Now!

Visit StarWars.com/TheHighRepublic for the latest news

© & TM 2021 Lucasfilm Ltd.